David Hall was Fred Dibnah's TV producer for many years, as well as a close personal friend. He made all of the most recent television series and is also the producer of *Fred Dibnah's World*. He is the author of *Fred: The Definitive Biography of Fred Dibnah*, *Fred Dibnah's Buildings of Britain* and *Manchester's Finest*, an account of his life in Manchester in the aftermath of the deaths of the Busby Babes.

Also by David Hall

Fred Dibnah's Industrial Age
Fred Dibnah's Magnificent Monuments
Fred Dibnah's Age of Steam
Fred Dibnah's Buildings of Britain
Fred: The Definitive Biography of Fred Dibnah
Manchester's Finest

FRED DIBNAH'S

MADE IN BRITAIN

DAVID HALL

CORGI BOOKS

TRANSWORLD PUBLISHERS
61–63 Uxbridge Road, London W5 5SA
A Random House Group Company
www.transworldbooks.co.uk

FRED DIBNAH'S MADE IN BRITAIN
A CORGI BOOK: 9780552161282

First published in Great Britain
in 2010 by Bantam Press
an imprint of Transworld Publishers
Corgi edition published 2011

Addresses for Random House Group Ltd companies outside the UK
can be found at: www.randomhouse.co.uk
The Random House Group Ltd Reg. No. 954009

The Random House Group Limited supports The Forest Stewardship
Council® (FSC®), the leading international forest certification organisation.
All our titles that are printed on Greenpeace approved FSC® certified paper
carry the FSC® logo. Our paper procurement policy can be found at
www.rbooks.co.uk/environment

Typeset in 11.5/14.5pt Times New Roman by
Falcon Oast Graphic Art Ltd.
Printed in the UK by CPI Cox & Wyman, Reading, RG1 8EX.

2 4 6 8 10 9 7 5 3 1

To Alf and Jimmy

Contents

Contents

Acknowledgements

With thanks to Fred's friends, Alf Molyneux, Jimmy Crooks and Alan Atkinson, and to my production team and film crew, Nigel Chatters, Leona Coulter, Jon Doyle, Kathryn Hall, Kate Siney and Rob Taylor, without whom Fred would not have been able to achieve his last great ambition. Thanks also to Mark Lesbirel at RDF Rights and to all at Transworld, especially Doug Young and my editor, Rebecca Jones.

Introduction

*We are all travellers in the wilderness of this world,
and the best we can find in our travels is an honest
friend.*

Robert Louis Stevenson

In the summer of 2004 I travelled around Britain
with Fred Dibnah and his recently renovated
traction engine to film the BBC television series *Fred
Dibnah's Made in Britain*. I had been making programmes with Fred for six years already, and during
that time we had become good friends. But when we set
out in May to shoot the first of the programmes, we
both knew that this would be Fred's last journey and
the last series we would do together. The cancer he had
been diagnosed with two and a half years earlier was
now terminal and he only had a few months to live.

The idea for *Made in Britain* went back to 1999,
when I asked Fred if he'd be up for a journey around

the country on his famous steamroller, *Betsy*, with his living van in tow. The series I had in mind initially would have seen Fred and the steamroller visiting castles, cathedrals and country houses as well as steam and industrial heritage sites. Fred was keen on the idea from the outset. He'd enjoyed the filming and the places we'd visited for the first two series, *Industrial Age* and *Magnificent Monuments*, and he liked the idea of combining this with a grand tour on his roller.

However, although my original idea was to travel around on *Betsy*, Fred had a different idea. The roller, he said, would be too slow and his traction engine far more suitable for such a journey. The traction engine was the heavy haulage vehicle of its day, a steam engine that towed heavy loads on roads. I knew that Fred had owned a 1912 Aveling and Porter engine for over twenty years. His plan was to restore it, but in the time that I'd known him I'd seen very little progress made. The as yet unnamed engine was little more than a rusty-looking boiler and what Fred described as 'a kit of parts' lying around in his shed, but he was determined. To finish rebuilding this engine after so many years and to set off on this grand tour would be one of the highlights of his career. He assured me he'd do his bit and get the engine on the road if I could do mine and have the series commissioned by the BBC.

Throughout the following year, the idea was developed further, as the BBC wanted a more focused series. Fred's traction engine was a time capsule of Britain's industrial past – an age when Britain was the 'workshop of the world' and the words 'made in Britain' were stamped on ships, steam locomotives, traction engines, mill engines, pumps, bridges and pit-winding engines all over the world. Every part of the engine had been invented and manufactured in the United Kingdom, so the idea was that Fred would travel the length and breadth of Britain under the power of steam to search out and celebrate the remarkable achievements of the inventors, engineers, craftsmen and industrial workers whose endeavours had made it possible for an engine like his to be built.

In each of the twelve programmes, Fred would visit a part of the country where an important contribution had been made, and through these twelve snapshots we would build up the bigger picture of the industrial activity that had shaped Britain. The skills and expertise were wide-ranging, from mining and smelt-ing the ore for the raw materials to the specialist craft skills of making parts such as pressure gauges, valves and bearings. Many of the skills, such as boiler-making, were still around in the 1970s but were disappearing rapidly, and on his journey Fred would seek out some of the little workshops where they still survived and share his passion for this great age of engineering. For Fred, it was perfect. It would give him the impetus he needed to get the engine finished and he could look forward to spending a few months on it travelling around and meeting up with some of his mates from the steam world who ran the workshops we would visit.

The idea was ambitious, but it wasn't to be, or at least not then. It was the time of Simon Schama's

History of Britain, and the BBC wanted a building history of Britain from us, so *Buildings of Britain* was commissioned instead and Fred's grand tour on the engine shelved for a while. Fred continued to work on the engine, but it wasn't a priority. Over the next two years we produced two more series and, as Fred's popularity increased, he got more and more theatre bookings. Added to that, another project was occupying a lot of his time – his plan to build a fully working replica of a coal mine in his back garden. When the BBC commissioned a film about it, *Dig with Dibnah*, it, too, took precedence over the restoration of the traction engine.

It was not until the end of 2003 that the idea for the grand tour on the traction engine came up again, just after we had finished *Dig with Dibnah*. The series was given the go-ahead by the BBC in early 2004, but by then time was very limited, because of Fred's health. He had first been diagnosed with cancer of the bladder towards the end of 2001, and although there had been remissions, he had by then been told that it was terminal and that he probably had no more than six months left to live. But however much he was suffering, Fred was determined to finish rebuilding the engine and to go on his grand tour.

It was a journey full of ups and downs, but Fred made it. Fitting the journey in around a filming schedule would have been a difficult project for someone in the best of health, let alone someone in Fred's condition. Added to this was the logistical challenge of driving a huge steam engine around modern Britain, with all the problems posed by traffic, road networks, hills and keeping the engine supplied with coal and water. It was a heroic effort and a few noticeable firsts were achieved along the way, such as crossing the Forth Road Bridge – the first time this had ever been done by a traction engine under its own steam. The highlight of the tour was a trip to London. Fred had been honoured with an MBE for his services to industrial heritage and broadcasting, and he went to Buckingham Palace to collect it on the engine.

As well as being an epic journey in search of Britain's industrial and engineering past, the journey was also about friendship and the men who really made this happen for Fred – his mining friends Alf Molyneux and Jimmy Crooks, and Alan Atkinson, who transported the engine around the country for him. Come rain or shine, they were there, giving their time unstintingly to make Fred's dream happen.

Above all, though, it was about Fred's sheer guts; about a man determined to achieve one last great ambition despite the pain he was in and however great the odds stacked against him. He had spent most of his working days dreaming about getting that traction engine on the road, and the joy of doing it seemed to outstrip the pain he was going through. Towards the end, he was really struggling, but there were places he wanted to go to and friends he wanted to see for the last time, and that kept him going.

Jon Doyle, the assistant producer on the series, summed it up:

You kept thinking, Why is he doing this to himself; why is he putting himself through this? Wouldn't he be better tucked up in bed? But you knew that was the last place that Fred wanted to be. There was no way he wanted that. He would rather have died on that engine than anywhere else. So no matter what he went through and how much it hurt, he was getting life; what life he had left came from the experience of getting out there on that engine and doing whatever he possibly could.

1

Building the Engine

Over a period of some forty years, Fred Dibnah demolished eighty-nine chimneys. His ninetieth, at the former Park Mill in Royton, near Oldham, was his last. It was the end of an era for Royton's textile industry, and for Fred. But being Fred, he'd had a new idea:

Really, me steeplejacking days are nearly over with. There's not many big chimneys like this left to knock down now. They do keep coming, but not quite as frequent as they used to. This of course will enable me to do lots of things that I've always wanted to do. Like now, after twenty-seven years, I've been able to finish me traction engine after all these years, and to celebrate this I'm setting off on a grand trip round Britain in search of everything that went into building and running an engine like this. It's a celebration of what a great industrial nation we were, because all the bits that went into it – coal, iron, steam, engineering and mechanics – are the things that made Britain a great industrial nation. When I bought the engine about twenty-seven years ago, I didn't really think it would take as many years as it has done. When I look at it now and see what I've done, I've almost made a new one. There's practically nothing left of the original. When it's screwed together, I think it'll actually be better than what it was in 1912.

A traction engine's a strange machine that were developed really from a lot of other engines. They started off in the 1840s, where all the effort were put in by either animals or the human frame. The men in the country, the blacksmiths and village mechanics, as you might say, decided that they would make a small locomotive boiler and then stick on top of it a crankshaft and a cylinder with a fly wheel, and place it on four wooden wheels so it could be used to drive threshing machines and big saws and all that sort of stuff. It could be used in quarries to crush stone; it could be used to work portable water pumps; it were like a general doer of all things on working sites.

Fred's Aveling and Porter convertible compound steam tractor was originally built for Somerset County Council in 1912 and configured as a traction engine. But by 1914 it had been commandeered by the War

Department, converted into a road roller and sent off to France. When it came back after the war it was acquired by Devon County Council and used as a road roller for the rest of its working life. In the mid-1960s, all the brass fittings were stolen when it was parked in a lay-by. It was then advertised for sale and tenders by sealed bid were invited. The successful bid was just £200, and it came from Peter Froud, a friend of Fred's. Fred always said that he was green with envy at the time. He'd just paid £175 for his roller, but knew the convertible tractor would have been a much better buy:

When I bought me steamroller I realized straight away I'd made a terrible mistake. I should have bought a traction engine. Steamrollers are very nice things, and everybody relates to them because steamrollers were the last steam-driven vehicles to be seen on any English highway as late as the 1960s, whereas steam wagons and steam traction engines had all disappeared. This meant that even by that time the money for a traction engine were getting a bit tall, so £200 were a real bargain.

Several years later, when Fred was a bit better off, he was in a position to buy a tractor, but by then prices had risen steeply. He knew Peter Froud was thinking of selling the Aveling, so in 1977, after a bit of haggling, a sale was agreed between them for £2,300, and Fred moved the convertible to his workshop at the back of his house in Bolton. The engine, numbered TA2436, looked to be in very good condition, and Fred was pleased with his new acquisition. It had nice lagging on the boiler, the belly tanks were all lined out and it'd had a smart paint job. On closer inspection, though, Fred found that the engine wasn't quite as good as it had first appeared.

'There were tell-tale signs for all to see,' he said, 'including a big L-shaped weld on the side of the boiler, right underneath the high-pressure-valve spindle. And the standard of the riveting on the boiler also left a lot to be desired.' It quickly became obvious to Fred that this boiler barrel wasn't good enough, and so began the twenty-seven-year slog to get the engine restored.

When we started filming Fred at work on the engine for *Made in Britain*, it was nearly complete, but he never tired of recounting the saga of its building:

When I first got it the BBC were filming, and I said to the producer, Don Howarth, 'If you give me eight grand, I'll be able to get it finished in six months.' Getting the engine all appeared in those early films: doing the deal, having a beer, dragging it in the shed and the irate wife never being able to go on holiday because of it. Then the beginning of the riveting; he filmed a bit of that, but not a lot. There's some archive film of that with me saying ridiculous things like, 'In two years we'll be steaming down the road,' and it's twenty-seven years on from there. Everything had been welded on – even the firebox, and the people who did it welded it in places where it didn't need welding so it caused me a lot of bother. I had to grind a lot of surplus metal off that I needn't have done if they'd done the job right in the first place. Then I found that the front axle was not original. It was from a Garrett No. 4 tractor, and the front wheels were also the wrong ones and were even different diameters.

I soon realized that what I'd bought were absolutely rotten, it were all rusty and all the rivets were pointed, so I started off twenty-odd years ago by making a new boiler barrel. I didn't actually roll the plates, I got that done at an engineering works, but I did all the riveting; the entire hole boring and the rivets. I made nearly all the parts for the engine myself, which is one of the reasons it all took so long. The gearing, all the cog wheels and all the transmission is all brand-new. I made a lot of the blanks myself with me own lathe. When I first looked at it, it didn't look too bad, but gears are funny things; if they're a little bit worn they make a lot of noise, and I don't like too much noise. So I ended up with a brand-new set of gears. Then there was the tender; it was a bit like a patchwork quilt. I've never been one of those men who likes things patched up, so I decided to make a brand-new one. With the various methods of getting plates red-hot and bending them round bits of iron, I managed to make a brand-new tender. All the bearings are

FRED DIBNAH'S MADE IN BRITAIN

brand-new, the cylinder block is new and it's got new piston rods, new valve rods and all new pins. But the biggest single job I had to do on the engine were the boiler.

There were much upset with it and a lot of trouble, and many setbacks that were no fault of me own, like cracks appearing in plates and things like that, but I soldiered on. You could have welded it up and made a bodge-up of it like lots of them are, but if it's had it I prefer to make a new one. Really, there are only three plates of the boiler that are original; three pieces of metal in the whole boiler are the original 1912. The rest of it is lying about the garden in bits and pieces. Then, of course, the tanks and the tender and all the gearing and all the bearings are all brand-new. And that's why I'm hoping it's going to run like a Swiss watch when we get it out of this shed and go up that hill on to the tarmac outside.

You've got to have a laugh, though; it has meant twenty-seven years and two divorces for me. Any man who's got a steam engine will tell you that you've got to have an understanding woman, otherwise you're in big trouble. It's really hard to reckon up the actual time I've spent on it, because there can be a period of six or seven weeks when you're working away from home and there's no time to bother with it. You get people writing these articles on how I did me traction engine up and they say things like 'I spent twenty-nine thousand hours on it,' but it's a bit of a weird thing how they can get it dead right down to the exact hour.

People buy them now, half a boiler and two wheels and no cylinder block, and start from there. It's amazing what wonderful achievements people in England have made restoring these things. I think they should get government grants or lottery grants, because it's ten times tougher than doing a motorcar, I can tell you. In my opinion, if you do one of these things up proper, it takes a long time if you're not a rich man. Even if you are a rich man, the hardest thing is to find the men who can do it for you, because the skills are disappearing fast. Even with this engine, living in this town now, I would be hard pressed to start again and do it, because half the firms that have helped me have gone, and the machinery is in India and China and places like that, which is bloody sad to me. I mean, the things that have been done for me here in this town, you couldn't get done no more because the people have gone.

Then there's the cost of it. Sometimes you go and get a price for something, and it's an arm and a leg and you think, It's going to bankrupt me. So you chew it over in your mind for three months, and finally and ultimately you come up with a solution. Necessity is the mother of invention, and I've saved myself literally thousands of pounds. If I'd had to pay for a lot of things it would have been a fortune. For the rubber tyres alone you are talking a thousand pound on each wheel if you pay for it at Dunlop. But there's ways and means you can find these things and get them practically given to you.

Money had always been tight and was one of the reasons that the rebuild of the engine took so long. But by 2001, with several new television series under his belt and a diary full of bookings for after-dinner talks, Fred was in the sort of position he'd always wanted to be in. He was completely independent, and he would have plenty of time between filming commitments and theatre bookings to devote his time to finishing the traction engine and starting work on building the replica coal mine in his garden. Life was looking good. The only cloud on the horizon was his health. Fred was suffering from abdominal pains and was admitted to Bolton Royal Infirmary for tests. After a series of X-rays and scans, the doctors discovered that his right kidney was not working properly and would have to be removed. After the surgery, he was told that the kidney contained a malignant tumour and the cancer had spread to his lymphatic system.

Fred wasn't going to be beaten by the cancer, nor was he going to be put down by the chemotherapy. He was as tough and stubborn as he'd ever been and wasn't going to give in easily. Within a day or so of the treatment, he was back out in his yard getting on with the work on the tractor and all his other projects. And that toughness saw him through. When his course of treatment finished he went for a scan, and the results were encouraging. The chemotherapy had been successful and Fred was given the all-clear. Life could get back to normal, and Fred was able to get on with the work on his tractor. By this time, Fred had a lot of friends helping him. Ian Thompson had been around, working in the garden, for as long as I had been going to Fred's. He stoked the boiler and generally operated as Fred's assistant – all on a voluntary basis. Then Alf Molyneux appeared on the scene. Alf was a retired miner whom Fred had first met in a pub he used to go to in Tyldesley, a small coal-mining community between Bolton and Wigan. Alf takes up the story:

Fred got chatting on steam, and it's infectious listening to him. He's such a nice chap and he was so easy to get on with. We got talking about pits, and he told me he'd got a pit headgear in his back garden. Being an ex-miner, I went to have a look, but it was on a day when he needed a bit of muscle power on the traction engine. I gave him a lift that first day, and that were it, I were trapped. When I first went he was relying on somebody calling and giving him an hour here and an hour there. There was nobody going regular like I started to. At that stage the original body of the tractor needed to be dismantled, and one of the first jobs I remember were stripping the boiler off the back end.

Alf had finished his career as a pit deputy. He was a few years younger than Fred, still strong and very capable, and as an ex-miner he wasn't afraid of hard, manual work; just the kind of man Fred needed. It wasn't very long before Alf was coming to give Fred a hand three or four times a week, and he started to bring his ex-mining mate Jimmy Crooks along with him. Jimmy had spent his whole working life in the coal industry and finished up 'a boss down the pit; a clever bloke', as Fred used to put it. Later on, when he was working on the engine with Alf, I asked Jimmy how he got involved, and he just pointed to Alf. 'This fellow,' he said:

There was one night me and Alf were with Fred, and he was on about getting his engine finished. He'd just found out then that he'd got cancer and he'd not got much time, so he was on about getting it finished so his two lads would be able to have an engine each. So we said, 'If that's all you want, we'll come and give you a lift.' We'd no idea about traction engines or boiler-making or anything at that time. We used to go out walking twice a week, and I ended up with a bad leg and we didn't go for a while, so we started coming here and this has taken over. It was in pieces in the shed when we started going.

Alf remembers those first days when he and Jimmy started going regularly to Fred's: 'We started piling into that engine with gusto, because he'd just been diagnosed and he said he wanted to get it finished. He was always talking about one for each of the lads.' But within a few weeks of Fred getting all this extra help, he had a major setback:

Everything was going very well; then when we'd just got six rivets left to do, a horrible crack appeared in between the four rivet holes where the barrel goes into the throat plate. That were really bad news, because this is the most complicated piece of plate on the whole boiler. The initial thought was that it were just a pencil line, but it weren't; it were a proper crack in the iron. It was most likely to have been caused by the way the thing was made in 1912. The only solution was to get it welded. So that's what I did. I called the welder, and while I was waiting for him to come, there was a terrible disaster in America. A traction engine blew up, killing five people and injuring forty. I thought, If that were to happen in England, it would be the end of the traction-engine movement, and they'd not allow us out on the roads any more. So while I were waiting for the welding to be done, I thought of having the engine X-rayed. A man came with his television sets and his probe and his gel, and he went round the seam of the rivets. As he did, his face was getting longer and longer. It were all cracked around the circumference where the rivets went in. All in all, there were twenty-seven cracks in the plate, he said, all invisible to the naked eye. This meant we would have to make a new throat plate, which would have been quite a feat.

'Making a new throat plate wasn't a job that Fred could do in the garden,' Alf recalled:

> He didn't have the machinery he needed for it, so he had to find somewhere to get the job done. He went to various places, and they couldn't do it either; the expertise had long gone. Then he dropped on an ironworks in Dukinfield, and he went there and had a word with the boss and the boss said, 'Go and have a word with such a body,' some old guy who had a lot of experience; and he looked at it and said, 'No problem.' I believe Fred had got an estimate from somewhere else which was hundreds of pounds, and when he enquired here it was 'Give us fifty quid,' or something like that, which suited Fred.

Fabricating the new throat plate was the biggest job Fred had to contract out during the rebuild of the engine, and he was full of praise for the Dukinfield firm of J. Bown & Co. who did the job. 'They were,' he said, 'the kind of outfit the steam men should support.' As far as Fred was concerned, they were top of the list of places we should go to film for the new series. For him, it was companies like this that had made Britain great, and he always lamented the fact that they had nearly all disappeared:

> In this modern and advanced age that we live in, it gets more and more difficult to find people who can actually do work like this. It's incredible

really; there's a heck of a lot of bodge-ups, and you can't really afford that sort of thing with a potential bomb, which is what an engine like this is, really. If I had to start again now to do what I've done on this locomotive boiler, I'd be in trouble. All the people who've helped me and done various bits of machinery for me have nearly all gone. Like the gearing with all the cog wheels on it, I made a lot of the blanks meself with me own lathe. And the reason it's taken all these years is the fact that the lathe is driven by another steam engine, and of course it means lighting fires and getting steam up like they did in the olden days. In them days they'd never let the fire go out, so they'd have plenty of power all the time, just like an electric motor. But of course all my machinery is antique. It does the job, but it's not quite as fast as modern electrically driven tackle. The thing is, the people who put the teeth on the blanks were loading all the machinery on to the back of wagons to be exported to India the week after they'd finished them. I don't know, they seem to be able to do the work in other countries, but not here. I think one of the biggest mistakes we've ever made is stopping bound apprenticeships for engineers.

Once the new throat plate had been made, Fred had to get it on to the end of the boiler and then rivet it to the boiler barrel. 'It was a tight fit when we put it on,' Alf remembers, and it took a bit of banging to do it, but these things need to be a decent fit. Next we had to make a hydraulic riveter to actually rivet the throat plate into position. Then Jimmy said we could do with a turntable, because you couldn't go swinging the hydraulic riveter round everywhere. With a turntable, we would be able to leave the riveter where it was and turn the barrel around, and lo and behold, next time we went Fred had made one from two pieces of kitchen worktop. We had a bit of assistance from a group in Wigan, some railwaymen, and they were using compressed-air guns, but Fred didn't want to do it that road. He wanted to do it more by hand, as they would have done it in the old days. That's the way we did the stays. You could do them with the gun, but they were all done by hammer, and there's some blows there – six hundred-odd hammer blows for one side of each stay. Once we'd got the throat plate on we got the whole thing on a set of temporary wheels taken from pit wagons and laid a track to push it in and out of the shed so we could work under the big crane to lift the flywheel on, and that sort of thing. I can't remember where we got everything from. It was cadge a bit here and cadge a bit there.

Jimmy was now going to Fred's two or three times a week with Alf. 'We kept adding to and adding to it,' he said, 'all the parts that Fred had already made for it. Then it got too big for the tub wheels, so we had to put another set of wheels underneath at the back. We got them from Astley Green Colliery Museum, on loan, supposedly. Then it came to putting the firebox in. All the stays had to be put in. Me and Alf would do five apiece. Then we put the boiler tubes in. Fred told us what to do. He demonstrated. Then he'd go and do something else and leave us to it.'

'We dropped lucky with the boiler tubes,' Alf said, 'because we'd been to the Bolton engineering works, Hick Hargreaves, just before they closed down, and there was a tube-bending machine there that they gave Fred and that made life a lot easier.' About this time, more helpers appeared on the scene, as Alf explained:

On Saturday morning I used to meet up with some mates who were all interested in mining, and we'd either go underground at Wet Earth Colliery or down some of the mine shafts on the moors up above Bolton. One Saturday morning I said to them, 'I'm going to Fred's. Come and have a look at his headgear.' They then started coming every Saturday morning, and it's then we decided we had enough men to start sinking the mine shaft. That was the plan. We did that a time or two. But in between that, especially when we got building the tractor up and doing all the riveting, there'd be plenty of bodies on a Saturday morning to lend a hand.

By the end of August 2003, Fred was making progress on all fronts with the engine and the mine, and he was busy with filming commitments and with theatre bookings. We were getting to the end of filming *Age of Steam*, but the BBC had commissioned another film about Fred's mine, and the filming for that had started. It was the first time Jon Doyle had worked with Fred, and he remembers well the scenes of great industry in his garden. 'At that stage,' he says,

> there was this amazing energy to get things done, but it was all interrupted by having breaks for pies and having a brew. It was a strange world of retired men, back in this industrial machine that Fred had created in his garden. It was always very entertaining and it never ceased to amaze me when I saw the sheer scale of the jobs Fred would do and the feats he would pull off. I remember seeing the engine very early on getting pulled out of the shed, and at this stage there were no moving parts on it. The first time I saw the engine, in September 2003, it had no wheels on; it was on tracks and they used to pull it out of the shed on them. To me, it was just a rusty-looking boiler. All the rest was in bits that were spread all over the shed: the wheels here, the gears over there and the chains hanging up from the walls. Then when they started to put them together there were parts that never seemed to fit properly because they'd all been made at different times.

To the untrained eye, the engine might have looked a long way from completion, but Fred knew that, after all the years of hard work, it was nearly finished, and with all the help he was now getting from Alf and Jimmy and the other members of 'Dad's Army', as his wife, Sheila, used to call them, Fred was confident he would have it on the road by the following spring. But his health was still giving cause for concern. He was going back to Christie's hospital in Manchester for check-ups, and at one of these his worst fears were confirmed. The cancer that had started in his kidney had now surfaced again in his bladder, where a large tumour had appeared. Fred started on another course of chemotherapy. But like the first time, he wasn't going to let it stop him doing the things he wanted to do. The doctors ordered complete rest, but Fred took no notice: he had his traction engine and his coal mine to finish.

But he was running out of time, and Alf and Jimmy knew that he wouldn't be able to achieve both of his ambitions. 'We kept trying to persuade him to finish the engine and leave the shaft,' Jimmy recalled,

but he was a stubborn bloke at times and if that's what he wanted to do, you'd have to do that. He had great plans for the mine, but I kept saying to him, 'You can't do it. It won't work.' But he kept going. We knew it would never get finished. But the engine kept getting bypassed because of it, and there were so many other jobs going on, like chopping trees down, putting the side of the big shed in and putting a new floor in ready for when the tractor was up and running.

But we also had some good laughs. Sheila kept

trying to make Fred a vegetarian, so Fred would have us in stitches, hiding his meat pie whenever Sheila was around.

At the end of 2003, when the idea for doing the *Made in Britain* series came up again, Fred was given an even bigger incentive to get the engine finished. It was just after we had made *Dig with Dibnah*, and it was the emergence of Alf in that film as the perfect foil for Fred that helped to get the series off the ground. Fred would need a steersman for the journey, and Alf had been very good on camera with Fred in the mining programme. With Alf on board as Fred's mate, the series was given the go-ahead. Fred was delighted – he would be able to achieve what had become for him one of his last great ambitions. The other one, getting his mine completed, had been temporarily thwarted when the council turned down his application for planning permission, but the prospect of this new series made up for that disappointment.

Everything was looking good. Fred's chemotherapy sessions seemed to be going well and we had high hopes that he'd be able to get the engine finished and be fit enough to embark on the tour. Fred himself was optimistic. Every time I went over to see him, he'd tell me about stories he'd read in the *Daily Mail* about some cure or other that had been developed in America. However, Fred's optimism and his joy at getting the series commissioned was short-lived. While I'd been discussing the proposal with the BBC, Fred was back at the hospital having check-ups. When he got the results, they couldn't have been worse. The cancer had spread, and it had got such a hold that the specialists had to advise him that chemotherapy wouldn't cure him.

It was early 2004 by now, and Fred only had a short time to live, but he was now a man with a very clear mission. 'As long as I can finish me engine off,' he said, 'it doesn't overly worry me about owt else, but I want to do me engine up and finish me pit if I can before I die.' He was confident that, over the course of the next six months, he would achieve the first of these ambitions. By now the engine was looking good, and despite all the setbacks he'd had, it was at last nearing completion. He'd reached the most exciting stage of the rebuild, with the wheels due to be put on, the cab attached and all the shiny green cladding and the polished brasswork to be put on.

We went over to film some of this for the first programme in the new series, and Jon Doyle remembers the scale of the work Fred was doing:

He'd start manoeuvring this 10 tons of iron up and down his garden and it felt like, any minute, it could have fallen down, but Fred was always in control of the situation. His ingenuity in getting a huge jack out to lift something up or using a block and tackle to move it around was very impressive. I thought it was amazing that a single person could find a way to solve such terrific and impressive engineering problems himself with just one or two other people there to help him. I'll never forget the sheer energy and the commitment from all the people around him, or the constant stream of passers-by who would drop in, and the fact that Fred would always have time to stop and have a brew with them, whoever they were and wherever they'd come from.

But Fred's willingness to drop tools to entertain anybody who cared to call in to see him wasn't so good when he was racing against time to get his engine on the road. By spring, the work still wasn't finished. It would need another few months' work before it was ready for the road. Once it had been finished, the journey itself and the filming, we estimated, would take at least four months. Fred was determined to carry on and do it, but he was becoming weaker all the time. His friends rallied round, and the garden became a scene of constant activity. 'He really wanted to get the engine done and do the tour,' Jimmy said. 'He talked about it a lot. But we couldn't get him to get on with it. We wanted him to abandon the shaft job and get on with the engine, but he wouldn't have it. He kept saying he was waiting for this or he was waiting for that. There was always something. But we don't know what he kept waiting for.'

By the time we started filming, the engine was 'a kit of parts', like pieces of Meccano that were all ready to be bolted together. The wheels had been replaced with a suitable Aveling pair and new bearings fitted. The tender, belly tanks, boiler barrel and ash pan had all been replaced with newly manufactured substitute parts. Before all the bits were screwed on, however, Fred was able to fill the boiler. He got it up to 175 pounds per square inch (psi), and there were no leaks, which was pretty good, said Fred, 'considering it is a homemade boiler, made in me backyard. It looks very rusty at the moment, but that's very good for it. Leaving it standing like this helps to seal the rivets up.' Fred explained a bit more about what was involved in these tests he was doing:

When you've made a new boiler, it's got to be tested, and a good way of testing it, the recognized way, is a hydraulic test. This means you fill it right up to the top with cold water till there's no air or anything in it, and you start pumping it up to one and a half times the working pressure, which in the case of this boiler is 300psi, which is quite a lot of weight and pressure from the cold water. Of course, cold water is harmless, and if it did blow apart it wouldn't be an explosion, because cold water doesn't expand. It just gives up when the pressure has been released. Now if you did the same with steam, you'd be pushing your luck. But there's another way of doing it. If you fill the boiler right up to the top with cold water and then light a fire, cold water expands when it gets hot and this builds up a pressure without the steam, and that's the way I'm doing it. The thing is, I've done it before, so I know it's going to be OK. I've now got this boiler full of water, and we've had it up to 125psi and there've been no leaks, which is pretty good. Very shortly we'll get it up to the full hydraulic test pressure at 300psi. The next thing is to shot-blast the engine and paint it matt black and roll it into the shed and start to assemble it. I'm really, really looking forward to that – after so many battles.

The shot-blasting was to get rid of the rust. After that, Fred got a man from Preston to come and paint the tender and the water tanks. 'Then,' Jimmy recalled, 'we started on the living van, re-timbered a lot of that. Then we had to find brakes; we couldn't get brakes for it. When we did finally get them it was all right going forward, but it wouldn't go back because the brakes kept locking.' By this time, Alf had been bitten by the steam bug. He'd never been into steam before, but after working with Fred on his engine, he'd bought his own little model steam engine which he worked on in his own back shed at home. As he worked on Fred's engine with Jimmy, I asked them both how much time they were spending at Fred's. Alf told me it varied:

We always come Mondays and Thursdays, and usually on Saturday, and then other than that, if he says he could do with a lift, I might have an extra afternoon with him. Then I just come in sometimes for a chat because he's such a nice chap to know. In one sense, I wish I'd known him years ago, but in another sense no, because I'd have probably finished up working with him on chimneys or something and I'd have missed out on my own career in the mines, which I always enjoyed. I hardly knew what a nut and bolt was when I started helping Fred, but his enthusiasm rubs off on you and you learn as you go along. He was always a very easy chap to work with, very easygoing, and I've learned a lot off him. He was a good teacher. But he used to teach himself as well. Often he'd read a book in the evening about some mechanical problem he'd come across and then he'd have a go at it the next day. The other thing was, he was never afraid to ask. He might be in a factory somewhere, and he'd talk to mechanics and he'd ask their opinion about a problem he was coming up against, or he'd ring one of his steam buddies and ask them. One of the things that always came across when working on the engine was that he was a perfectionist. You'd put a rivet in, and if it weren't quite right, it was drill it and get it out. But if you did do something wrong, he wouldn't start shouting and bawling about it. He'd just say, 'No. That'll not do,' and you had to do it again. So you quickly learned only to do it once and do it right. If we hadn't got in with Fred, though, we'd probably never have taken any notice of traction engines and all that. But it's got infectious, hasn't it?

Jimmy agreed. 'Especially when you look at what we've done. This was just a pile of scrap when we started.' As he spoke, I looked at the engine, which

Jimmy was busy rubbing down. It was now looking as though it was nearly ready for the road. The boiler had been painted matt black and the tender and belly tanks were a beautiful, high-gloss green. The engine itself was no longer a kit of parts, as all the gearing, pistons and drive mechanisms had been fitted.

Fred came into the shed and rubbed his hand appreciatively over the tender's paintwork. 'That's nice and smooth, innit?' he said. 'Smooth as glass. And we'll soon have the wheels on. Don't worry.'

Alf looked at the footplate. 'There won't be much room for you here, Fred, when I'm driving this,' he said with a grin.

Fred laughed and looked at the flywheel. He was still interested in the paintwork. 'Saved us a lot of messing getting somebody in to do it,' he said. 'It's nice when it gets to this stage. Anyway, I'll go and put the kettle on.'

'That's a good idea,' Alf said. 'That's the best idea you've had all day.'

Fred left Alf and Jimmy looking at the engine. Alf was getting excited about the thought of getting the engine out on the road. 'Wait until we're bombing down the road,' he said. 'That will be a delightful day. That will be a day to remember. It really will. But like I said, there's not a lot of room on it. With the steamroller, we can all hang on the back, but I don't think there are a lot of places here where you can hang on to the side.'

Alf pointed to the stays in the boiler:

These stays, believe it or not, there's 56,000 hammer blows in this line of stays, inside and out, and the same again on the other side. A chap came down one day and we were banging away at these, and he said, 'How many hammer blows does that take?' I said, 'I don't know, because we've never counted.' So we counted just one and then multiplied it by the number of stays. When Fred did the first stay he said to me, 'This will be your job.' So I did one and said, 'How does it look?', and he said, 'It could do with a bit of an adjustment.' So I gave it a few more knocks, then on to the next. He reckons now I'm his expert stay knocker.

'Stay knocker extraordinary,' Fred announced with a laugh as he came back into the shed with the brew. 'Where can we put this bloody thing?' he said, as he struggled to find a clear surface to put the battered old tea tray down. Eventually, he found a trestle to rest it on, but by this time the tray was swimming with all the tea and coffee he'd spilt. Fred might have been able to rebuild his engine, but organizing a brew was a different matter.

There were a lot more brews before the big day dawned when the engine could be steamed up for the first time. But was it going to work? Fred looked on proudly as his Land Rover was used to pull the engine out of the shed on the railway track and shared his thoughts:

This is it, really. After twenty-seven years and two divorces, I've finally got the thing back together. Some periods I were full of despair, particularly with the saga with the throat plate. But practically what you're looking at, other than the casting of the cylinder block and the crankshaft and the flywheel and the two plates on each side of the boiler and the one over the top, the rest of it is brand-new. We've had the boiler in steam before, but today is the day we're going to light the fire and see if it will all go round; that's the important thing.

With the engine out on the drive, Fred made one or two final small adjustments to the valves as he was getting steam up:

It's been like a long, hard twenty-seven years, I'll tell you. And every time, there were some unforeseen disaster. But I'm not the only guy doing this. There's dozens of them all over England in little sheds, trying hard with very little money. In my opinion, instead of giving it to these men with tight trousers who dance on stages, they should give a bit to the lads who are mending traction engines, because they are an unbelievable tourist attraction. I mean, in Dorset, there's a guy there who has I don't know how many million people come every year to a traction engine rally from all over the place.

By the time he'd had a break for the pies at lunchtime with Alf and Jimmy, the engine was steamed up.
Fred climbed up on to the footplate. 'Here we go,' he
said. 'Handle forward. Regulator open.' The engine
mechanism started to turn over. Fred beamed with
satisfaction at seeing everything in motion for the first
time and looked down to Alf, who was standing by the
side of it.

Alf's face was wreathed in a big smile. 'It's like a
Rolls-Royce,' he said. 'Magic!'

'Yeah, I'm quite pleased with that,' Fred replied.
'Really, when you think, all them years, and never
really knowing whether we were going to make it or
not. When you think we nearly made a new one.'

'We have made a new one,' Alf contended.

'No,' Fred said, 'there's a few bits that belong to Mr
Aveling and Mr Porter.' Fred stepped down from the
footplate to stand beside Alf and look at the engine.
'It doesn't seem that long ago that we were banging
away with the hammers,' he said. 'And now the worst is
over with. All we've got to do now is put the rear end
on and the wheels and the pipe work. When you think
we've had this boiler in three pieces and it's always a
bit of a worry whether you've got it back together
right.' Fred got back up on to the engine and gave one
long, triumphant blast on the whistle. But why had it
taken so long, I wanted to know. Fred had an instant
answer:

If I had an electric motor instead of a steam
engine driving me machinery, it would've taken

43

maybe a year or two less. But the other thing is that as soon as you light fires in boilers they seem to have some fatal attraction for people, who just come from nowhere. And of course, you can't stop talking, can you? You've got to talk to them. So I would say about half the twenty-seven years has been taken up with talking and not doing the job!

The engine was nearly finished but so, it appeared, was Fred. He continued to visit Christie's hospital for palliative care. However, on one of his visits there, he was given some information about two new drugs that were being tested, and they asked him if he would be prepared to take part in the clinical trials for them. I learned about the proposal the next day, when I was over at Fred's. When I arrived, he got me a brew and then showed me the papers he'd been given at the hospital. 'It's for some new-fangled Josef Mengele stuff they want to pump into me,' he explained, 'and because it's never been tested on humans before, they don't know the effects, but so far it's worked on animals.'

Whatever Fred's description, it was clear that here was a possible new cure that Fred was being offered. It sounded as though it might be a lifeline for him. Every time I'd seen him over the previous few months, Fred had told me about some new miracle cure for cancer he'd read about. Could this be the one that would work? The tests the hospital had asked him to take part in would take up most of the summer. They would involve frequent visits to Christie's hospital, with some overnight stays. Fred was thinking about it. Clearly, the trials offered him a glimmer of hope, but he wasn't too keen, especially as the doctors had emphasized that the tests were unlikely to be of any direct benefit to him. He would, they had explained, be taking part in the interests of medical research that might benefit cancer sufferers in the future.

Fred was weighing all this up against the fact that the one great ambition he had left to achieve before he died was to get the engine around the country for the new series he had been offered. He knew that time was short, and that if he didn't get it done that summer, he would never be able to do it. What if we tried to fit the filming around the tests? But Fred wasn't happy with this idea. What if the course of treatment had such bad side effects and made him so ill that he couldn't finish the filming schedule? What if he became bedridden and couldn't go to Buckingham Palace to receive the MBE he'd recently been awarded?

We talked it through, but I could see Fred had already made his mind up. He wanted to live the rest of his life doing exactly what he wanted to do, and that was travelling around Britain on his beloved steam engine, not being laid up in a hospital bed. He was determined to steam ahead with his farewell to his millions of fans, even though he was critically ill. He knew it would have been a difficult project even for someone in the best of health, but he was absolutely insistent.

I was uncomfortable with this. I sat at Fred's kitchen

table and tried to reason with him. If there was the slightest chance that the drugs he had been asked to test could give him even six more months to live, he should take part in the trials. I felt we needed to postpone the filming until at least he'd given it a go, but Fred wanted to get on with things as quickly as possible. Any delay now, he felt, would mean it would be too late. I said I'd try to find out a bit more about the drugs, and asked Leona, the researcher working on the series, to find out what she could. The results were not encouraging. Both drugs were in the very first stage of being tested on humans, and it was unlikely that there would be any benefits for those taking part in the trials. When I reported our findings to Fred, he almost seemed relieved. We were going to go ahead. Everybody close to Fred at the time assured me that this was what he really wanted. Finishing the engine and making this journey would give him a focus. It would be something to keep him going and keep his mind off the end. It was now a question of getting it done, so that Fred could achieve one of his last wishes.

By now, Fred had a fixed urinary catheter in place. This was bad enough in itself, but it was also causing him to catch bladder infections, so he kept having to go to the Royal Bolton Hospital for tests and for treatment to replace it. 'It was,' Sheila recalled, 'a strange, topsy-turvy time. One day we'd be off to Christie's, having more tests, being prescribed more medication, then the next day he'd be bounding round the garden with the strength of ten men, working long hours to get the engine finished.'

One of the final jobs that needed to be done before they could go out on to the road was to create somewhere for Alf to stand. The footplate had been designed only for one-man operation, but Fred was going to have Alf up there with him all the time as steersman. 'We made a platform for me to stand on for steering,' Alf remembered,

and it was just the right height for me. There were always that danger of your foot going in the big cog, because that weren't guarded, so Fred put a little lip on the front of the step so as you could put your toes against that and you couldn't go forward. Once we'd got that done, I remember the very first time we went out on the road. Fred said to me and Jimmy, 'There's a piece of plywood there, put that down at the front and I'll just run on to it.' So he did that; just poked it out of the shed. Then he said, 'There's another sheet there,' and I said to Jimmy, 'Just watch, he'll be up the drive and out on to the road next,' and he were. When he went out on to the road, the chains for steering the engine were very slack. He turned right at the top of the drive out on to the road. He was going along, and for some reason decided to turn right, where there was no road to turn into, and he nearly went through a bloody fence.

Fred wasn't going to let a little thing like this worry him. The long, difficult work of restoring the engine was nearly over. 'It's all practically finished now,' he said. 'The only things left to do are cosmetic, like the lagging round the boiler, beautifying it, in a way, but now we've got it to this nice stage where it will run, we might as well do all the testing before we put any guards on anything. Even when they made them, they used to take them out on the road and bang them through their paces before they put the finishing touches to them and the classy paint job that made them look a million dollars. So that's what we're going to do.'

2

Testing Times

The day had finally arrived when Fred was going to be able to take his tractor out on to the road and drive it around Bolton. 'Before we set off on this journey,' he said, 'I want to do a few road tests with it around the local area, and visit one or two people who've helped me with machining and engineering the bits that I couldn't really do myself. This should be good fun, I think. I'm looking forward to a fair turn of speed and no noise at all, silent as a Rolls-Royce.'

Fred's sons, Jack and Roger, lived on the Isle of Man, and his eldest, Jack, had come over for the big occasion. As Jack lit the fire and began to get steam up, Fred noticed there was a leak in the boiler. You could hear the irritation in his voice when he said:

Why is it that we steamed this boiler up about

fifteen times when it was just a boiler and it didn't leak? Then you put it back together again and everything starts leaking. If you could get at these leaks without half dismantling the engine it would be all right, but they're all in places it's impossible to get at. Still, it's basically all right, so we'll go and have a bit of a run round the neighbourhood to see how it performs.

But getting a traction engine out on the road isn't like getting your car out of the drive. There's hours of preparation involved, as Fred explained:

Being a traction-engine driver weren't an easy business. It weren't just a matter of climbing on the thing and setting off down the road. There's a lot of preparation before the thing even moves. Number one, you'd got to sweep the tubes. On average, there's thirty to forty 2-inch tubes running through the boiler of a traction engine, and if you don't clean yesterday's soot out of them, they don't steam very well. So that's one thing you've got to do bright and early. Then you've got to procure some sticks and an oily rag and get the fire lit and make sure there's enough water in the boiler. If there's no water in the boiler, you're in trouble. Then while the fire's raging away and boiling the water in the boiler, you proceed to go round with the oil can and, God forbid, there's dozens of little oiling points. Some only require oiling about once a week, but there's a lot of it needs doing daily when you're out on the road. Or maybe twice a day, and then you have to stop somewhere and oil it all again.

The whole procedure takes a couple of hours before we are actually able to set off. I can't think of anybody who's ever done it any quicker. Really trying and having done it for nearly forty years, it's still very temperamental. One day they'll steam really quick, the next it can take you hours. A lot depends on the weather as well; if the wind's blowing or it's raining. The coal's another terrible thing. Sometimes you get really good coal and it'll go for miles without putting any coal on, as though it's radioactive, and other coal's terrible. You open the door and shove it in, go about a mile down the road, open the door again and there's nothing there. It's all gone. There is less and less good coal. The people you buy it off don't really know where it's come from or what it is. It's marketed as steam coal, but you don't know until you've tried it out.

After two hours of preparation, the engine was ready for the road. With Jack on board as steersman, Fred drove it up the slope of his drive past his pit headgear and the green living van that he planned to tow around the country when the grand tour itself got started. At the top of the drive, Jack expertly negotiated the tight left-hand turn to get the engine through the gates. Father and son steamed off down the road, past the big Victorian houses that had been the homes of Bolton's mill owners. Just after they'd gone through the first set of traffic lights, Fred brought the engine to a halt opposite his local newsagent's. Jack ran over to the shop and came back with a packet of Polo mints for his dad. Fred never went anywhere without his Polos, which he crunched continuously, and today wasn't going to be an exception. After putting a mint in his mouth he was on his way again, down the hill towards the next set of traffic lights. He was out on the road on his engine for the first time, and it was going well. So what was it like to drive an engine like this?

Driving a traction engine is a fairly simple thing really. There's very important things you've got to watch, like the water level in the boiler. If you're an absolute raw recruit or a beginner and you put in for your driving test on the traction engine, the man who comes to do the test is happy as long as you can get round a corner, do a three-point turn and stop the thing. There's a lot more to it than that, though. I mean, they don't ask you about what would you do if the water's disappeared out of the bottom of the glass, which is very important, because a steam boiler is basically a bomb. This means that it's vital that it's kept full of water. If you don't have water in it, it can explode.

If you do reach that situation where you are out of water and there's no way of getting any water in the boiler, drive it up a banking so the front is up in the sky, so what water there is in the boiler will flood the top of the firebox and keep the fuseable plug in one piece. This is a fail-safe device within the firebox, a bronze plug with a lead core. If there is no water covering it, the lead melts and what's left of the contents of the boiler puts the fire out. But you're in a hell of a mess if you let that happen. It doesn't do the boiler any good. It doesn't do anything any good, so the water level is one of the all-important things.

To make the thing go, the equivalent of the accelerator in a motorcar is what's called the regulator. This is just a handle that basically opens the steam valve that lets steam into the cylinders or, in the case of the throttle on a car, lets petrol into the carburettor. It's exactly the same principle really. But an internal combustion engine is a very feeble thing compared with the power of steam. Steam is instant, but with a car you've got to get the revs up.

Then there's the braking system. There are no air brakes. Basically, the brakes are just big blocks of wood inside the rims of the rear wheels rubbing on two brake rings. The most sophisticated tractors, like this one, have sometimes got a flywheel brake. We've also got a foot brake, which is very helpful, because it stops it pretty quick. But the thing you've got to watch for is when you're approaching traffic lights and minding your own business and everyone's in a big hurry, like they always are. They want to pass you, and there'll be three cars stopped at the traffic lights and the guy behind you thinks there's enough room to get in there before you, so he pulls right in front of you, which is deadly. You've got to take violent action and put the engine in reverse. Then you've got to be smart because sometimes, if it's got full steam on, the bloody thing will start going backwards and there's somebody up your rear end. It's quite frightening. A lot of people who own these things don't go on the road. They're scared of actually getting among the modern traffic. But I've always found that if you don't do anything daft and you take your time, you're all right.

I've never had any real trouble in the middle of cities or towns, because you're going so slow other people can steer round you. The thing that causes the trouble is mainly the lax observations of motorists and other people. They're coming along, and they see this unusual machine, and their concentration goes. They'll stop at traffic lights, and some other guy at the back will see the same vision, and he'll forget that the traffic lights are on red and that there's a car there stopped and BANG. And really it's nothing to do with you at all. You're in the nearside lane; you're going 3mph, getting ready to stop, and yet there's been five grands' worth of damage done at the side of you because of lack of observation on the part of the motorcar driver.

When Fred was building the engine, the local scrap-metal merchants provided a lot of the materials he needed. 'If Fred could cadge things,' Alf said, 'that is what he would do. That's how he got on and got the engine built.' Fred himself said, 'There's ways and means . . . Various benevolent people have been very kind to me.'

One of Fred's favourite pastimes was to journey down to the local scrapyard, where you'd see him rooting around all sorts of boxes and skips, searching out little bits of brass and copper. The people who owned the scrapyard obviously thought a lot of him, because they never charged him, or if they did, it was coppers. So the first place he planned to visit that day was the local scrapyard. He wanted to let them see the finished engine, but he wasn't just going along for the ride. There were other reasons for his visit, as Fred explained. 'We're on our way to see a scrap-metal-dealing company who have a particularly fine set of weighing scales, where we can put the engine on and weigh it to the last couple of ounces. It's very important that you know how heavy the thing is. And it's always worth a visit, because when you get there, you never know what you're going to find.'

Fred made a right-hand turn across the oncoming traffic into the scrapyard. It was a big place, with piles of metal stacked all round the edges of the yard and a Portakabin office with a weighbridge in front of it. Fred drove the engine straight on to the weighbridge, parked up and went into the office. Jason, the scrapyard boss, told him that the engine was just over 8 tons.

'Just over 8 tons,' Fred repeated. 'Aye, well, that's all right! It won't take as much coal as the steamroller. You don't want paying, do you?'

Jason laughed. 'Do you ever pay?' he replied.

'There's a lot of your scrapyard in that engine, you know,' Fred said. 'Various pins, and all sorts of bits and pieces.' And he was still on the cadge, looking for a bar to make a driving pin for one of the wheels. 'Right!' he said to Jason. 'I'll just go and see if there's a piece of 3-inch bar down the end of the yard. See them pins in the back wheels, them big shiny ones? Well, there's one short on the other side. It doesn't really need it unless you are in the muck and you get stuck. So I'll go down there and have a look round, and if there is a piece, I'll come back and show it to you, like I normally do, and you'll wave to me through the window, then we'll disappear quick. All right?'

Jason was used to Fred's way of doing business and readily agreed to let him have a root around his yard. Fred left the office and started to search through a pile of scrap. As he did so, he talked about some of the things he'd got from the yard:

There's quite a lot of this engine and the things I used for building it has come out of this scrapyard. Even the hydraulic riveter; those great thick lengths of tubing for making the hydraulic riveter all came out of here. They're very good to me here. They never charge me; very benevolent people they are. That's why I've come, actually.

On this occasion, Fred didn't find what he was looking for, so he waved cheerily to Jason and drove the engine out of the yard and into the traffic that was flowing outside. Next stop was the place where Fred got most of the copper and brass for the engine. It was only just around the corner from the first scrapyard, but this place was a modern warehouse unit. As Fred steamed up, Mike, the owner, was standing in the car park ready to greet him. 'We brought some of your brass back!' Fred said as he climbed down from the engine.

'It's a fair machine!' Mike said admiringly, standing back and taking a look.

'Oh aye,' Fred said. 'There's a lot of your brass on here. I'll point a few bits out.' Fred walked round the engine with Mike by his side, pointing out all the brass and copper that he had contributed to the engine. 'The bottom of the whistle; a lot of the union nuts; they've all come out of your bronze bin. The metal that the lamps are made out of. All the metal that the taps are made out of all came out of this scrapyard. One of them lubricators on the crankshaft came from here. And there's a tap round the corner what we get the washing water out of; that's come from here. All the brass nuts and bolts have come from here. Even these greasers come out of this scrapyard, you know. People throw away stuff that they think is never going to be of any use in the modern world, but people like me can put it to good use in the old world!'

But Fred was always on the lookout for anything else that looked as though it might be useful for him, so he went into the warehouse and searched through containers filled to the brim with brass and copperware. It was an Aladdin's cave for Fred, packed full of treasure. 'We'll have all of England jealous if they see this lot in here,' he said. 'It's our secret collection of jewels and everything splendid.'

When Fred drove back home, there was a lot more traffic around. This was difficult for him, because everything about the engine was still very new. One of the things he was having to get used to was the speed. The traction engine went a lot faster than his steamroller, so there was a big learning curve for Fred. It was a much more fiery beast than *Betsy*. Then there was the newness of some of the parts. He found it difficult to change gear at first, because the gears were so new there was no wear on them. The edges of the cogs were newly machined and their edges were sharp and angular, so they didn't mesh together very easily. In spite of this, when Fred got back home after his maiden voyage he declared that he was very pleased with the engine: 'Today's been 99 per cent successful,' he said. 'The leaks are a bit worrying, but they're not that serious. Then there's one or two odds and sods that need seeing to, and then we'll be ready for our world tour, I would think! The only thing about it, though, is that in top gear it goes very fast, much faster than the steamroller, and I'm afraid to say, I'm not quite used to that yet. In fact, I nearly crashed through the neighbour's fence with it when I was getting it out the other day.'

As his dad talked about the engine, Jack drove it

over to a fire hydrant just over the road from Fred's
Victorian house and he and Alf began to fill the tank
on the tender with water. 'How do you know when it's
full?' I asked.

'When I get wet through,' was Alf's swift reply. 'I
had a shower this morning, but I might be having
another shortly, and this'll be a cold one.'

Fred came over to join them and explained that the
mechanical lubricator wasn't working properly. 'Even
when they first made this thing,' he said, 'it's likely that
the lads who took it out on a test run would have to
put up with all these sort of things that we're having
to put up with. I mean, basically, there's nowt wrong
with it. It bombs along at a great speed, the springs
work and the rest of it, mechanically, all works well. I
can't think of anything wrong other than the fact that
the gears are too bloody good a fit, so you can't get it
in gear. But when you think how nice it will be when
it's worn that bit; it'll be perfect. I mean now, low gear
you can get in, but high gear's a bit tough.'

Overall, the first day's road trials had been a great
success, and it was time for a celebratory drink. Ian
was standing by with a carrier bag full of cans of
Guinness. When Fred asked Jack to go over to the
house to get some glasses, Ian said they could drink it
out of the can. 'Oh no,' Fred responded. 'It's horrible
that. It's uncouth drinking out of tins. It's like drinking out of bottles.' Jack brought his dad a glass, and as
Fred poured his Guinness, Alf commented, 'A long
twenty-seven years, Fred.' As Jack and Alf drove the
engine back to the place where it had stood for so long

in the garden, Fred drank his Guinness and looked on contentedly. He had some more road tests planned for the next day. And this time it was going to be Alf's turn to get up there beside Fred and do the steering.

Next day, when we arrived at Fred's, the engine was steamed up and ready to go. Fred explained that on this little trip he was going to a local engineer's where they had machined the gears for the engine. It was the sort of engineering that was just too big for Fred to do with the machinery he had in his shed.

When Fred and Alf arrived at Metric Engineers, it didn't look like the sort of place that would disappear any time in the near future. It was a modern engineering works in a new industrial unit which had some very up-to-date machinery. As they drove into the yard at the front of the works they were met by the managing director, Malcolm Anderson, and Brian Haley, who did all the work on Fred's gears.

Malcolm wanted to know what sort of speed Fred could get out of the engine. 'We've had it up to 12mph this morning,' Fred told him proudly. 'It was quite hairy at that stage. It depends who's steering it. But yeah, it's quite good. I'm quite pleased with it. But it's got a few leaks. I think it needs a dose of porridge or something. Quaker Oats and red lead, they recommend, so I'm going to have a go at that. All where it leaks you can't get at it. They're all in right awkward places.'

Then Brian asked a key question which nobody had asked before. Did Fred like this one better than the other one? Fred deliberated. 'I don't know really.

I'm more confident with the other one, driving it. It's a bit hairy, this one. It doesn't stop, you know; with the brakes screwed on and everything, it's still going!'

'You'll get wet if it rains in this one,' Brian observed, alluding to the fact that the engine didn't have a cab. But Fred said he wouldn't. 'I'm going to make a roof for it,' he said. 'But I've not got a lathe long enough, so I might come to see you again.' Fred had been coming to Metric Engineers for many years for help and Alf listened as the three men talked about the jobs that had been done for Fred's engines here. Then they talked about Fred getting into trouble with the tax man for getting one job done in exchange for him bringing his ladders along and cleaning all the guttering out on their works. Bartering like that wasn't allowed, he was told. He should have invoiced them for his services and they should have invoiced him for theirs. 'What a world we're living in,' Fred observed.

Malcolm and Brian walked around the engine with Fred, looking at the parts they had made for him. They'd made the big iron rim on the flywheel, then Fred had got it red hot and shrunk it on in his garden. The biggest component they made for Fred was the gear wheel. Then they took it to the gear cutters, who put all the teeth on. 'And then,' Fred said, 'the gear cutters went bankrupt, so we can't go there any more.' Brian said it was because they'd done all that work for Fred for nothing.

After a bit more banter about payment for jobs they had done for Fred, he was on the scrounge again. He was still looking for the 3-inch rod he'd been searching for at the scrapyards the day before and wondered what they'd got in their scrap bin. There was clear affection for Fred and admiration for his engineering skills and what he had achieved in his back garden. 'Soon sort you out with that, Fred,' Brian said.

Fred turned to me and pointed out the gears. 'Brian here did all of this,' he said. 'And on the other side there's a great big one he made, and the actual worn-out original one is still hiding in a corner in this engineering works. We should go in and have a look at it to see what a mess it was when I first got this thing.' Inside the works, they found the old gear wheel standing against a wall in the corner. All the teeth around the outside of it were so worn down they looked round. 'I don't want it back, you know,' Fred said as they walked towards it. 'Yeah, when I think that, when I got it all them years ago, the teeth were all like that on every wheel. You can tell how many thousands of miles it must have done. They must have lost three-eighths of an inch off each side that's worn away. It's no wonder it sounds so much quieter now.'

On the way back home from Metric Engineers, it started to rain. Very soon, the engine was driving through a real downpour, and Fred and Alf were getting very wet. There was no time now to build the cab before setting out on the grand tour, so the engine driver and his steersman just had to hope for a good summer. But a bit of a soaking wasn't a problem for Fred. The engine was now doing 12mph. Fred was very pleased with its performance, and he was getting used to travelling at these high speeds. 'Basically, when you're steaming along the road, if the road's a good one and wide enough and everyone's getting by you, you can relax. It's a bit like driving a canal boat. The steering's very similar, a bit this way and a bit that way, but there's no signalling system on it. You've got to hang outside and put your hand out, like they did in the olden days.'

The only thing that Fred still wasn't happy about was the leaks. He thought they were getting worse. They were not dangerous, he said, but the trouble was trying to get rid of them. 'If I could get at them with a caulking chisel I could stop them in two minutes, but they are in such awkward places that if you start with unorthodox caulking, like trying to go round corners, you could make it worse than what it is already, so we might as well wait and see what Malcolm, the boiler inspector, has to say when he comes to see it. But there's nothing that is very serious, and at least mechanically it is very good.'

Over the next few days there were some last-minute preparations for the big trip. No living van can go out on the road without a touch of the sign writer's artistry, so Fred had got the best man he knew to come and do the job. It was a beautiful spring morning and, as the sign writer carefully painted 'The D'Arcy Lever Coal and Terracotta Company' in gold lettering on the side of the van, there were plenty of little jobs to keep everybody else occupied. Alf was busy cleaning the smoke tubes. As he pushed the long-handled wire brush down the length of each of the tubes, he explained that they get full of soot and you've got to keep them clean or else you start losing all the efficiency.

As we filmed Alf at work, Fred came over to join us. 'I've got the number plate on,' he said. 'First registered in 1921 by Devon County Council.' I asked him if he had to pay the same road tax as for a car, and Fred launched into a bit of the history of the traction engine:

You don't pay any tax now. We're actually exempt. Up till 1921, there was no taxation on traction engines and road rollers. Then they decided they should all be registered. Steam-rollers were five shillings; agricultural traction engines were the same as a farm tractor. It all rolled on like this for many years. Then in nineteen-fifty-something they abolished the tax on steamrollers. No doubt the paperwork cost more than the five bob they got in revenue, so they kicked it into touch. The thing is, they kept traction engines the same as farm tractors. Steam wagons and road locomotives, which is what this is, were the same as a motor car if they weren't being used commercially. If they were actually being used commercially, they had a rough trip. They had to have a different licence for every county they passed through, and some authorities wouldn't even allow them to go through during the hours of daylight. They had to go through in the dark, which was unbelievable hassle for them. I think the authorities were rather silly treating them like this, especially when you think they were the best road haulage vehicles we had, right up until modern times. All the heavy stuff that's scattered all over England like Lancashire boilers and blooming great cast-iron anvil blocks for steam hammers were all dragged around the country by traction engines. The motor wagons of the period around 1920 didn't have half the guts that one of these things had. But by 1930 the diesel engine was catching up, and they made a diesel tractor that pulled 100 tons, which put paid to these men overnight. For 100 tons you had to have two of these things, one at the front and one anchored at the back to stop it when you came to a big hill, because there were lots of terrible disasters going down big hills.

Just having lived at the end of traction engines being used commercially, some of them were in a hell of a state. The council steamroller would be encrusted with so much grease, coal dust and oil that you couldn't see any of the rivets or anything like that. You look back at the picture books, and every time they stopped they had the oily rag out, giving it a rub. But that came to an end. The last steam vehicles to be used on the road commercially were steamrollers, and that's why kids now refer to a diesel roller as a steamroller, because they don't know the difference. The thing is, they kept them going up to the mid-1960s, because the old guys who drove them were ready for retiring, and they'd come to an agreement with them that when the tubes went in the boiler, that was it. The drivers were finished, and they sent their rollers off to the scrapyard and that were the end of it.

The road tests had been a great success, but Fred's engine still wasn't quite finished. Although it could be driven along the road, there were important jobs that still needed to be done. 'There should have been guards on it covering the gear wheels,' Jimmy recalled. 'We took the old ones to a place at Atherton to have some new ones made, but we didn't get them in time. But we only took them a week before we started on the road. Health and Safety would have had a field day if they'd seen it with them gears whizzing round. Me and Alf kept saying, "Let's get all these things done, and then we can try it out."' But Fred couldn't wait to get out on the road with it and he talked about it all the time:

We're ready now for a good run outside pulling the living van, because really we've never had the van behind it. A few weeks ago, we towed the Land Rover with it some distance, and it performed very well. I reckon that was a couple of ton. The living van, even though it looks very bulky, is only made of sticks of wood, and there's not much weight in it. The wheels are exceptionally beauti-ful; they've got double roller bearings in them. When you jack it up and spin one of the wheels round, it keeps going for about three minutes before it finally stops. It's dead easy to pull, whereas the running gear of a Land Rover must be awful – all them gears and prop shafts and all that, trying to drag round. The thing is, we can't go anywhere without the living van, because it's like a support vehicle. We've got the tool box, the coal, the brewing-up tackle, the beds – everything you need is in the living van, and you can't play about with one of these without any support vehicle. A lot of them have their wife or their uncle coming behind, and everything's chucked in cars or a two-wheel trailer, but that doesn't quite look right. And if it comes on raining, you've got your own mobile home and you can just stop at the side of the road and have a brew until the rain stops.

Journeying the length and breadth of Britain, the traction-engine men of old would have been on the road for days at a time, and the living van would have been their home. This is the way Fred wanted to do things on his journey. It's certainly the way he would have done it five years earlier, when he was still in good health.

When we were planning the logistics of the journey and the way it would be filmed, I discussed this with Fred. First of all, did he really want to do the whole journey for real and stay in the living van? 'Aye, well, I would,' he said, 'depending on whereabouts we were and the degree of safety for the engine. I wouldn't just leave it at the side of the road. Some engine men in the olden days used to just jump off and leave their engines by the side of the road and go straight into the pub. I've seen that happen when I were a little lad. Their engines were all filthy and oily, and nobody cared about anything. With the steamroller, over the years, I've slept at the side of the roadway. You just pull up when you're tired and worn out and call in the pub for a pint or two and then retire to bed in the shed.'

As I talked to him, it was clear that Fred would like to have stayed in the living van in a lay-by or outside a pub each night, but we agreed that, given his state of health and the demands of a filming schedule, he would need to be booked into hotels with the rest of the crew and secure parking would have to be found for the tractor. Then we started to look at the rest of the logistics for filming with a traction engine. Arrangements always have to be made with places we film well in advance, and schedules have to be kept to. But how fast would the traction engine go? How much coal would it need, and where would we get it from? How many water stops would the engine need? Because it was new and Fred hadn't been out on it before, it was all a bit unpredictable. He'd only really got the roller to go on: 'The steamroller will do about 12 miles on a tankful, and then you're at rock bottom – boiler's empty and tank's empty – but this is a different kettle of fish. According to the book, it says it's capable of doing 50 miles on one fill-up of water. But we shall have to see.'

Fred reckoned that the engine would do at least 12mph, so we based all our schedules on that speed, and he thought the journey would take about four months. 'You don't want to be rushing,' he said. 'You know, there's some quite long journeys involved in it, but it'll be uneventful, other than waving to people as they pass by, which happens a lot. Then there's always the unplanned; things happen, like getting invited into people's houses, which can be quite dangerous. You end up pouring whisky down your throat. It's happened to me before. "Just bring it round to our house," people would say, "so we can take a picture of it in front of the house," and then you ended up at a party. I've even been invited into weddings.'

We also needed a low loader to transport the engine between locations. I talked to Fred about it, and he recommended Alan Atkinson. Alan was a long-standing friend of Fred's, a fellow steam enthusiast from Preston, who owned a roller and a steam wagon. His company, Atkinson Trailer Hire, had just the sort of vehicles we needed, and Alan had, in the past, transported Fred's roller to various rallies up and down the country. When we asked Alan to provide the transport for the tractor, he was pleased to join the team.

The low loader would cover the long distances between locations, but there was still going to be a lot of driving for the tractor, and getting round under the power of steam wasn't going to be easy. An engine like this wasn't really designed to be driven in modern-day traffic. Fred explained the problem:

When these engines were made, the traction engine were basically king of the road. They were the biggest things that came down the street at any one time, and everything got out of the way of this thunderous monster that 'ad smoke billowing out of it. But as time 'as gone by and we've got into the modern world, you've got to be on your toes in modern-day traffic, because these things don't stop quickly. You need a few yards to stop if you're going at 7 or 8mph.

In the olden days, the driver's instruction book of Norman E. Box's Lancashire Steam Road Rolling Company, Broadheath, Manchester, actually tells you which towns won't let you do what. Some towns wouldn't let you go through during the hours of daylight. You had to wait outside town till it were dark before you could pass through with a traction engine or a road roller. It also told you when you were able to use the horse troughs in each place, because in them days there was an abundance of horse troughs. There's hardly any mention of hydrants. They had to ring the borough engineer and say, 'I work for Norman E. Box Steam Road Rolling Company and can I come through Heywood or wherever on the twenty-third of what have you?', and it's got in the book, 'Approaching Heywood at the summit there's an horse trough that can be used for filling up traction engines.' It's all in the book. There's unbelievable things in it, like 'In case of an accident, on no account must you speak to the police. Ring head office straight away.' That's incredible. You mustn't mention anything to the cops.

We've no problems with that, and we won't have any problems getting water. We're going for a new pipe for the water lifter before we set off, and we've got a stand pipe for hydrants. Now, you're supposed to have some sort of licence for messing about in hydrants, but I think, if we can have a talk with United Utilities, who I think are in charge of hydrants, we'll be OK. Them hydrants are very important things. If you live in a house and the water people haven't been round and lifted the lids off the hydrants near you for ten years, all the mud off the road, with the traffic and rain, washes down and goes through the little holes on the top. Eventually they finish up filled up with mud right up to the top, and it can be years before anybody goes near the damn thing. Then you arrive on your steamroller and you lift the lid up, and it's just mud in there. It's very unpleasant. So you roll your sleeves up and put your hand down and feel if there's anything at the bottom, and there you can feel the cock that works the hydrant. So what you do then is put the tap handle down, turn it on and blast all the mud out, so you've actually done the fire brigade and the water company a favour, because when you've done this and turned it off in a neat and orderly manner and you've only had a few gallon of water, you've cleaned out the hydrant for them free of charge.

Any man with a steam engine that needs a drink when he's going along the road should be allowed to get a bit of water free of charge. That to me is fair and a good service to the water company.

I do know one lad who got fined. He lifted the lid off to put the key on in the middle of Lancaster and the bloody thing broke and water was squirting up into the sky in the middle of Lancaster, but he'd got the road blocked, so he had to move off and leave it in full flow. He couldn't do anything about it, so I think they sent him a bill for a few quid.

In planning the trip we also needed to know about coal: how much was going to be needed and where we were going to be able to get it. Again, it was a bit of an unknown thing for Fred, because he'd never done any real journeys on this engine. He only had the roller by way of any comparison:

From here to Manchester on the roller you'd get through about two and an half hundredweight of coal, so I would think this, with a good fire on it, would get practically all the way to Manchester. It's got a very big firebox, and the reason for this is that it was made for the export market and they might have had to burn any old rubbish – wood, straw, anything you could shove inside it that would burn. So if we get stuck miles away from any coal supply we'll be able to burn wood, any-thing – rubbish, fences!

Fred was clearly looking forward to his grand tour

and couldn't wait now to set out. The idea of going to Buckingham Palace to receive his MBE on the engine was particularly appealing. 'I don't know what the Queen will say,' he grinned, 'even though there are pictures of Aveling and Porter machinery at the front of Buckingham Palace. That's why, on the brass plate, it has the royal letters patent. Aveling's rollers rolled all the gravel at the front of the palace in the 1890s or 1900s.'

The traction engine was now ready for the road. As Alf cleaned out the smoke tubes in preparation, he reflected on the work that had been done on the engine:

The more you get into it, the more you get interested in seeing it actually running. We've now got it on the road. It's had a test run and it runs all right, no problems, and it's beautiful and it's an achievement. And it's enjoyable with Fred on the platform driving. He's very easy to get on with. No problem. Never fell out or owt like that.

Oh aye, and now I'm going on this holiday with him. Aye, he's invited me to accompany him. That'll be a once-in-a-lifetime opportunity. I'm really looking forward to that. I'm the steersman! I've no doubt he'll show me how to drive the thing properly in the course of the next weeks and months. I've already had a go at steering, and I've been on the steamroller with him as well, but I think there's a bit more love in this, because I've actually helped to put it together, and it is a marvellous machine. Everybody who sees it says so. Everybody loves it. 'Course I'll have a running commentary off Fred. I'm really looking forward to that. That'll be something else. That really will.

But before Fred could set off on the grand tour proper, there was an even more important hurdle to overcome – the boiler test. It was scheduled for Tuesday 4 May – the week before the start of the journey. Fred was up early to get the engine steamed up in time for the arrival of the boiler inspector. He'd got the engine parked outside his shed, and as he lit the fire in the early-morning rain, he talked about the inspection:

This is the big moment. After twenty-seven years of uncertainty, hard labour and some horrible periods, we've finally got it so that it will run, and this morning is the big test. The boiler inspector is coming here to see it blowing off, and if he's happy he'll authorize us to go and get the thing insured. It's already passed its hydraulic test, which means we pumped it full of water up to the required pressure, and the inspector has already given it a thorough examination when he came here for the first part of the test and stripped the kit right down. That was a long process that involved removing the mud holes and using mirrors to look inside the boiler. The inspector works for the insurance company, and what he's doing this morning is the steam test, which involves steaming the engine up to full pressure and checking the safety valves blow at the correct pressure. Once he's done this he'll be able to give it the final go-ahead.

Fred was trying not to show it, but he was worried about the engine passing the boiler test, because he knew that this was make or break for the whole show. He was under enormous pressure, and everybody who was there to film the morning's events remembers he was very panicky. Nobody had ever seen him like this before. Then, just before the inspector arrived, there was a particularly tense moment for Fred. He looked distraught as he explained what the problem was:

We've got some steam coming from underneath the lagging on the cylinder block which should not be. It could be one of two things: a crack in the cylinder block, which is disastrous, or water that's accumulated on a ledge when we hydraulic tested it. I've been frightened like this before, when I were a beginner. On me roller I had all the lagging round the boiler, and I'd done a hydraulic test, and then there was steam coming out everywhere. It turned out it was all the bloody water trapped inside the lagging that was turned into steam by heat from the boiler. I'm hoping that this is what has happened here, so I'm going to just lift up the lagging and see where that steam's coming from. If it's coming out of a hole, we're in trouble.

Fred looked worried as he investigated. 'I've got to look in here,' he said, taking the cover off the cylinder. There was great relief written all over his face when he found a little pool of water about half an inch deep. This indicated that it was a false alarm. Fortunately, there was no problem. 'There's no leak,' Fred announced. 'The steam's coming from water that has accumulated under the boiler.' It was no great surprise that there wasn't any major problem at this stage. Fred was a good boiler-maker, acknowledged by many in the boiler-making fraternity as the best amateur in the country. He had a great fund of knowledge and expertise, and as he waited for the pressure to build up, he shared some of it with us:

A lot of people have the idea that there is sealant on all of the seams on a boiler, but this isn't the case. Instead, all of them have to be caulked. The business of caulking the seams on a boiler is one of the most important parts of the boiler-maker's job, because a boiler is made up of iron plates that have rivets holding them together. There's nothing in between the plates, so however tight you get the two plates pulled together with the rivets, you still get minute gaps between them. The boiler-makers of old used to leave their new boilers out in the rain, and of course rust and God's natural ways filled the joints and made them steamproof. But this could take months and months, and the business of caulking speeded it all up. What you do is put a blunt-ended chisel on the joint and tap it with a hammer. The secret is tapping gently; not too much, because if you 'it it too hard you're forcing the plates apart, which is bad news, so it's a business of just lightly tapping. In the days of Robert Stephenson, they would have to do exactly the same, but they had a much rougher trip because they hadn't got wonderful rollers for forming all the plates. If you go to the museums and look at these early locomotives, they did it all with big hammers. You can see they are all cobbled over with big hammer marks. It must have been very difficult for them; they must have had many a royal battle trying to stop the leaks, and of course they put chemicals in, and horse urine and stuff like that, to get the corrosion going and stop the leaks.

As he talked, Fred was constantly checking the pressure gauge on his engine. He explained that the insurance man would want to see it blowing off at the safety valves at 150psi. 'Just at present,' he said, 'the safety valves are screwed down to withstand 300psi, so when we get to our required pressure, I'll start slackening the nuts off and then we'll start blowing off.'

It was late morning when Malcolm Finlayson, the boiler inspector, arrived. It was still raining, and as he walked down the drive under a big golf umbrella, Fred went to greet him. There's quite a lot of paperwork that comes with a steam engine, and all of this has to be checked before an engine can be insured. Malcolm had already inspected it all, so he handed it back to Fred. Then, not wanting to duck the issue, Fred took the inspector to see the worst of the leaks. It was one that had been just about impossible to get at with a caulking tool. Malcolm had a look at it. He wasn't unduly worried about it, but he did say that it would have to be sealed up. Fred thought he'd got the answer to the problem. 'Well,' he said, 'we'll give it a dose of Quaker Oats and what have you or something like that, and see what happens.'

Once the inspector had looked at the leaks, it was time for the main part of the inspection. 'We'll go and have a look at the needle,' Fred said, 'because it must be getting towards 150 now.'

Malcolm looked at the pressure gauge. 'Yeah, you're almost up to pressure now,' he said to Fred. 'You just have to set the safeties to 150, and if you release the pressure we'll see what happens.' They had to wait around until the pressure was right, and Fred seemed to be getting a bit impatient. If the engine didn't pass the boiler test, there would be no road trip and no series. It would have been the end of Fred's dream. But there was no need to worry.

Fred adjusted the safety valves so they lifted at the correct pressure of 150psi. Everything worked perfectly, and Malcolm was happy with what he saw. His last job was to have a look at the front tube plate to see that there was no water fizzing out from there. Fred opened up the inspection door on the front of the boiler and Malcolm shone a torch in and had a good look down into the heart of the boiler. Again, he was happy with what he saw. Fred's workmanship was perfect. 'There's nothing there, Fred,' he said as he turned from the engine. 'That's OK, there's no leaks at all there. And that completes it really. If you do those small alterations and get that leak stopped, you should be all right; I should be able to sign you off.'

'Now then,' said a happy-looking Fred. 'It's pie time.'

After the pies, Fred rubbed the engine down and reflected on the significance of that morning's events:

Now that we've passed our boiler insurance test, it's very good. I didn't really have any doubts, but you don't know about the inspector, whether he's going to let minor leaks go or whether he's going to insist on them being mended before he issues you with a certificate. But he's a good boiler inspector; he's a nice chap. He looked at the leaks, as I call them. A lot of people would maybe go, 'Tut tut,' but as far as boilers go it's not that bad; it's not squirting out steam, only little blobs of water, which eventually will seize up. They'll stop when a bit of rust gets going. When they made these boilers in the olden days they used to leave them out in the rain for a week or two to let the rain run round all the edges of the rivets so they got the rust going and then they cleaned them up and painted them. When you look at pictures of Horwich Locomotive Works, there's row upon row of brand-new boilers all out in the rain, and you can tell they are brand-new, because they've all got white lines painted on them marking out when they made the thing. They were obviously there to get the weather into the minute crevices. Really, a hole with a blob of water on it is as big as a fly's leg, it's that fine. And, naturally, holes like that would seize up pretty quickly.

After the boiler test, there was one more job that Fred had to do that afternoon before he could set off. To keep their tanks full of water, the traction-engine men of old used to use a water-lifter suction hose. This enabled them to get water from any horse trough they went past or from lakes and roadside streams when they were out in the country. Fred needed to get one for the journey, and he explained where he was going for it:

Before we set out on the journey proper, I'm going to have to go down to Manchester to get a water-lifter suction hose that I'm having made for the engine. The place I'm going to this afternoon is S. Redfern & Co. They manufacture large industrial hoses that are custom-designed and hand-made. The actual hoses that were made for traction engines were wire and fabric with a spring inside them, and you really need one of these things. You could be in the country and a long way away from any hydrants, and if you hadn't got this facility it were bad news. When you need water and there are no hydrants around, you stop anywhere where there is water that can be sucked up. It's the engine itself that does the work. The steam in the boiler goes into the water lifter and sucks up the water out of a river or a pond. But it's limited, because I think it's only about 25 feet that atmospheric pressure will push water up a pipe. The hoses you need to do the job are pretty hard to find, and we are very lucky having Redfern's on our doorstep, where they make them. The water-lifter suction hoses they make are designed for steam traction engines, and I believe they're the only company left still manufacturing them. They use traditional manufacturing methods, making the hoses in more or less the same way as they did seventy or eighty years ago.

Fred headed off to Redfern's in his Land Rover with Alf and Jimmy to see his hose being made. While they were there, they found out a bit more about the manufacturing process from supervisor Maurice Fox. As they watched an operator wrapping layers of rubber and nylon fabric around a steel tube, Maurice explained that they bought in the rubber in sheets and cut it on an ancient machine called a bias cutter. Their machine is the only one of its kind to have survived the Manchester Blitz. At this stage, the rubber is not in a cured state, which means that it has not been vulcanized. This is done after the rubber and the nylon fabric have been wrapped around the tube. Then the hoses are placed on trays in a steam autoclave, the doors are closed, the pressure is raised and it takes one to two hours to vulcanize. When it is removed, they take the cloth wrapping off, and the steel tube that the rubber has been wrapped around is removed, leaving the vulcanized rubber hose. All that remains to be done after this is to attach the appropriate connecting fittings for the specific engine the hose has been made for.

After the explanation, Fred, being Fred, had to have a go at making the hose himself. With the operator standing by, he wrapped the tube for his own hose by operating the hose-making machine – the machine that turns the steel tube round. It was like a lathe, specially adapted, with foot pedals to stop and start it. No trouble for Fred, and he was soon wrapping the steel tube with the rubber strips as if he'd been doing the job for years.

The hose they were making for Fred had an internal diameter of an inch and a half, and Fred had brought a couple of connectors along with him to fit this size. The problem was, he hadn't been able to find a nut that would fit either of them. 'Not to worry,' he was assured by Maurice. 'I'm sure we can find one for you.' The idea was that Fred would be able to take the completed hose home with him, but after searching their stock, they couldn't find any connectors that were suitable for Fred's engine. They promised to have one for him by the next day.

When we got back to Fred's, he said he would now go ahead and have the engine insured. It was only then that I realized that he'd had the engine out on the road for the road tests around Bolton without any insurance, and we'd been filming him on it! I didn't dare contemplate what the consequences would have been if he'd had an accident. Fred was never a great one for paperwork, and he still needed to do a lot of tinkering about with the engine before he set off on his trip. The insurance needed to be sorted out urgently, so Fred gave the engine number and the insurance company details to my daughter Kathryn, who was the production manager for the series. I was confident that she would get it all sorted out in time.

3

First Days on the Road

It was the second week of May 2004. Having passed its boiler test and performed well on its road tests around Bolton, Fred's traction engine was now ready for its grand tour. But first of all there were some more local trips to make. Coal would power the tractor's journey around Britain, but as there weren't any coal merchants left in Bolton, the destination for the first day out on the road was an open-cast mine between Wigan and St Helens.

According to the filming schedule we had drawn up for the day, we would be travelling from Fred's house in Bolton to the Crock Hey Open-cast Mine near Ashton-in-Makerfield. On the way, we would be stopping in Westhoughton and Abram at old pits. The plan was for Fred to stop at the sites of these closed-down collieries and tell us something about the history of coal mining in this part of Lancashire. Then he would stock up with coal for his journey at the open-cast mine before driving the engine back home that night.

The following day, Fred was going to set out from home again, to visit Astley Green Colliery Museum, and return home that afternoon before heading for Cumbria the following week on the tour proper. Each of the return journeys we had planned for these first two days was about 30 miles long. Fred estimated that, even if the engine only did 10mph, he'd be able to do each journey comfortably in the day and do all the filming that was needed at each location.

It all seemed feasible but things got off to a bad start. The coal that was going to be collected for the trip had to be stored in the living van, so that morning, the engine was going to tow 'the shed', as Fred always called it, for the first time. But first Fred had to get the van out of his garden, where it had been standing for over a year, and that wasn't easy. The van was parked on a ledge just above his pit bank. It was tricky to move it because there was a big drop on one side and the ledge projected at right angles on to Fred's steeply sloping drive. He was going to hitch the van up to the engine to pull the van off the ledge and turn it on to the drive to get it out on to the road. It shouldn't have been too difficult, especially with Alf and Jimmy on hand to help, but it was. There was a problem with the brakes, and this started to cost us valuable time. Fred had fitted new brake linings, and when the van went backwards as he tried to manoeuvre it off the ledge, they were locking on. He couldn't get the van off the ledge and on to the drive.

Fred couldn't believe it. Everything about the engine was in good order, but here they were being delayed because the brakes on the van wouldn't work. For over an hour, there was a lot of pulling and shoving. But everything had to be done carefully: one false move and the van would have toppled over, and we couldn't afford any damage being done to the van.

Fred produced an oil can and applied some oil to the brake linings, which helped. It unlocked the linings, making the van much more manoeuvrable, but there was still the problem of negotiating the turn from the ledge on to the drive. It was all getting a bit tense, and the clock was ticking on, cutting down the time for our journey to the open-cast mine. Each time Fred tried to pull the van, it looked as though it was in grave danger of turning over. Then Fred had a brainwave. He produced a block and tackle from his shed, hitched it to the living van and attached it to a tree on the opposite side of the drive. It did the trick. With one big pull, he got the engine on to the drive.

From there, it was easy, and at last, after a two-hour struggle, the van was out on the road. As he parked the engine with the living van in tow outside his house, Fred said, 'I'm knackered, and we've not set off yet. But, after a few trials and tribulations, at long last we're ready for our epic journey. The first thing we need is plenty of coal. It used to be full of coal mines round here. Now I've got to go all the way over to the other side of Wigan to get my coal.'

It was twelve o'clock before they got going: three hours behind schedule. Sheila stood at the front door and waved as they set off. Alf was at the wheel as they drove past the railway station and out to the other side of Bolton. The traction engine was a fine sight. Cars hooted and passers-by waved as it chugged across town, but they soon had a problem. Whichever way you go out of Bolton, it's all uphill. It was an early test for the engine, and straight away it was struggling. A long line of cars built up behind as it crawled up the hill past the gable ends of the red-brick terraced houses and on past the mosque on the way up to Daubhill, or 'Dobble', as Fred and Alf always pronounced it. It laboured along St Helens Road at not much more than walking pace; not a very good start.

Jimmy was crawling along behind in his car. He'd got his hazard warning lights flashing to warn drivers of the slow-moving engine ahead, but the irate drivers at the end of the half-mile queue that had built up didn't need any warning of the hold-up. Crock Hey mine was only about 14 miles from Bolton, so on paper it looked as though it was going to be simple enough to get there and back in a day, but it was already clear that, at this rate, we would never do it. The earlier plan to stop off along the way at the site of a couple of former collieries was certainly going to have to be shelved.

This was the engine's first real test, so a few teething troubles were to be expected, but this was slower than anybody could have imagined. Only a mile and a half from the centre of Bolton, Fred could see that some roadside adjustments were needed. He brought the engine to a halt. Pressure was low, and it just didn't have enough power to get it up the hill at anything other than a crawl. Fred looked disconsolate. 'We've run out of steam and run out of water,' he said. 'I mean, that's a big hill for a traction engine. From now on, it's all downhill and it's fairly flat, so if we can get the boiler full of water again we should be in with a chance. But it's performing very poorly even with 150 on.'

Then Fred remembered that on the road tests they'd had a bit of a problem with the mechanical lubricator, a device fitted to a steam engine to feed lubricating oil into the cylinder. 'Did we ever do anything with that mechanical lubricator?' he asked. ''Cos it isn't working! There's no oil going in the cylinder, so it's, like, running dry. It's not good, you know. If you did that with your motorcar, it wouldn't get very far. It'd start making squishy noises and stop.'

Fred got down from the engine and took a spanner from the tool box to make some adjustments before setting off again. But they'd only got a few miles down the road when they had to stop once more. They'd reached Atherton, about 4 miles from Bolton. Close by was the site of Pretoria pit, the scene of Lancashire's worst ever mining disaster. Three hundred and forty men and boys died there in an explosion four days before Christmas in 1910. It was the third worst mining disaster in British history. Today, all that remains is a memorial on the site of the colliery. Fred wanted to go to pay his respects and to tell the story of the disaster and of the bravery of the rescuers. But there was no time to make the short detour.

Instead, I told Fred, we would go there and film with him later in the year so that it could be included in the series.

The engine was standing by the side of the road, in a residential area. Soon a small crowd had gathered around, and a friendly local policeman and woman drew up in their van to have a chat. Fred wanted to have another look at the mechanical lubricator and decided that, this time, it would be better to get the ladder out of the living van to have a proper look at it. As Alf went for the ladder, Fred got down from the engine, laughing. 'Traction engine,' he said. 'Donald were right, you know. Should've sold the lot and bought a stamp collection. You can carry it about in your back pocket. An' it's worth just as much money.'

For the benefit of the police and the growing crowd of onlookers, Fred explained that he was having trouble with the mechanical lubricator. 'It's not functioning,' he said, 'and that could make it hard work for the pistons and the slides, so we're going to lift it up a bit and see if it makes any difference.'

Progress was now a little bit better, because the big hill was behind us and the engine was now travelling on the flat. It was a warm, sunny afternoon, and it was all waves and smiles from the passers-by and toots on car horns as Fred and Alf made their stately progress past the rows of terraced houses that lined the roads between Bolton and Wigan. Fred was even beginning to enjoy himself. 'This is the life,' he shouted above the noise of the engine as he steamed along. 'Life on the open road. You see why they invented diesel engines. These things weren't really designed to be driven in traffic like this. And 11 tons moving at around 10mph doesn't stop in a hurry.'

Fred was being a bit generous in his estimate of the engine's performance, as it still wasn't going at much more than walking pace. But whatever the speed, it was hot, thirsty work; time for some refreshments. Fred spotted a pub that he'd been to before. 'It's all right here,' he said as we approached. 'I once camped out here with Sue [his second wife].' He parked the engine up by the side of the road opposite the pub and sounded surprisingly upbeat about the progress they were making. 'Things aren't going too bad,' he said. 'We're still having a bit of bother with the mechanical lubricator. It's the ball that works the ratchet wheel. There's not quite enough travel in it. If it moved a bit further, it would go in the next notch.' But how was it looking now for getting round Britain was what I wanted to know. 'It might take a bit longer than we thought it would,' was Fred's reply. 'The thing is, I've really not got used to it yet, but there's definitely something mechanically wrong. It should go better than it is doing. On the level, it's all right. It bounces along. But as soon as it comes to a hill, even with full pressure on, it slows up, and that's not a good sign at all.'

It was time to go over the road to the pub and sit outside in the sun with a well-earned pint. 'How many miles have we come?' Alf wanted to know. It was generally agreed that they must have come 8 to 10 miles. By this time, we were scheduled to be at the open-cast mine we were heading for, but we were nowhere near it. Instead we were close to another of the colliery sites we had planned to visit. Fred had always had a great interest in mining disasters, and Maypole Colliery at Abram was the site of another of them. On 18 August 1908 there was an explosion there, caused by a mixture of coal dust and gas. Seventy-five men and boys died, and only seven bodies were recovered. The remains of the others are still underground. There were whole families in which all the menfolk were wiped out. Buildings over a mile away were shaken by the blast, which completely destroyed the engine house and blew the headgear away. The only way of dealing with the fire that raged below ground was by flooding the pit, and over 100 million gallons of water were poured down it. Fred wanted to visit the site to have a look at the stone memorials to the disaster victims but, again, time was against us. We would have to come back later in the year.

Fred was disappointed, but as he sat in the sunshine with his pint, he was able to look on the bright side. 'All things considered, we're not doing too bad,' he said. 'It's only half past three. But 10 miles on that thing and, believe me, you're ready for a pint, even though it's very quiet and you can talk and all that. One thing I don't like, though, is the springing. The steamroller is dead smooth, but that thing, when you go over a bump, it really shakes you up.' In spite of the lateness of the hour and all the problems they'd been having, Fred was still optimistic that they'd reach the open-cast mine. 'They might all have gone home,' he said, 'but we'll get there. Bloody good pint this.' But

Fred wasn't as happy with the performance of his engine as he was with his beer. It was his first proper day out on the road, the day he'd been looking forward to for so many years, and the engine had been a disappointment, as he made clear when he talked about its performance:

> To me, it's gutless. Mind you, it's made to run on 200psi and we're running it on 150, and I've had words with various people who say it's bad news when you've not got 200 on. They don't want to know. I rather think that thing would go anywhere with 200 on, but we haven't got it, so we've just got to struggle a bit at least while we've got these little blobs. I'm going to put another packet of Quaker Oats in it. It has a tendency to bubble up and it goes into all the little orifices. At least, that's the theory. Even as far back as Richard Trevithick, his boiler needed a dose of red lead and oats. Potato peelings are all right as well.

By the time Fred had finished his pint, a crowd had gathered around the engine parked up on the other side of the road – a bit of excitement for everybody on a quiet summer afternoon – and the cameras were all out as the engine chuffed off down the road. But they didn't get very far, and they'd only gone a mile or so when they had to stop again.

It was another small hill that was causing the problem, and the engine just hadn't got the power to get up it. 'I've never been as embarrassed in my life,' Fred said as the engine ground to a halt yet again. 'The steam-roller would have been halfway up the hill by now.'

It was tea time and they were still 4 or 5 miles away from the open-cast mine. This time, Fred just couldn't get the engine going. The problem was that it had come to a stop in top gear. Fred decided they would have to put the blower on to raise the pressure and get a bit more power. That extra 50lbs, Fred said, would definitely make a difference. But how soon would he be able to get the extra on and get it up to the 200psi he wanted? Fred shook his head wearily. He just didn't know.

Then a surprise visitor came to join the crowd that had gathered. It was Stuart, the owner of the open-cast mine they were heading for. He'd shut up shop for the day and come home for his tea so, even if they reached the mine, they weren't going to get any coal that day, especially as there was another hill ahead. Fred asked him if there was a good pub near his pit. The reply was in the affirmative, so the next thing Fred wanted to know was whether it had a good car park where they'd be able to park the engine for the night. Again the answer was yes. That was good enough for Fred. He knew now where he had to get to before nightfall. 'We'll see you about midnight then!' Stuart joked.

'Eh?' Fred questioned. 'It's not that bloody far, is it? Have you come across those old workings yet?' Fred got excited when Stuart told him they had. 'Hey, that's interesting,' he said. 'Old workings. Ones that nobody's been to in a hundred years. Yeah, we'll go and have a look. That'll be good, that. We'll see you tomorrow.'

But Fred clearly couldn't contain his excitement at the thought of seeing these old workings. 'Are they good?' he wanted to know. 'Can you see the tunnel? Are they full of water?' He was full of questions for Stuart, but he couldn't get away from the problems he was having with his engine. He turned his attention back to it and announced to the crowd that had gathered round, 'It's very poor. The bloody steamroller would lick the arse off it. There's something up with it somewhere. We're going to have to look into things.' Then, looking at the pressure gauge, he told everybody, 'Another midge's wotsit and it'll do.'

Stuart was still standing by the engine. 'You didn't know we were coming, did you?' Fred said to him. 'It was supposed to be a surprise visit!' Then, turning to me and the crew, he said, 'He gives me coal, this lad, you know. I don't have to pay for it, he gives it me. He's got a big mountain of it: a coal mountain.'

When Stuart took his leave, the engine still hadn't built up enough pressure to get started. 'Might as well have a rest,' Fred said philosophically, but after another couple of minutes they were ready to move off. Fred knocked the blower off and got the engine started. Then with a healthy chuff, chuff, chuff, it was on its way up the hill with a queue of cars crawling along behind it. But again it didn't get very far, and this time the problem was much more serious.

By this time, we'd covered about 10 miles, and the engine was out of water. It was a problem that needed urgent attention. Fortunately, Fred spotted a fire hydrant over on the other side of the road. He had to get the engine across quickly against the flow of tea-time rush-hour traffic. Then, as Fred brought it to a halt, it was action stations for everybody.

'Get all the tackle out quick,' he yelled. In less than a minute, they'd got the pipe and all the connections out, taken the cover off the hydrant and got the pipe attached. Soon the water was flowing into the tank on the back of the tender. But there was water every-where, with as much coming up from the end of the pipe, like a fountain, as was going into the tank. The problem was that the nozzle Fred had made was too big and it wouldn't fit into the hole that went into the tank. With water gushing up all over the place, Fred explained how close they'd been to disaster:

There's a safety plug at the bottom of the boiler, just above the firebox. If we'd not managed to fill up in time, it would have melted and put the fire out. This would have meant we wouldn't have been able to move the engine from here until the plug had been replaced, and that's a big job. We could have blown the plug out and we'd have been here all night. You'd get sacked on the railway if you did that. You can get away with a few do's with no water over the top of the plug, but one day it'll have you, and that's it. Terrible. We should have a dipstick, really, to check the water level, but I've not got round to that yet.

As they filled the engine, the traffic crawled past on

the narrow road, and a crowd of onlookers collected on the pavement. There was clear excitement not just at the sight of this strange, smoking monster, parked on the road outside their houses, but because such a well-known personality was driving it through their neighbourhood.

Cameraman Rob Taylor remembers the chaos we caused with all the traffic, and the people coming out of their houses to talk to Fred. It was also the point at which some of the production team and the crew began to realize that this shoot wasn't going to be like anything else they had ever experienced. 'As they filled the engine,' Rob recalled, 'there was a moment of realization about what was in store for us. It was at that point on this first day out on the road I realized that it was going to be quite an epic getting this traction engine around the country and having to refill it a few times a day. I suddenly realized the scale of the task that lay ahead of us.'

Production assistant Kate Siney said later, 'I think that's when I realized how popular Fred was. There was this massive queue of traffic behind, but as soon as they got to the engine and realized who it was, nobody seemed to be bothered that they'd been stuck in traffic for the past half-hour. They just waved at Fred and seemed quite happy that they'd be late home from work because of him.'

Fred loved the crowds, and as Alf and Jimmy got on with the job of filling the engine, he chatted to his audience and signed autographs. 'The man's a star!' one of the crowd said, happy to be in Fred's presence.

Alf and Jimmy had other concerns. It was getting late, and there was still the question of where the engine could be parked for the night.

Jimmy had lived near Wigan all his life, and he'd worked at many of the mines around there. He knew it all like the back of his hand, and as he and Alf filled the tank, he gave him some directions to a nearby pub. He knew it had a big car park where Fred might be able to park the engine up for the night. With the tanks filled, pressure up and all the gear stowed away, the engine was ready to move off for the last stage of that day's journey – to the pub.

Fred and Alf were soon steaming off into the distance. The trouble was, we had stayed by the side of the road where the engine had filled up to film it driving away down the road. The crew car and Jimmy's car were both parked over on the other side of the road, about a hundred yards back. By the time we had packed our kit up and got back into our cars, the engine had disappeared out of sight and, unknown to us, Fred and Alf had decided to turn off the main road just after they'd set off. Nobody knew where the pub was that we were heading for, other than that it was over the other side of the M6 near a place called Billinge, so we drove off in that direction, confidently expecting to catch up with the engine. But a couple of miles down the road, there was no sign of a traction engine ahead of us or, more to the point, a queue of traffic behind a traction engine.

The next hour was spent driving up and down what seemed like every road between Ashton-in-Makerfield, where we had stopped, and Billinge. I lost count of the number of times we crossed and re-crossed the motorway. What made the whole episode quite surreal was the fact that Fred and Alf both had their radio mics switched on, so every so often, as they came into range, our sound recordist would pick up snippets of radio mic signal from them. All of a sudden, he'd say, 'I can hear them. They must be close.' But no sooner had he said it than they'd disappear again. Each time he heard them, we thought we'd tracked them down, but tantalizingly, the voices faded away as we drove out of their range. It was bizarre: an 8-ton traction engine with a big green living van in tow seemed to have disappeared into thin air!

Eventually, we found the pub. It did indeed have a big car park, but there was no sign of our engine in it. By now, it was around half past six, and we needed to get the parking for Fred and the engine sorted out. When we asked the landlord, he didn't seem too keen; in fact, he didn't seem too friendly at first. Time to find another pub perhaps, but more importantly, time to send out search parties to find Fred and his disappearing engine.

We retraced our steps, driving back in the direction we had just come from. Reaching a roundabout about half a mile from the pub, we stopped to look down each of the roads leading off it, and there in the distance was the puff of black smoke indicating that the engine was there. Fred told us that they'd turned off the main road because that was where they thought the pub was, but they'd found themselves in the middle of a small housing estate and got lost.

By the time we'd led Fred to the pub, it was seven o'clock. It had been a long hard day, and it had all been a bit of a disappointment, not just for Fred but for us as well. It was time to find somewhere to stop for the night, and we were pinning our hopes on the landlord we'd just encountered being accommodating. As he pulled to the side of the road just before the entrance to the pub car park, weariness and disappointment were etched all over Fred's face as he summed up the day:

There's something amiss somewhere, you know. It should go better than it is doing. Number one: the mechanical lubricator's fell off altogether now; it's hanging on top of the boiler. We should have the big firing shovel like the one I have for the steamroller, but we've forgotten that, and we've forgotten the big rake. With all the excitement, we've forgotten half the tackle. You cannot rake the fire with what we've got. The thing is we've hardly any coal left.

There was a bit of a debate about how far we were from the open-cast mine. If they could get the engine as far as the mine the next morning, they'd be all right, but they were so low on stocks they might have to have a bag delivered to the pub before they could steam up the next morning.

But there was only one thing on Fred's mind. 'It doesn't want to steam up,' he said. 'We were stuck on that big 'ill back down there for about an hour. I want to have a look inside the valve chest tomorrow.' Jimmy agreed. He too thought it was the valves that were causing the problem. 'In the morning, when it's cooled down,' Fred said, 'we can have a look in there and we'll soon see if there is anything wrong. But we're going to have to get the lubrication sorted out as well. I think if we got to the coal mine with it, we could take the lubricator off there and mend it. Because it'll be safe to leave it there if we need to.'

Jimmy remembers that first day on the road. 'Everything had to be spot on for Fred,' he said. 'I think that's why it was such a big disappointment to him when it wouldn't perform at the beginning. The trouble was, we should have had more time beforehand. We should have been working on the tractor instead of digging. But Fred got involved with his mine, and he left the tractor to carry on with that.'

Fred cheered up considerably when he saw the pub landlord approaching with a couple of pints. 'Would it offend you,' Fred asked him, 'if we parked our machine at the end of your car park?' It was a bit of a tense moment, but the landlord replied immediately, 'No, of course it won't. No, that'll be fine.'

'We'll sleep with it tonight, you know,' Fred told him, 'and we'll come and have a pint with you. We can't leave this thing. It's took twenty-seven years and two divorces to get it to this state.' The landlord laughed, gave Fred one of the pints he'd brought over and took the other over to Alf, who was still standing by the engine. Fred quaffed his pint appreciatively.

'You can see why so many people come here,' he said. 'It's nice ale that. Bloody lovely.'

As Fred enjoyed his pint, the landlord pointed out some space at the far end of the car park and said he could park the engine and the living van there for the night. Fred explained that they were having some problems with the engine. 'I want to take some bits off,' he said, 'and have a look inside its belly.' That would not be a problem, the landlord said, then went back inside. Fred stood in the middle of the car park, pint in hand, reflecting on the day:

It's not performed as well as I thought it would. It's only teething troubles, I think. It's like there's something come loose somewhere. It goes better backwards than forwards. There's something amiss, and tomorrow, when it's all cold, it's only five minutes of a job to take the valve chest covers off. Possibly the lock nuts have moved. There seems to be a clicking noise that shouldn't be there. And the fact that the mechanical lubricator isn't working ain't doing it any good. We've got to keep putting it in the displacement ones, and they're only for giving it a quick drink every now and then. They're not really for continuous zooming along. The rod has come out of the little thing that's on the eccentric rod. The threads weren't very good when I did it and I expected having trouble with that. It actually works on the back stroke, pulling back, so it's trying to pull the screwed bar out of the end of the thingy. So we've got to take that off and get it home and fettle it up somehow or other. Or if somebody round here has got a welding set, we could get it welded on, and it doesn't matter about the threads then.

Alf, however, had enjoyed his first day on the road. 'It were brilliant,' he said:

I suppose if it had run perfect first time, that would have been great, but it was still good. Fred was disappointed, though, because we had to keep stopping to get the pressure up when we shouldn't have had to do that. We should, as long as we kept feeding the fire and kept it filled up with water, we should in theory have been able to go all day. Having said that, there were some good scenes when we stopped. The kids at that school in Ashton, and then there was the nursing home as we were approaching Hindley, where they started bringing the residents out on Zimmer frames and wheelchairs to sit on the lawn looking at us while we was blowing pressure up. That was great.

For Alf, the fine weather that we were enjoying added to the pleasure. It was a warm spring evening as Fred, Alf and Jimmy manoeuvred the living van around the car park to get it parked up at the end of that first day. The sun was going down behind the trees that lined the pub's bowling green as they unhitched the van from the engine and, with a bit of pushing and shoving, got it into a parking space at the end of the car park, with the engine tucked in by the side of it.

No sooner had they got it into place than a small red pick-up truck drew up with a couple of bags of coal in the back. Alf examined the coal, casting a seasoned miner's eye over it. 'It's good coal,' the truck driver said before Alf had a chance to deliver his own verdict, and he carried the sacks over to the engine and tipped the coal into the empty tender. 'We burnt a bit on the way here,' Fred observed, 'but we're all right now. That's plenty for getting us to the coal mine.' As the sun set, Alf got the ladder out of the living van and climbed up to polish the brasswork on the chimney. Fred was feeling a lot happier now. 'The end of a perfect day,' he said contentedly. 'We've found a nice pub that does grub. And it looks nice and safe for the engine.' And with a 'Goodnight, see you later,' he disappeared into the living van.

Alf and Jimmy went home and left Fred with the engine, but they were back early the next morning to help get it ready for another day on the road. The coal they had been given the night before wasn't very good quality, but it would be enough to get them to the mine. As they were working on the engine, the man who had delivered the coal the night before arrived with his mate. They watched as Alf and Jimmy polished the brasswork and Fred tinkered with the mechanical lubricator that had given him so much trouble the day before. The coalman asked Fred if his coal was burning all right. Always polite and not wanting to offend his benefactor, Fred said, 'It's OK – a bit smoky but it'll get us to where we want to be.'

The two coalmen stood and looked at the engine admiringly. 'Poetry in motion, isn't it?' one of them said. Then there was a barrage of questions for Fred, who was very happy to answer them all. 'What sort of weight is it? It's not power-assisted steering, is it? Has it passed an MOT?' Fred launched into a long answer to that last question:

Well, no, that's the funny thing, they never actually ask you about its mechanical condition, they're only interested in the boiler blowing up. And of course, there's some of them are positively dangerous when it comes to going down big hills and all that. The only criterion for getting it insured is the boiler certificate. Nobody asks you about the state of the gears, or the brakes and all that. Some of them have no brakes, like Fowler ploughing engines what they ploughed the fields with – 22 ton and no brakes, but they are so low-geared, if you shove the regulator, they just stop. With this, you've got to have the big blocks of wood. Otherwise, it can be quite dodgy, especially on hills. If you're halfway up a hill an' it's not having it in the big wheel, you've got to stop. But the top priority is, everything that's hanging on the back has got the brakes screwed on and blocks of wood under every wheel, so there's no way when you pull out of cog that it can set off backwards down the hill.

'So it's only two gears, has it?' the coalman wanted to know.

'Yeah,' replied Fred. 'Slow and very slow!'

'And what about pulling capacity?' his mate wanted to know. 'What will this thing pull?'

'When it were made,' Fred told him, 'it were designed to pull about 30 ton, but I doubt whether it would now.'

After the visitors had left, there was time to spare before setting off, as the engine was getting up to the right pressure, so Fred got a battered old garden chair out of the living van and sat out enjoying the morning sunshine. Alf and Jimmy were cleaning up around the traction engine. As Alf swept the ash on to a shovel, the head of the brush fell off. Alf burst out laughing.

'It has to be Fred's, this,' he joked as he studied the end of the brush. 'Anyway, where are we now?' he asked Jimmy.

'Billinge,' Jimmy replied.

'Billinge?' Alf questioned. 'Well, where's this bloody Dire Straits place he keeps on about?'

'Which Dire Straits?' Jimmy asked.

'The Dire Straits that Fred keeps saying we're in,' Alf replied.

As Alf and Jimmy carried on with their banter I sat down with Fred and talked to him about all the troubles of the previous day. He said:

When we arrived here last night in dire straits, the engine didn't want to run smooth and nice. We knew that a thing called the mechanical lubricator weren't really working but all through the day we'd been looking at the wrong end of it. When we got parked up here and the engine cooled down we were able to have a proper look at it. We found that, at the end that's connected to the eccentric rod, the threads that went into the rod were stripped, so instead of doing a proper pull back, it shoved it forward but it wouldn't pull it back, 'cause it works on the backstroke. We hadn't been able to work out why the ratchet wheel weren't going round till we discovered this. We discovered it purely because it came out completely and ended up lying on top of the boiler, so we knew there was something seriously wrong. Anyway, we then dismantled it and we found a friendly person in the neighbourhood to take it to a little engineering man who fettled it up for us. So now I don't think we'll have any more trouble with it.

The only other problem I think we'll have now is the fire being clinkered up, because we've not brought the rake with us. This is because we've not got any cab on this. I'm so used to the steamroller with a cab, and that has all the irons hanging on it. But on this, because I've not had time to build a cab for it yet, there's nowhere to put anything. The other thing we've forgot is the tube brush. With a single-cylinder traction or steamroller, they're so violent that when you open the regulator out of gear, *whoof whoof whoof*, and all the muck in your tubes gets blown out over your neighbour's washing. With a compound like this it's more gentle, and it doesn't blow the muck out of the tubes, so every morning it's important that you sweep the tubes. You can, if you're desperate, do it with a piece of rag tied to a stick. I've done that before with a piece of privet hedge, in the olden days, when I first started being a steam-engine enthusiast.

I'm not happy with its performance, though, as far as power is concerned, compared with me steamroller, which will go up a mountain with 50lbs on it. But this thing, you've got to have 150, and if you go any lower than that, it's a waste of space, bad news. Whether I've done something wrong in reassembling it or not, I don't know. What I do know is that I have a friend who is what you might call a steam-engine-valve wizard. He's very clever, and it's like going to see a specialist; it's better getting a few opinions on what might be wrong with it. I've spoken to people on the phone who've got the same thing, and they say, 'Below 150, they're a waste of space; they won't do nowt.'

But I'm hoping for better performance today. Yesterday was a day that was fraught with every sort of difficulty and problem. I mean, it's the longest journey we've been on it, and I think, really, considering we didn't leave till lunchtime and we were here at seven o'clock, and it's what – 10, 14 mile, or something like that, with all the things that went wrong, I think we did bloody well to get here.

'So hopefully it'll be a bit quicker today,' I ventured.

'Maybe, yeah, I can't promise you though!' Fred said with a laugh.

It was now nearly time to go. Before long, the engine was steamed up, and Fred manoeuvred it to hitch up the living van, but everything about the engine was still very new to him and he wasn't comfortable with it yet. 'I've not got used to all these handles yet,' he said. 'The steamroller's very simple compared with this. And everything is on the wrong side – opposite to where it was on the roller.'

Finally it was time to move on. They were a day late, but they only had another 2 miles to go from the pub, so it wasn't going to take them long to get to the opencast mine. Although there is very little sign of it now, this whole area they'd been travelling through had been at the heart of the Lancashire coalfield. It was one of the first areas in Britain to become heavily industrialized, due to its cotton mills and coal mining, and mining played an important part in Lancashire's economic development. Now, there were no pits.

The decline of the industry was rapid. In the immediate post-war period from 1945 to 1951, coal mining in Lancashire had looked secure. A worldwide sellers' market and the return to peace-time conditions produced a high level of activity and a temporary boom in Lancashire's coal industry. But this period of intense activity was short-lived. In 1950, there were 70 collieries employing 55,000 people, and approximately 12,500,000 tons of coal were produced per annum. After 1951, the industry began to decline, and the number of pit closures increased sharply from 1958. By 2004, when Fred was setting out on his grand tour, there were fewer than 500 people working in the mining and quarrying industries combined, and one of the only places left where coal was still being extracted was the Crock Hey open-cast mine to which we were heading.

The short journey to the mine was uneventful and, as Fred drove past the great piles of coal stacked up near the entrance, he gave two triumphant blasts on the whistle. He brought the engine and the living van to a halt on a weighbridge in front of a huge coal mountain.

'How much does it weigh, Stuart?' Fred shouted as the owner came out of his office.

'It's 11 tons,' Stuart called across.

'The engine is 8 tons, so that means the living van is about 3 tons,' Fred said. 'This morning, believe it or not, it's performed very well. We bombed along nicely. We've not run out of steam; we've not run out of oil. So that's a good thing. That's why it didn't want to go yesterday. There were no oil in the cylinders and we kept priming and washing out what bit there were, and now it's running OK.'

As he was saying this, Fred stopped short. 'Oops, wait a minute!' he exclaimed. 'Oh, what have I done? I've done something very silly. I've got carried away, and the bloody boiler's going to be full up to the top, and as soon as we move, it'll be *whoof whoof* out of the funnel. That's with not concentrating, you see.'

Fred had injected too much water into the boiler,

and now water was being sucked into the cylinder with the steam, and that's not very good for the engine. So he had to open a valve near the bottom of the boiler to get some of the boiling water out. As he did this, Fred disappeared in a cloud of steam.

Once the problem had been sorted out and the cloud of steam cleared, Fred stood by the side of the engine talking to Alf. 'Just think,' he said. 'The coal industry in Lancashire were mainly round here, Wigan and Abram and Leigh. And slowly but surely, in the 1960s, it all but disappeared, nothing at all left of it.'

'I think,' Alf said, 'there were a spell when everyone would be connected in one way or another to the coal industry. Right down to the shopkeepers.'

The main reason they had come to Crock Hey was to collect a load of coal for the first part of their journey, but there was no way that Fred would leave the site without having a look at the workings, so Stuart gave them a guided tour. After a short walk, they came to the workings, which looked more like a quarry than a coal mine. They were dominated by what looked like a great cliff face where the rock and the earth had been dug or blasted away. At the bottom, a huge mechanical digger was at work clearing earth and loading it into the back of a big four-wheel-drive truck.

Stuart led the boys into the old workings of the coal mine that had once been here. The passages they were walking through had once been underground, but they were now in the open air; the surface of the old mine had been excavated so that the remaining coal could be extracted from ground level. It was as if the top of the coal mine had been sliced off, and as we stood above the passages to film the boys walking along them, it was like looking down into a sectional drawing of a coal mine.

As they walked, they chatted about the mine. When Jimmy said he thought the workings would have been wider than they were, Stuart explained why they were so narrow: this mine had been worked without props, and the miners had taken as much from the passages and made them as wide as they'd dared without any support. Looking up on to the cliff face, Alf spotted clear signs of a coal seam halfway up. There were a number of different coal seams around Wigan, and Stuart explained that this one was the Wigan 5-foot seam.

When they had completed their tour, the main job was to get the storage lockers at the back of the living van filled with as much coal as they could. But Fred disappeared again with Stuart, leaving all the donkey work to Alf and Jimmy. Alf opened the door into the storage compartment near the back of the van, and he and Jimmy peered in. The door was small, no more than 3 feet wide by 3 feet high, but the storage space it opened on to was big, stretching all the way across the back of the van.

'How are we going to get the coal in there, Alf?' Jimmy asked.

'With difficulty, I imagine,' Alf replied. 'We're going to have to find something to push it to the back. But I've no doubt Stuart or somebody will find a couple of mugs to load it.' As he said this, Alf laughed and pointed to himself and Jimmy. And that's exactly the way it was. They went over to one of the coal mountains and Alf started to shovel as Jimmy held open a large bag.

Alf stopped shovelling and turned to the camera, saying, 'If it were making pots in a pottery or gears in an engineering workshop, the boss would be having a do. Because it's shovelling coal, he doesn't want to.' Alf and Jimmy worked on. The bags piled up, but there was no sign of Fred.

When it looked as though they'd got enough bags to fill the storage space in the van, Jimmy hauled himself up and, with a nimbleness that belied his years, wriggled into the cupboard where the coal was to be stored. As Alf carried the first bag over and lifted it up to the cupboard, Jimmy, crouched down inside, took it from him and pushed it to the far corner of the storage space. It was reminiscent of the cramped conditions on the coal faces that the two friends had worked on, and it was time for a few mining jokes. 'The sprinklers aren't working in here,' Jimmy said.

Alf looked into the dark hole and, quick as a flash, responded, 'And if I catch you without an oil lamp again you're in trouble.'

It was hard work, but there were no complaints. 'Where's Fred?' I asked them as they were getting down to the last couple of bags. 'Fred?' Alf replied. 'Jimmy said he went down to the pub half an hour since. He should be back now, because that's the last bag.' But behind all the joking, we all knew that Fred was no longer physically capable of doing this sort of heavy work. Throughout a long, hard-working life, Fred had never been afraid of physical graft, but now he just wasn't able to do it. Without the support of friends like Alf and Jimmy, the planned journey wasn't going to be possible.

By the time the coal had all been loaded and Fred had reappeared, the engine was steamed up and they were ready to set off for their next stop – Astley Green Mining Museum, one of the few places to survive to tell the tale of coal mining in the area. It houses Lancashire's only surviving pit headgear and engine house. The colliery began its life in 1908 to exploit coal reserves in the south Lancashire coalfield. It had a life-span of only sixty-two years, finally closing its gates in 1970. The coal seams at Astley Green are very deep and overlain by 100 feet of wet and unstable ground. This made the sinking of the shaft very expensive, and the construction of the pit tested mining-engineering ingenuity to the very limit. The shaft dropping method called 'Drop Shaft', which involved forcing an iron cylinder with a cutting shoe down into the ground, was used successfully for the first time in the UK. Peak colliery output was 2,800 tons a day in 1967, and at one time, 2,300 men worked there. Alf remembered it well, because it was a pit he had worked at for a time.

It was early afternoon when the engine began its journey to Astley Green. Crock Hey was surrounded by woods that were carpeted with bluebells, and the engine made a fine sight as it chugged through the sun-dappled greenery. Things were looking good.

It was quite a long drive to Astley Green, much of it along the East Lancs Road, the dual carriageway that was once the main road from Manchester to Liverpool. It was very busy, with fast-moving vehicles speeding past the engine in the outside lane, but there were several sets of traffic lights, which were posing a bit of a problem for Fred. He was still not used to driving the engine, and he was having trouble judging stopping distances as he approached the lights. This meant he was constantly having to plan ahead, adjusting his speed as he tried to calculate whether the lights were going to be on red or green when he got to them. So he'd be making his way carefully towards them, allowing himself plenty of space to stop, and then somebody would overtake and cut in and Fred would have it all on to stop the engine without ploughing into the back of the impatient motorist who'd cut him up.

Fortunately, there were no big hills on the road, and Fred was feeling a bit better about the way the engine was performing. It was still slow, but not quite as bad as it had been the day before, and there were not quite as many stops. The mechanical lubricator had been fixed, and that was making a big difference, but all of our timings were way out. In the projections I had made with Fred, the estimate for this sort of journey was about an hour and a half. Instead, it took all afternoon. It might have been going a bit better than the day before, but the engine and living van were still crawling along at no more than 3mph and having to stop every mile or so. I followed in the production car with the hazard warning lights on, and a constant line of vehicles sped past us in the outside lane. As the afternoon wore on, Fred got more and more dispirited. Ever the perfectionist, it hurt him that this machine, which he had devoted so much of his life to rebuilding, was not performing properly.

It was early evening before the engine arrived at Astley Green; too late to do any of the filming that had been planned for that day. But that wasn't the only problem. The long hours spent on the footplate of the traction engine over the previous two days had clearly taken their toll on Fred. He'd not really left Bolton yet, but it was already clear that he was too ill to spend so much time driving the engine. As he climbed down wearily from the footplate, he looked up at the rusting pit headgear that dominated the skyline. 'I climbed up there once,' he said wistfully.

I remembered the occasion well: the first day's filming I'd ever done with Fred was here at Astley Green. No sooner had we arrived and started to unpack our filming gear than Fred had shinned up to the top of the towering hulk of ironwork. Not much chance of that now, I reflected.

The plan had been to do all the filming at Astley Green and then drive the engine back to Bolton that evening, but there was little hope of getting all this done. It was far too late: it would have taken till past midnight to drive the engine back, even if Fred had been in a fit state to do so. Fortunately, the big old colliery gates were locked each night, which meant there was secure parking for the engine. Alf and Jimmy got the covers out from the living van and put them on the engine before driving Fred back to Bolton.

These two days had been a useful trial run for the main part of the filming, and we'd all learned a lot of lessons, not least of which was the fact that we would have to reschedule everything for the rest of the shoot. Our estimates had been hopelessly over-optimistic, but it was too late to cancel the following week's shoot, when we were taking the engine up to Cumbria. The decision was made to go ahead with the filming the following week but to postpone everything that had been arranged from then on and take a two-week break to give us time for a bit of a rethink and Fred time to do some much-needed fine tuning on the engine and hopefully finish some of the jobs he hadn't previously been able to get done. There were still no guards to cover the gears and other moving parts, and the engine still had no cab. They were also still short of some of the key accessories they needed for the sort of journey they were about to undertake. One of these was the suction hose that Fred had gone to make a couple of weeks earlier. The fittings were proving to be difficult to get hold of, so Fred was having to set off on his journey without the hose, all for want of the right connection. There were some big challenges ahead in the hills of the Lake District, but Fred had some good friends there, and he was impatient to get there and show them his engine.

4

Repairs in the Lakes

The other essential material that had to be dug from the earth in the manufacture of an engine like Fred's was iron ore, so the next stage of the journey involved going from Lancashire to the Cumbrian coast to visit the last deep-working iron-ore mine in Europe, Florence mine at Egremont.

Without iron [Fred explained] it wouldn't have been possible to build an engine like mine. It's just about 100 per cent iron; the wheels, the boiler, the firebox, the cylinders and the motion gear, cranks and shaft are nearly all iron. The advancement of iron smelting and the steel-making process throughout the nineteenth century made the mass production of steam locomotives, winding engines and traction engines possible. Huge lumps of iron were used in engines like mine, and the high-quality tools needed to build the engines were made of steel. Cumbria is a region that is not often mentioned when we talk about our industrial heritage. But the area we now think of as the beautiful 'unspoiled' Lake District is also an area fabulously rich in the raw materials used in the construction of my engine. West Cumbria's ancient volcanic landscape is richly endowed with deposits of coal, iron ore and lime – all the essential ingredients for steel-making. The steel-works at Workington still produces railway lines; its rail track is still exported all over the world. And it all started because the West Cumbrian iron ore, the red stuff, is amongst the finest-quality iron ore in the world.

On Monday 17 May, one of Alan Atkinson's low loaders arrived at Astley Green to transport the engine and living van to Cumbria. Because it was the first time this had been done, inevitably it all took a long time. One of the major delays was caused by the fact that the engine couldn't be winched on. It had to be steamed up so that it could be driven on, but then the fire had to be allowed to die down and the engine had to cool off before the low loader could set off to transport the engine. It was something I hadn't realized when we were doing the scheduling, and it was to have a major effect on the time everything took for the rest of the shoot.

The plan was to transport the engine to a place called Lowick Green, about 4 miles south of the bottom end of Coniston Water. From there, Fred was going to drive the engine to Torver, about halfway up the lake, and stay the night with an old friend, Dick Ransome. Dick had been the engineer on the steam yacht *Gondola*, which is owned and operated by the National Trust, and had been its manager for fifteen years.

The crew arrived at the rendezvous point at the appointed time, but there was no sign of Fred and his engine. We hung around for several hours, but it was lunchtime before the low loader arrived. As they inched the engine off and started to get steam up, I went off to Ulverston to get sandwiches for everybody. When I returned, there was a surprise. Fred's eldest son, Jack, had arrived with Dick Ransome. Fred was delighted, not just to see Jack, but to have him around to help out with the engine. But even an extra pair of hands doesn't make things happen any faster with a traction engine, and it was well into the afternoon before it was steamed up and ready to go. Fred got up on to the footplate and Jack joined him as steersman.

The engine pulled out of the lay-by where we'd been parked. The road was narrow, twisty and undulating and, sure enough, as they headed for the Lakeland fells another queue of cars soon formed behind. Fred was enjoying himself, as he gave his report on the day's events: 'My eldest son Jack's come over from the Isle of Man to give us a lift on this trip. And really, the way we're going on, I think we need all the help we can get. But while we're up here, we're calling on a mate of mine, Mr Richard Ransome. Dick is a fellow traction-engine owner and steam-engine enthusiast, and we'll be able to do some running repairs in his workshop, because this thing's giving me trouble and I'm a bit disappointed in it.'

But Fred wasn't just disappointed, as cameraman Rob Taylor recalled. 'I remember Fred being quite embarrassed that we were filming and it didn't work, and he was Fred Dibnah, Mr Steam, and it was all on camera not working. I don't think he was that keen at that time. He didn't want us to make a big thing of it not working.'

We'd decided after the trip to Astley Green that the engine needed to go back to Fred's yard and have more work done on it, but realistically, it would have needed three months, not two weeks, and I knew he would never have got it done. If we'd put everything off for that long, Fred wouldn't have been fit enough to do the trip. The battle Fred had with himself was not wanting the engine to be seen in the state it was in but at the same time wanting to get round and do the tour. The main problem he was having with the engine was lack of steam, and Fred thought he knew the reason for this, as he explained when we made the first of many stops that afternoon:

I think I've put the cylinder block in one of the pistons a bit too far forward. I know for a fact that the high-pressure piston is covering the port-holes up when it's in the forward position, which means that, when it's supposed to be working, the steam can't get at it properly. So what I'm going to do is, when I get to Mr Ransome's, I'm going to ask him – no, I'm going to beg him – to use his workshop and shorten the piston rods by about a quarter of an inch. When we get there we'll take the end cover off and wind the crankshaft round. When we do this, the piston will go back and we'll be able to see how much we've got to cut off. You can't do any harm on the back stroke. There must be plenty of room there. But that's the only thing I can think of that is making it perform very poorly. The bore is all right. The slide valves are all right. But the piston is going too far up the bore. And there's not enough room to let the steam in and shove it back again. But there's nothing terrible we can't mend. I don't think we'll have any bother sorting it out when we get to Dick's.

But Fred had to get to Dick's first. The hills of the Lake District were proving to be a real problem. Long queues of traffic were building up behind the engine, and when he had to pull over to the side of the narrow road again for another stop to get pressure up, Fred started to express some worries as to whether it would be able to tow the living van as far as Dick's:

Well, there's another big 'ill yet. It would make it on its own, even if it can't make it with the van, and I suppose we could get a friendly farmer to tow the van for us. But I don't think it's wise to try and move it anywhere else until we've done something to try and get it to run better. In

121

bottom gear this is slower than the steamroller. It's really painful in bottom gear. And on the steamroller there are no springs and it's a dead smooth ride. This in bottom gear is jumping up and down.

Fred didn't mention it, let alone complain, but in his condition this constant bumping up and down on the engine was causing him a lot of pain and discomfort. He didn't want to talk about his illness with me, for fear I might cancel the filming. But with the engine, progress was painfully slow on the hills of this winding little road, and by late afternoon we'd reached the point where the road meets Coniston Water, still about 5 miles short of Dick's house at Torver. At least the scenery was good. But I knew that didn't mean much to Fred. Throughout the years I'd spent travelling around Britain with him, he'd never been very impressed by any of our scenic wonders. 'Mountains,' he used to say, 'they all look the same, and one tree looks just like another. I don't know what people see in them. Not like a good chimney.'

When we finally got to the lake, Fred stopped to have a chat with Dick, and help was at hand. One of Dick's mates came and rescued the engine by hitching it up to his Land Rover.

'Just a bit of insurance, Fred, isn't it?' Dick said reassuringly.

'Yes,' agreed Fred, 'and when we get there we're going to do some running repairs, aren't we?'

'Absolutely.' Dick nodded. 'Make it well again. It's

all research and development, isn't it?'

Fred and Jack climbed up on to the engine and steamed off by the side of the lake with the engine running light. It was a beautiful, early-summer afternoon, and with Jack up there beside him steering, all was well with the world. Everything was a bit easier now, without the living van in tow, and they travelled at a decent speed along the side of Coniston Water towards the Old Man of Coniston and the other high Lakeland fells that surround the top of the lake.

It wasn't long before they were pulling into Dick's yard, followed shortly afterwards by the living van, towed by the Land Rover. Fred was now convinced that his diagnosis of the problem was correct. If, as he thought, the piston was covering the inlet into the cylinder, it meant that the engine would go along all right on the flat, when the momentum of all the weight in the engine carried it forward. But as soon as it got to a hill and started to slow down, the piston was going slowly right to the end of the cylinder and was covering the port for so long that it wasn't letting enough steam in. He was confident he'd be able to get it sorted out here in Dick's workshop, and as he wiped the engine down, he outlined his repair plans for the following day:

In the morning, when it's cooled down, we're going to have to take the cylinder end covers off and weigh up how much we can take off the end of a piston rod. It's not hitting end. It's stopping short by a midge's wotsit, and it's not

123

letting the steam in to push the piston back. I'm 99 per cent sure that if we shorten those piston rods by about three-quarters of an inch, it'll be a different engine altogether. So hopefully Dick will help me, I know he'll help me. I know he will do that, because I've known him a long time.

As Fred talked, Dick came over with a can of Guinness for him. 'Why have you not got one?' he asked Dick.

'I don't drink it,' Dick replied. 'I'm a bitter man myself. I'm not really a stout fellow.' Then, looking down at himself, he laughed and added, 'Well, I am. Anyway, good health, Fred.'

As Fred drank his Guinness, Jack moved the engine to where it was going to be parked up for the night and, with the help of Alf and Jimmy, started to put the covers on. That evening, Fred, Jack and Alf stayed with Dick, and they contacted another old friend of Fred's, asking him to come over to see if he could shed any light on the problems they were having.

We woke up the next day to a glorious morning in the Lakeland fells. The sun shone down from a clear blue sky on the grassy slopes of Torver High Common and the lofty ridges and crags of the Old Man of Coniston. Fred was up early, and when I came over from the pub the rest of us had been staying at, he'd already got the cover off the valve chest. Jack and Jimmy were moving the flywheel round by hand, which was, in turn, pushing the piston along. Fred was peering into the valve chest, but he looked up to report on the decision they'd made the night before. 'We've got Roger Mallinson coming, who's quite an authority on steam engines. He actually makes steam engines for rich people's steam yachts – you know, for Lake Windermere and everywhere else – and he's a clever lad. He knows his stuff. I think he'll agree with us that the high-pressure piston is completely strangling the port where the steam comes out.' Fred then went back to his inspection until Roger arrived.

Fred had great respect for Roger's engineering expertise, and he was cheered up considerably when Roger had a look at the engine and gave his verdict: that it wasn't in bad condition. But, like Fred, he was worried about the way the piston was covering the port opening in the cylinder. After some deliberation, they decided that the problem was being caused because somebody had made a new piston that was a bit thicker than the original, and that there was a simple solution. They could make the port opening bigger, which would allow steam to get into the cylinder in front of the piston.

With the problem diagnosed, Roger invited Fred to accompany him on a cruise on his steam boat, *Shamrock*, one of the oldest in Britain. He'd had it since 1976, but when he bought it he had to redesign and rebuild its engine from scratch. The sun was still shining, and an afternoon's excursion steaming on Lake Windermere would give us a pleasant break. Fred knew what the problem was now, and what needed to be done. The job wouldn't take long, and could be done later that afternoon, so we left the engine and travelled by car to Low Wray, on the north-western shore of the lake.

Shamrock was moored at a little wooden jetty outside a neat boathouse in the trees by the side of the lake. Roger had got steam up and was ready to set off as we arrived with Fred. It was like stepping into a time warp. Already on board were Roger's brother, Miles, and his wife, and they were dressed for an Edwardian outing on the lake – striped blazer and boater for Miles; long dress and a parasol for Mrs Mallinson. Roger himself was resplendent in his Edwardian captain's uniform.

As soon as we were all on board, Roger put the engine into reverse and, with a toot on the whistle, reversed out on to the lake. The engine was almost silent as the boat glided to the centre of the lake. As Roger steered, Miles told Fred the story of the boat. She had been built in 1906 by Shepherds of Bowness and owned by a cotton millionaire. When the owner died, he left her to his engineer, Mr Ashley, but he couldn't afford to run her as a pleasure boat, so he used to hire himself and the boat out to wealthy families who came to Windermere for the summer. After the Second World War the number of people who could afford to do this shrank, so Mr Ashley's son put the boat into the ownership of the Bowness Bay boat company, and they removed her lovely steam plant and had a diesel engine fitted. The company stopped using the boat at some point, however, and by 1976 she was lying derelict. She'd been like this for some years when Roger obtained her, and he spent almost three years restoring her to her former glory.

Miles also happened to be an expert on the earliest machines to play recorded music, and when he'd finished his little history of the boat, Fred said, 'I believe you've finally mended my gramophone.'

'Oh, I did,' Miles answered, producing an ancient-looking phonograph from under his seat, 'but it isn't a gramophone. It's a phonograph with cylinders, not discs.' For our benefit, Fred explained that he'd brought this old phonograph for Miles to have a look at the last time he'd been on a trip on this boat. 'It was in a bit of a mess, to put it bluntly,' Miles said. 'Fred said, "Do you think you could do anything with this?" and I looked at it and said, "It's a hell of a challenge, but we'll have a go." And here it is. It's a 1905 Edison James Mark B phonograph.'

Miles wound the machine up, saying, 'And it's clock-work, of course.' Then he brought out a shiny horn, which he attached to the machine. 'And it's got a lovely aluminium horn,' he went on. 'I've fitted a new gear and a new spindle and a bottom pulley for you, so it's all working now.'

'Like our tractor,' Fred said. 'It's nearly all new.'

Miles got one of the cylinders out. 'And what are we going to play?' he asked, looking for the title on it. 'Yes. "The New Colonial March". The cylinder is made of wax, and this is also 1905. The machine's American, or it was originally, but the cylinder with the music on it is English. And we'll see if it'll go.'

Miles put the cylinder on the machine and started it off. The stillness of the lake and the gentle *phut, phut,*

phut of the engine was broken by a lot of crackling and hissing, before a plummy voice announced, ' "The New Colonial March", played by the London Regimental Band.' A rousing march rang out across Lake Windermere. Is this how it was all those years ago when Beatrix Potter stayed here, possibly going for excursions on this very steamboat? The music summoned up images of glorious summers past – Fred's time, I thought; the time when he always said he would like to have lived. Never had he looked more at home. 'Ah, it's wonderful,' he said when Miles asked him if he liked it. He sat back, his troubles far away.

We couldn't stay out on the boat all afternoon, though. There was work to be done on Fred's engine back at Dick Ransome's. Roger steered back to the little jetty by the boathouse and drove over to Dick's yard. He got to work on the port at the root of all the problems with all the precision of the skilled engineer that he was, and by the time the work was finished, it was getting late. Just time for a meal and a few pints down at the local pub, then an early start the next morning. We had a very full day ahead of us.

The low loader had gone back to its depot in Preston after the engine had been unloaded on the first day, but it was back bright and early the next morning, ready to transport Fred and the engine to the Florence mine at Egremont. We were scheduled to start filming there later that morning. However, Fred didn't want to leave Dick's until the engine had been tested, to make sure that the repairs had done the trick.

After the usual two to three hours to get steam up,

the engine was ready for the road. Again, it was a beautiful, clear morning; every ridge and gulley on the Old Man of Coniston stood out in sharp relief. But Fred had far more important things to concentrate on. Was the engine going to work any better?

Alf and Jimmy hitched up the living van; Fred climbed up on to the engine, with Jack beside him, and pulled it out on to the road which they'd struggled along two days earlier. He got into top gear and drove up and down. He was soon smiling. To his great joy and satisfaction, the engine was performing the way he had always hoped it would. The adjustments Roger had made to the cylinder had worked, and for the first time it felt like a vehicle he could take real pride in.

When Florence mine was working at peak production between the 1920s and the 1960s, it supplied the steel-works at Workington that became world-renowned for the production of railway lines, manufactured with West Cumbrian ore. From Torver to Egremont it was about 35 miles, and the original plan was that Fred would drive. But we had abandoned this plan when it became clear that the engine wasn't capable of great speeds. Instead, the low loader had been booked to transport the engine there.

Iron-ore mining was one of the great industries of West Cumbria, dating back to Roman times. But it was not until the 1830s, when deep mining began in the region, that this valuable mineral was mined here on a significant scale. It brought waves of workers from the tin mines of Cornwall and the copper mines of Ireland, as well as immigrants from Poland and Italy.

As steel production developed, the demand for iron ore expanded enormously, particularly in the 1850s, when the railways were built, reaching its height in West Cumbria in the late 1870s and 1880s.

In this period, there were 300 iron-ore shafts in this area and the industry employed more than 5,000 people. The average annual iron-ore output in the early 1880s was 1.5 million tons. The best-quality iron ore to be found anywhere in the world is haematite, and it is this that is found in the limestone layers of the West Cumbria landscape. Because haematite is high in iron and low in phosphorus, it is particularly good in the production of pig iron, a crude iron containing high levels of carbon and other impurities tapped from the blast furnace and left to set in rough blocks, which is ideal for conversion into steel using the Bessemer process.

Henry Bessemer introduced his revolutionary Bessemer converter in June 1887. The Bessemer process is a highly economical and efficient way of making steel, in which the carbon, silicon and manganese impurities in cast iron, which make it brittle, are oxidized and then removed by air being blown through molten cast iron in a furnace. Iron could be converted into steel at a fraction of the cost it had been done previously, and the process took just twenty to thirty minutes, instead of ten days! Before the Bessemer process, there was no steel suitable for structural use in the manufacture of ships, girders, bridges or railway lines, among other things.

Because the iron ore produced in the area is a

distinctive red, the miners became known as the Red Men of Cumberland; coal miners were known as the Black Men. There was always a friendly rivalry between the two, coal miners taunting the iron-ore miners for being 'soft' and boasting that they could lift shovelfuls of coal that were 2 to 3 feet in diameter. The Red Men said that if a shovel that size was full of iron ore, you wouldn't be able to lift it off the ground. (Iron is considerably heavier than coal. If a fist-sized chunk of coal fell on your helmet, it would have no impact, but if the same-sized chunk of iron ore fell on your helmet, it would knock you over, and if you weren't wearing a helmet, it would kill you!) As we waited around for Fred and the engine to arrive, we found out that Florence was the largest iron-ore mine in Europe still working. But the whole place was a shadow of its former self. It was still a commercial operation, the ore mined being used to make pigments for dyes used in paints, but there were only three employees and they produced 500 tons of iron ore each year. Florence mine was all that was left of a once-great industry.

This was the sort of thing we should have been finding out in the course of filming, but two o'clock came and went and there was no sign of Fred or the engine, and no news from them. We stood around and waited, and as time dragged on, it started to get embarrassing. Filming involves a lot of people and punctuality is of the essence. Kate Siney remembers the problems we had with sticking to any sort of schedule: 'It was my first job in telly,' she said. 'It was hard to schedule anything, and everything was late, and I left and went to work on other programmes thinking that's the way it always was, that you just did what you could – but nothing could be further from the truth. Everything has to be on time.'

I couldn't understand why it was taking so long to transport the engine the relatively short distance from Torver to Egremont, and frustration mounted as precious filming time slipped away. It was well on into the afternoon before the low loader carrying Fred and the engine got anywhere near the mine. The reason for the delay, I found out, was that they'd been driving past the road to Ravenglass, home of the Ravenglass and Eskdale Railway, which had always been a great favourite, not just of Fred but of Jack and his younger son, Roger. Jack had wanted to visit the railway, so they'd made a short detour. It was a place where Fred had spent many happy days with his lads, and it had been difficult to drive past for what was likely to be the last time without taking a quick look. The trouble was, they'd not seen very much of it, because after they'd turned off the main road to go into Ravenglass, there had been a low bridge, and the low loader with the engine on the back of it wasn't able to get under it. They were stuck, and it took the driver a long time and a lot of skilful manoeuvring to get back to the main road.

Once they got close to the mine, the engine had to be steamed up in order to get the shots of it arriving. Fortunately, this time, this didn't take long, because the engine was still warm from the driving it had done that morning. Fred drove it off the low loader and, with Jack by his side as steersman, he made his grand entrance, up the hill from the main road and past the pit headgear that dominated the scene. He was met by a welcoming party consisting of the mine owner, Gilbert Finlayson, and the two miners who worked there with him, but as he drew up outside the single-storey building that housed the office and the lamp room, Fred's first concerns were for the engine.

'I'm still not very happy with it,' he said, 'unless it's me misjudging the product. Compared with the steam-roller, that would have waltzed up that hill with cobs of coal coming out of the funnel. But this is still idle, lazy. It'll do it in bottom cog coming up that hill pulling this thing, but this were made for pulling about 15 tons. The van weighs a couple of ton. It's nowt. There's still something, somewhere, wrong. Anyway, we're here.'

Gilbert listened to Fred's complaints about the engine, then walked up to it to greet him.

'Well, Fred,' he said. 'We thought you were never going to land. We've been waiting a couple of hours for you! I'm pleased you've got here, though; we're ready to go down the pit now.'

Fred played the part of the traction-engine driver who had driven the engine the whole 35 miles from Torver. 'It's a long way from, from erm, where've we come from,' he said. 'I've forgotten it's been that long! They're not known for speed, these things. Yeah, but we did get here, that's the main thing. It doesn't like hills, this thing, you know.'

'We've got a cap lamp and a helmet for you,' continued Gilbert, 'and there's a big hill to get down underground. We're going down to see the men working the mine in the old-fashioned way. This is hard-rock mining. First, holes are drilled into the rock using compressed-air drills. I'm going to give the men a hand to charge the holes with high explosives. I'll try not to get my cap blown off!' Once everybody was kitted up with a lamp and helmet, we made our way to the mine entrance and down the long incline that led to the workings.

'Bloody chemotherapy,' Fred said as they made their way down. 'Buggers your circulation up. I find it very hard walking. I used to be like a gazelle. But I'm bloody knackered now.'

They carried on walking, further down into the workings. 'Keep your heads and your backs down, lads,' Gilbert exhorted them, before telling his visitors a bit more about the iron-mining industry in West Cumbria: 'You know, we were a great big mine industry round here; we had between two and three hundred iron-ore mines.' Fred wanted to know how many men had worked there. 'Well,' Gilbert replied, 'there'd be – in this bit alone, at the start of the Second World War, there'd be about a thousand men.' Then stopping by one of the old shafts, he went on, 'We've got eleven shafts here. And this is the site of number-three shaft. This one was sunk in 1905.'

Fred was fascinated by anything to do with mining, and he was soon putting the discomfort he was feeling out of his mind and questioning Gilbert about the operation. 'When you were sinking this drift out,' he wanted to know, 'how much powder would you use?'

'Well,' replied Gilbert, 'you went for a 5-foot advance every shift, and you would use 20–30lbs of explosives – fairly high explosives. And, of course, detonators. The men worked in companies which would have been either twos or threes, and their daily routine would be to do the blast at the end of the shift, then there would be a chance to get the fumes clear before the next day's shift. We favoured spraying into the air a mixture of compressed air, water and castor oil, of all things. It's a great medium for clearing the dust.'

'Castor oil, eh?' quipped Fred. 'Yeah, keep you regular that, won't it?!' Then he remembered something he had seen the last time he'd visited the mine. 'Have you still got that exotic—' He broke off when he spotted what he was looking for. 'Oh, they're here, see!' It was mushrooms he'd been looking for, growing in the dark. 'They're in fine growth there, aren't they?' he said. 'Have you tried any in the pan?'

They moved on, going deeper into the mine, and Gilbert resumed his commentary: 'And this is where we come to the ore. Remember, as well, of course, that there were those two or three hundred mines, perhaps all owned by different companies. And all selling to different ironworks. And they were vying with each other for quality and price. It was a very competitive area to be in, and a competitive industry to be in.'

Carrying on still deeper, they came to a squat-looking machine like a small bulldozer. Gilbert explained that machinery like this in the mine was powered by compressed air. 'It's got a bucket on its front,' he explained, 'and it loads into its own body.

And when it's full we travel it back to the top of the ore pass, and we can tilt the body up, the rear door opens and the load drops into the ore pass. Marvellous machine, isn't it? All our ore went to be made into pig iron and then steel. Some at Workington and some down at Millom, which was a one-industry town.'

As he talked, Gilbert spotted some of the iron ore he wanted to show to Fred. 'Fred, come and have a look at this in the roof here,' he said, pointing to a vein that sparkled in the light of his cap lamp. 'It's as good an example of kidney ore as you'll see anywhere in the world. Almost good enough to make haematite jewellery out of. But it's a little bit like onion skins. Thin layers. We need thick layers to make good jewellery. We don't get much of that nowadays.'

It was gone six o'clock by the time we got back up to the surface. The day had been far too long for Fred, and it still wasn't over for him, because he had an appointment at Christie's hospital in Manchester at eight o'clock the following morning that he had to get back for. Jimmy was going to drive Fred back to Bolton that night and then bring him back up to Cumbria after his appointment. But Fred was worried about his engine: he didn't think the site was secure and he was reluctant to leave it for the night, so Alf volunteered to stay in the living van as night watchman.

The crew packed up and headed off for the pub we were staying in at Egremont. I set off to take Jack back to Dick Ransome's, where he was spending the night.

I'd been so taken up with the filming and all the concentration involved in getting the best part of a day's work into a few hours at the end of the day, I'd almost forgotten that Fred had brought Jack along with him.

The quickest route to Dick's was over the steep Hardknott and Wrynose passes, but I couldn't chance going that way, because I'd not expected to be doing any driving that night and I was very low on petrol. Better to take the longer route that went through a few small towns and villages, where I might find a petrol station open. But it was too late; any that I passed were closed. By the time I got to Dick Ransome's, it was nearly ten o'clock and my petrol gauge was on empty.

When I explained my predicament, Dick said that there was a petrol station in Coniston, which was only a couple of miles up the road and, if I hurried up, I should just get there before they closed. With Jack safely installed, I raced up by the side of the lake and made it to the petrol station. Then, with a full tank, I headed for the high Lakeland passes to get me back to the west coast – and what an unforgettable drive it was. With the high fells that surrounded me illuminated by the last rays of the sun as it set in the west and an empty single-track road winding ahead, I sped up and down the one-in-four gradients on each of the passes, twisting and turning around the sharp bends. I've never done any rally driving, but I thought this is what it must be like: I felt I was going to take off from the crests of some of the hills. Up from Little Langdale and over Wrynose, with the bulk of England's highest mountains, Scafell and Scafell Pike, up to the north at the head of Mosedale. Past the Roman fort at the top of Hardknott before swooping down the switchback all the way to Eskdale and the run alongside the famous little railway.

I've never driven so fast on narrow mountain passes like this before, and I haven't done so since. Looking back on it now, I'm sure it had something to do with the slowness and delays and lateness of everything to do with the engine; some sort of release from the frustration I felt at everything taking so much longer than any of us had anticipated. Anyway, whatever it was, it was an exhilarating drive, and I got back to Egremont by ten thirty. The good people at the pub had kept the kitchen open to make sure I didn't go hungry. Alf was there, and as I had my meal we got him a taxi to take him back to the engine and his bed in the living van for his night-watchman duties.

Next morning, we filmed him as he polished the chimney on the engine and gave us his view on these early, somewhat trying days of Fred's grand tour:

I'm just finishing Fred's top off. He likes his brass and copper polished up nicely. And then later on we're going to get steam up and shoot off to Workington steelworks, where all the iron ore from Florence went to. The engine is running a lot better than it was. We did those running repairs at Dick Ransome's. We've got some proper steam coal. Hopefully, that will make a big difference. But it was running better yesterday, and it'll have a good trial today when we steam off to Workington. I think Fred is a bit disappointed with it, because we can fire the steamroller up and it will run all day as long as you keep giving it coal and water. And I think he expected the same out of this straight away, even though, he'll tell you himself, we're bound to have little teething problems. Also we're not running at full running pressure as yet because of the leaks. But I think they've stopped now. So hopefully at some stage we'll be able to up the pressure slightly and run at higher pressure, and that will help tremendously. So we're getting there.

And was polishing the engine part of Alf's job, I asked him. 'It looks like it,' was his reply. 'I've a bit more yet to do before he comes, because he likes to see it gleaming. There's the copperwork to do, the whistle, wipe the paintwork over, and then we're ready for off and getting it all dirty again, ready for polishing tomorrow!'

We left the engine and headed for the steelworks in order to set up there before Fred arrived back from his hospital appointment. Ninety-five per cent of the United Kingdom's railway network was rolled at Workington, and there's probably not a railway in the world that doesn't have tracks with the name 'Workington' stamped on them. They had a saying around here that the railway tracks exported from Workington 'held the world together'.

The blast furnaces at Workington were capable of producing between 50 and 70 tons of pig iron every few hours, and the molten pig iron was taken from the blast furnaces to the Bessemer shop in 50-ton ladles transported on special railway wagons. Rails were made at Workington for 127 years – but by the time we were filming, they were no longer smelting iron there. The Bessemer plant had been closed and almost every trace of the old steel-making process had gone. Most of the steel was rolled in a modern, computer-controlled rolling mill, but what Fred was interested in was seeing the old hand-rolling mill, which was still used for small light and narrow-gauge railways.

We set up and started filming while Fred was still back in Manchester having his chemotherapy treatment. Sheila had taken him to the hospital and Jimmy was waiting at the house to drive Fred up to Workington straight after his appointment. We set up by the rolling mill in time for Fred's arrival at the works. It was exactly the same as the one in the ironworks on the Blist's Hill site at the Ironbridge Gorge Museums; the one that Fred had watched as a boy at Walmsley's in Bolton, which had been its original home. It was the one he had enthused about so many times; the one we'd filmed him with at Ironbridge for the Industrial Age series, when he did his magnificent action replay of what it had been like when he'd seen it working at Walmsley's. This one at Workington was now the only one left in the country that was still in operation. Fred hadn't seen anything like this in action since he was a boy, and I wanted to capture his first reactions when he saw it.

The camera started to roll as he walked in, but when

he saw the rolling mill he was subdued. Two or three years earlier, there would have been no stopping Fred from getting the tongs from one of the workers and having a go at handling the white-hot metal as it came through the rollers himself. But not now – though it was hardly surprising after his chemotherapy treatment a couple of hours earlier. He livened up a little bit as he talked to one of the workers about how hot it was working right on top of the heated bars of steel all day, and he remembered that, in the rolling mill in Bolton, they'd had a Spitfire propeller hanging from the ceiling to cool the place down.

After lunch in the boardroom at the steelworks, we went back to Florence mine, where Alf had got the engine steamed up, ready for us to do some driving shots. With Alf back as steersman, they went out on to the dual carriageway that ran past the mine. As we stood by the roadside and filmed it steaming past, the engine seemed to be running a lot better, something Fred confirmed when he brought it to a halt at the side of the road:

It's running very well, actually. Yeah. I'm getting a bit more used to it. On reasonably level roads, it's all right. It's when you come to a big steep one, it's like motorcars: you have to change gear. The steamroller I had for forty years is low-geared and you don't have to change gear. It's like having one of them cars with a V8 engine. You just keep your foot down. It's getting better, but one of the problems with this is you can't fire it on the move. We might be able to do it with a short-handled shovel. I've made the footplate 6 inches longer, so how the hell the guy who drove it before managed I don't know. He must have had to stop every time he put coal on.

By the time we'd filmed the engine driving up and down the road and got shots of it arriving at the mine and leaving, it was late afternoon. It had been another long day, but there was more still to be done. We had arranged to film Fred having a chat with some retired steel workers at a pub near Workington, but we had to stay with the engine until it had cooled down enough for Alf and Jimmy to get it covered up for the night. Then it was back up the road to Workington.

In 1962, the steel industry employed around 5,000 people in Workington alone. When we filmed, there were just 200 steel workers left in the town. Most of the old working ways had gone for ever, but down at the pub, Fred was meeting some of the former workers there. Tom and Phil Baguley, Andrew Melville and Ronnie Tinnion had all worked in the Bessemer shop, and we wanted to find out what life there used to be like. First of all, they talked about the rolling mill that Fred had looked at that morning.

'It was a bloody sorry day when they took the old steam engine out from that mill,' Tom said. 'It was dead reliable. My grandfather was the roller in that mill, and during the war he worked permanent nights and he worked six nights a week. In the old days, they had to manhandle the pieces on the rollers with a fork about 12 foot long. And as the tail end came out, these lads with tongs used to grab it and whip it into the next pass, and away it would go again.'

'I'll tell you summat,' Fred said. 'The lads who did that made it look dead easy, but they'd give you the tongs and say, "Have a go," and bloody hell, it weren't that easy. It's quite frightening if you watch it. If you realize what could happen to you if owt went wrong.' Fred went on to introduce Alf and Jimmy, saying, 'These two lads were coal miners.' This led Tom to talk about some of the miners from the local West Cumbrian collieries:

'The cobbler and his last' is a very old saying. It's what you get used to. Now, we had the Solway colliery, and it closed. And we lads, we worked in the Bessemer. And these colliers got a start in the Bessemer shop and do you know how long they lasted? One day! And their reason was, 'It's too dangerous here.' And a lot of these were miners that were working 3 miles under the sea. It was the sparks they didn't like, especially in the Bessemer when it was turned over and emptied. Belts were taboo in steel-working, you know. And the reason was that, if you were caught in the sparks, you could shake them down if your trousers were loose. One lad was actually killed because metal hit him and it had nowhere to go because it was held in by his belt, so belts were out. Wellies were out as well, because the sparks could get inside them.

Ronnie picked up on this, saying:

Any of your body that is normally exposed to the air, like your hands and face, heal fairly quickly if you get sparks on them, but Tom here had his feet burnt rather badly, and there's not much flesh there, so they're notoriously slow at healing. I was one of a group who was injured in 1962 when a ladle of iron fell. A shackle was being used which wasn't really supposed to be used, and that is what caused the accident. It was only a small emergency ladle with 4 ton in it but, of course, when it came down there was molten iron everywhere. I was in charge of the job at the time, and I got knocked down in the rush. You sort of automatically put your hands out to save yourself and, even though I was an under-manager, I'd never been frightened to use a shovel and I had fairly horny hands. But I remember the skin started peeling off like blotting paper, and I'd only got my first car about three weeks before, and I thought, Oh Christ, how am I going to be able to drive the bloody car?

Ronnie went on to tell another story:

Boys came to start work in the Bessemer when they were fourteen or fifteen, and one of the first jobs they had was taking the sample from the pit side to the laboratory for chemical analysis. And what they used to do was carry it with a bent bit

Above: After Fred had demolished his last chimney, he was ready to take to the road on his recently restored traction engine.

Right: The Aveling and Porter convertible steam tractor was originally built for use by Somerset County Council in 1912. Fred bought it in 1977 and spent twenty-seven years restoring it to its former glory.

By Royal Letters Patent
NO 7838
AVELING & PORTER
LIMITED
ROCHESTER
KENT
England

Above right: There were plenty of last-minute adjustments on the big day, before Fred could run the engine for the first time.

Below: Fred's hydraulic riveter and overhead crane, which he used when building the engine, stand tall beside his shed.

Above left: Fred was proud that he had made nearly all the parts for the engine in his back garden himself.

Above: After twenty-seven years and two divorces, the restored engine was ready for the road.

Below: The first stop on the long journey was at Crock Hey Open-cast Mine near St Helens, to load up with coal.

Above: Teething troubles: Fred endures one of many stops that he was forced to make during the first few days on the road.

Left: Fred's mate Alf Molyneux saw the opportunity to accompany him as steersman as the trip of a lifetime.

Below: Alan Atkinson and his low loader transported the engine on the long hauls between locations.

Above: Battling the hills of the Lake District so early on the tour, before all the running-in problems had been sorted out, was a major challenge for the engine. Fortunately Fred's eldest son, Jack, is a skilled mechanic and was on hand to help his dad sort out some of the problems (*left*).

Fred was pleased that Roger Mallinson, who he regarded as 'something of an expert on steam engines', was able to help him get the engine back on the road for a visit to Florence Mine, Egremont, where Alf swapped mining stories with the guides (*inset*).

A sunny afternoon on Lake Windermere: a steam launch, an Edison phonograph and the company of old friends . . . no wonder Fred looks the picture of contentment!

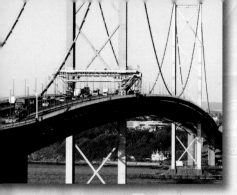

Left: Crossing the Forth Road Bridge was one of the highlights of the tour.

Below left: Fred enjoys a brew with Gordon Newton at Israel Newton's boiler works in Idle, Bradford.

Below right: Not so long ago there were hundreds of boiler works all over Britain, but today Israel Newton's is one of the few that remain.

At Ryhope Pumping Station, Sunderland, the Victorian engine house provides the perfect backdrop for Fred's engine and living van.

of wire, maybe about quarter of an inch in diameter. Well, this little chap, George Dickinson, wanted a Jimmy Riddle, so he went behind a tin shed, and he had this bloody thing in his hand, and he happened to catch it, you see, and of course he burnt it. So he went down to the ambulance station and he said, 'Oh, I've burnt me pencil.' So they bandaged it up, but they didn't leave him a hole at the end!

There was laughter all round at the plight of little George Dickinson before Tom spoke of his admiration for the skills of some of his former work colleagues:

There was a chap who was the blower in the Bessemer and I had terrific admiration for the skills he had. He was the guy who looked at the flames to see if the ore was right. At one time, the management brought a computer in to do the job, but it failed; it couldn't match what this lad was doing. He could look at some iron being poured out of a storage tank that we called a mixer and he could actually tell you the analysis of it by looking at the sparks. I did admire that man, George Goodall, because I've met a lot of steel men, and in my book, he was the best steel-maker ever.

'The heat and the light from the flame from the Bessemer was terrific,' Ronnie went on to say. 'Before the war, you could actually read a newspaper in the town of Workington from that flame. During the war, they weren't allowed to work the Bessemer on the night shift because the flames were a guide to the German bombers.'

Fred was fascinated by all these stories. Working men like these were his real heroes, and he never tired of talking to them about the jobs they did when Britain was still a great industrial nation. By the time we were ready to go, it was past eight o'clock, but our hotel was only about five minutes' drive away. The trouble was, the engine was parked at Florence mine, about 15 miles back down the road, and, again, Fred didn't think it was a secure enough location. He was worried about his engine and living van being vandalized, and insisted on going back there to stay in the van rather than at the hotel. Alf volunteered to go with him and have another night in the van, so he and Fred had something to eat at the pub and then I drove them back to Egremont.

Next morning, the low loader came to pick up the engine. The original plan had been to take it up to Scotland, where we were going to continue with the next stage of the journey. But because of the problems Fred was still having with the engine, and the difficulty of working out any sort of schedule we had any hope of being able to stick to, I'd decided to take a two-week break. This would give Fred the chance to get the engine back home to do some more work on it, and us the opportunity to revise the schedules yet again.

While the engine was being transported back to Fred's, we all went to Astley Green Mining Museum to pick up on the filming we'd been scheduled to do there a couple of weeks earlier. When we arrived, Fred recalled the scene when he had visited the colliery soon after it had been closed down:

> The scrap men had been, and all the windows in the engine house were broken. The rain were going in at one side and out the other, and they'd nicked all the brass off the winding engine. It looked very sad, and only beat the scrap man by the skin of its teeth. But now, thanks to the work of the enthusiasts who came along to rescue it, it's almost ready to run. They've got a Lancashire boiler for it, and they have a grand collection of odds and sods. They've also got a steam hammer and about five or six steam engines, all connected up to a big vertical boiler. But what a task these lads face! I know how much time it took for me to get this engine of mine done, but a whole pit – well, that's really something else.

The museum the enthusiasts run houses Lancashire's only surviving pit headgear and engine house, both of which now have listed-building status. But it was what was inside the engine house that saved the place. The massive steam winding engine inside wound 8 tons of coal up the shaft next to the engine house every two minutes at up to 58mph from half a mile depth, and it was the uniqueness of this engine that brought demolition to a halt. The number-one engine is a 3,300hp twin-tandem compound, and it is Europe's, possibly the world's, largest surviving steam winding engine. It was manufactured by Foster, Yates and Thom of Blackburn and was commissioned three months after the *Titanic* went down in 1912.

As we were setting up for filming in front of the headgear and the engine house, a wedding party walked over to Fred. They were holding their reception at the pub that overlooked the museum, and soon Fred was posing for photographs with the bride and groom. The bride's long white wedding dress trailed over the dirt of the colliery yard, but she didn't seem to mind. These were special pictures she was getting for her wedding album. She wanted Fred to join the wedding party in the pub and have a drink with them, but Fred declined politely, explaining that he had work to do. When we started filming, he talked to Alf and Jimmy about the mine and its history. 'Lady Pilkington, of Pilkington glass fame, cut the first sod in 1908,' he said. 'But then they had a lot of trouble when they sunk the shaft, because of water. So the whole thing is seven-eighths lined with cast-iron tubbing, and it's over 800 yards deep.'

'I can remember riding in here,' Alf recalled. 'I've rode this shaft. I worked here for a spell in the 1960s. I believe they're in the process of getting monies together now to get the headgear repainted and re-furbished properly.'

'Better hurry up,' Fred said. 'You can see a few holes in it!' Then there was a general discussion about the fact that it was worth saving. 'After all,' said Fred, 'this is the last one in Lancashire apart from ours. It's gotta be worth a big grant from the lottery people to keep it stood up. If you wanted to open a ballet school, there'd be millions for you, but not to paint something like that, which has kept a lot of families in bread and butter for a long time.'

Fred remembered an interesting tale about a miner who was doing some work on the shaft when he fell off the top of the cage. By pure chance, he landed on top of the other one, which was coming up, just as the two cages were nearly level in the middle of the shaft. Alf remembered the incident because it had happened when he was working there, but it wasn't something he really wanted to talk about, other than to say he didn't think that man ever went down that shaft again.

When we got into the engine house, the interior was quite a sight, big enough to accommodate a couple of tennis courts, with a lot of room left over. The engine it houses is a real monster, but as Fred and his mining friends looked at it, its great hulking mass stood silent. What a sight it must have been during its working life, turning the 100-ton drum in the middle, wound round with the steel cables that went over the pit headgear to wind the cages up and down!

'Aye, it's a fair machine this, isn't it?' Fred said. 'They only ever made three, you know. One for here, one for the Yorkshiremen and one for Africa, but this is the only one that's survived. I should think it's one of the biggest steam winders in the world.'

'They could do with putting a bit of oil on it, couldn't they?' Jimmy observed. 'It's a bit rusty.' Then, as the three friends walked along by the side of the engine, they talked about the size of it. Everything about the engine was huge. It had four cylinders, two on either side of the drum that dominated the centre of the engine house. 'Look at that bloody connecting rod,' Alf said. 'Fair job, ain't it!' They admired the workmanship and the sheer scale of the engineering behind it.

'They're fair castings, them,' Fred said. 'How'd they get them from Blackburn to here? Traction engine, I imagine,' he said, answering his own question.

'But how would they have got this thing in here?' Jimmy wanted to know.

Fred had been having a good look round, and he thought he'd got the answer. 'I've been round the back of the engine house,' he said, 'and there is a big doorway down at the bottom, and if they took the engine to pieces, that hole is big enough for even the biggest pieces.' By this time, they were in the middle of the engine house between the cylinders, and Fred decided he was going to have a closer look.

'What're you doing getting in the bloody cylinder?' Alf asked with a laugh.

'I'm just looking at the ginormity of it all,' Fred replied. 'You could have a game of tennis in between these cylinders, couldn't you?'

The power to turn the winder came from sixteen Lancashire boilers, but all of these had been early victims to the scrap man. When the preservation society took over, it managed to get hold of three similar boilers, in the hope that one day they would be able to raise steam again. Fred went out of the engine house with Alf and Jimmy to have a look at them.

'They don't look in too bad nick, do they, really?' Fred said. 'They're all three of them different, though.' Then as he walked around the boilers and studied them, he observed, 'There's been a few men killed with these, you know – rolling around, you know.'

'You don't know what's wrong with them, do you?' Jimmy wanted to know.

'Well, it's easy to get inside them,' Fred replied, 'then I could tell you what's wrong with them. You just have to undo them, then you can get right along the bottom, in between the two fire tubes. Then, on the top, there's another big door that you can get in, and you can walk along the top. The thing is, you've got to look for big, deep-pit holes.' Fred peered into the dark interior of the boiler, pointing things out to Alf and Jimmy. 'Inside here, there's two pieces of angle iron, then a bloody great lump of inch-thick plate. And then, if you look on the outside, there's more of it, isn't there? Can you see it on the outside? Well, them are called gusset stays, and they stop that weak area there from being pushed out. A mammoth piece of boiler-making. But let's go for our tea.'

It was the end of our first week on the road. We'd known all along that it was going to be difficult, but nobody could have anticipated quite how difficult. The engine was certainly performing better after the work at Dick Ransome's, but anything would have been better than those first couple of days we'd been out with it, and it was still painfully slow. Everything was taking so much longer than expected – getting the engine steamed up, cleaning it down and sheeting it up at the end of the day, loading and unloading it on to the low loader. The logistics of trying to arrange a filming schedule around a traction engine were difficult, and timings were impossible to keep to, but when this was added to making sure the central character in the films, a very sick man, was looked after, I wondered if it was going to be possible to carry on.

In all of this, Fred's health and well-being had to be of paramount importance and, although he was bravely trying to hide the fact from everybody, he was clearly suffering. Fred knew that this was going to be the last time he was going to see old friends like Dick, and he was unhappy that the demands of the engine and the filming schedule hadn't given him enough time with either Dick or Roger Mallinson. But he was determined to carry on. There were more old friends to see on this trip, and small firms that had helped him with parts for the engine or with advice. For Fred, this was a way of saying thank you.

In order to go on, there would have to be a big rethink about schedules, about the number of places it would be possible to visit, about the distances involved and the amount of driving Fred would be able to do on the engine. Then, given Fred's worries about security, there was also the question of finding secure parking for the engine each night, somewhere Fred would be happy to leave it. The next stage of the journey was going to be a long one, up to Bo'ness on the Firth of Forth, where we planned to visit a foundry to see how the castings for an engine like Fred's would be made.

Before attempting that sort of distance, we really needed to take time out. The problem was, we all knew our time was limited. Fred's health was deteriorating rapidly, and his illness was making some of his actions unpredictable. For example, when Jack had turned up on the shoot unexpectedly, Fred, naturally, had wanted to make sure he was kept happy and so had tried to take him to the Ravenglass and Eskdale Railway, and we had to find a way of taking this sort of thing into account.

The effect of the drugs that Fred was taking, and the pain and discomfort he was suffering, meant that he was beginning to lose his grip on reality a little. For years we'd worked together, and Fred was always the easiest person in the world to get on with; never any complaints about anything and always happy to go along with whatever was required for the filming. But when he got back home after the Cumbria trip, he kept telling Sheila that I had 'buggered off for the night with the film crew and left him stranded in the middle of a field with Alf, the engine and the living van and only two sandwiches to eat between them'. He was, of course, talking about the night at Egremont when he had insisted on going back to stay in the van at Florence mine. Sheila said later that, while Fred had said this in earnest and had seemed very annoyed, she had found it difficult to believe, as she knew how much Fred thought of me and how well he had always been treated when we were filming. When I explained what had happened, she accepted it straight away.

What this incident made clear was that, in rescheduling the filming over the next couple of weeks, finding somewhere with secure parking for the engine each night had to be a prime consideration. Fred had to be happy that his engine was safe. His dream may have been to sleep in the living van by the side of the road, but he was in no fit state to do this.

While we reworked the schedules, Fred had the traction engine's teething problems to attend to. Top of the list was stopping the leaks from some of the rivets on the boiler and, being Fred, he'd got his own methods. He put various concoctions into the boiler, including porridge oats, red lead and large quantities of urine, which he'd collected in a bucket at the back of the shed. These were old recipes he'd found out about from studying the methods of traction-engine drivers of the past. Sheila recalled how he came into the house one day during this period saying, 'Bloody 'ell, cock, water's pissin' out of the boiler on that thing. Get me some eggs, will you, when you go out next, about a dozen should do. I'm going to put them in the bugger to see if it stops the leaks round the rivets. No matter how you caulk it, you still need some corrosion to make it perfect, but we haven't got time. Oh, and get some porridge oats, that might do the trick as well.' Sheila got all the ingredients, and Fred poured them into the boiler, but much to his frustration, the recipe didn't work and the boiler still leaked. More drastic measures were called for.

When I went over to see how he was and how the

engine was progressing the following week, he told me all about what he'd been doing: 'Them eggs were a load of crap,' he said, 'but I had a better idea. It occurred to me that it would give an unbelievable seal, like it did in the old days, if we filled it with cow piss.' He went on to tell me how he'd been in touch with the local abattoir to deliver about 40 gallons of it to him. They'd arranged to bring it round for nothing in a 40-gallon drum, but then they'd rung him and said they wouldn't be able to do it because of 'bloody Health and Safety rules'. Undeterred, though, Fred had started thinking along similar lines and had a plan.

'If you need a piss while you're here,' he said, 'nip round the back of the shed and piss into that big blue container round there. When it's full, we'll put that in the boiler. It should do the trick.' Sheila told me later she was a little concerned about this, as Fred was using it all the time, and the hospital had told him to avoid bacteria where possible. But nothing was going to stop Fred getting his engine in the right fettle to continue his grand tour.

5

A Bridge Too Far

It was Tuesday 8 June when we picked up on the filming again. The revised plan was to transport the engine to a point in the Scottish Borders where I would get some shots of Fred on his way up to Bo'ness on the Firth of Forth before putting the engine back on the low loader to continue the journey to Bo'ness. Now that we were more aware of the amount of time everything to do with the engine took, we had allowed the whole day.

When Alan Atkinson arrived at Fred's that morning to pick up the engine, Fred was in good spirits. The rest had been good for him, and for the engine. But no amount of work on it was going to make it any quicker to get it on to the low loader, because an unforeseen problem had emerged. The low loader had a winch and, under normal circumstances, the engine would have been winched on and they would have been on the road in no time. But it wasn't just the engine that was being transported, it was the living van as well. The winching point on the engine was at the back, which was where the living van was attached, so that couldn't be used, and in any case, in order for them both to fit on the low loader, they had to go on forwards, but there was no tow point on the front of the engine strong enough to pull both. They would have to be driven on instead, and of course this meant that every time the engine was going to be transported it would have to be steamed up and this would add another couple of hours' waiting time to the schedule.

This problem with the loading was completely unexpected, so again it took much longer than I had anticipated to get it to our pre-arranged rendezvous point at Abington Services on the M74. I hung around there for a few hours until eventually the big green cab of Alan's truck came into view with Fred's engine and living van perched on the back. It was around two o'clock and they'd already spent six hours getting the engine steamed up, loaded and transported. Once they'd arrived, the engine had to be steamed up again and driven off the low loader, which meant that it was nearer to four o'clock before we were ready to do any filming. As Alf and Alan got the engine ready for the road, Fred explained why we were in Scotland:

We're now in Scotland and we're heading for a foundry to find out more about the casting process and foundry men. Castings are a very important part of a traction engine. The cylinder block, the cylinder end covers and the pistons are all made from cast iron. Even the hub caps over the wheels are made from cast iron and the business at the front where you've got the steering gear is made from cast iron.

By the time the engine was ready for the road, eight hours had been taken up that day getting it steamed up, driving it on and off the low loader and transporting it; all for a couple of minutes of driving shots. Already, the logistics just didn't seem to make any sense. But once the engine was on the road, a lot of the problems were forgotten, as it made such a fine sight chugging along by the sparkling waters of the infant River Clyde. There was little traffic to worry about and the gently rolling, seemingly empty landscape of the Lowther Hills made a tranquil contrast to Fred's iron horse as it puffed and clanked along. Startled sheep ran away up the green hillsides to get away from this smoking monster as it made its ponderous progress further up the valley. This is the way things should have been; the way things would have been if Fred had been in good health and the engine had been functioning properly: puffing along the back roads of Britain at the gentle pace of a bygone age.

Despite all the day's delays, Fred was in good spirits. The running repairs he'd done on the engine over the previous two weeks appeared to have been a success, and it was running well. Fred and Alf were enjoying themselves. The weather was good, and it was a fine open road with no big hills which followed the bottom of the Clyde Valley. The conditions were ideal for a traction engine, except for one thing – water. After an hour's driving, the tanks were running low. The river was close at hand, but they'd still not been able to get the connecting fittings they needed for the suction hose. If they'd had that, they would have been able to get water from the river, but without it, and with no fire hydrants out here in the middle of the country, Fred had a problem. Then he spotted a row of cottages by the side of the road.

Alf remembers the occasion well:

We were running short of water, and we were in the middle of nowhere. Then we came over a brow and there were three or four cottages on the right-hand side, so we pulled over. 'Have you got a garden hose?' we asked. Yes, they had. They fixed us up with water and asked us if we wanted a cup of tea. Fred said, as usual, '''Ave you owt stronger?', and out they came with four or so cans of beer. Then they said, ''Ave you got enough coal?' and they fixed us up with a bag of coal.

I remember it all as another idyllic scene. A warm summer afternoon, a picture-postcard location, a traction engine quietly hissing in the sun and four men standing by it chatting as they drank their beer. They talked about Glasgow and about some of the foundries and engineering works there. 'Glasgow was one massive foundry,' one of the men said. 'There were foundries everywhere there.'

'Best engineers in the world came from round here, didn't they?' Fred observed. After a long chat, and Fred convincing the men to sign his petition to allow him to continue work on his replica coal mine, it was handshakes all round, and with a blast on the whistle, a tankful of water and an extra bag of coal, Fred and Alf were on their way again.

The engine bowled along through the hills in fine style. Fred was much happier with it; there was no talk of selling it now. At last he could have some real pride in the engine he'd built. However, even though Fred, Alf and Alan had been up at the crack of dawn, it was nearly six o'clock, and they were still around 80 miles from their destination.

I drove on ahead to the Bo'ness and Kinneil Railway on the Firth of Forth, where the engine was to spend the next few nights. There was good secure parking for it there, so Fred would be able to leave it and stay in a hotel without any worries. There was also a plentiful supply of coal and water, and there were workshops and plenty of willing helpers if any running repairs were needed. However, some of the roads from Abington to Bo'ness were narrow, which made the journey for the low loader slow, and the boys didn't arrive with the engine until nearly nine o'clock. Again, it was too late for Fred, in the condition he was in, and when they arrived, he was exhausted. Fortunately, the restaurant at the hotel we were booked into was open until ten o'clock and we got there just in time to get a meal – but only just. In spite of all our efforts to reschedule and cut down on what we were hoping to achieve in a day, everything was still taking far too long.

Next morning after breakfast, I drove down to the railway with Fred and Alf. Alan had already set off with the low loader on his way back to Preston. At the railway yard, there were one or two enthusiasts and volunteers who lent a hand as Fred and Alf got the engine ready for the road.

The plan was to drive from the railway to Falkirk, which was about 8 miles away. I was going to get some driving shots along the way. When we got to Falkirk, we were going to meet up with the crew, who were travelling up from our base in Leeds that morning, and we were going to do some filming at the Falkirk Wheel.

The engine was steamed up and Fred was on his way by eleven o'clock. Progress was good, but sedate. The engine was certainly not bombing along, but it was going much better than it had been. Our route took us past the huge Grangemouth oil refinery. There was a nice shot to get of Fred's relic from the age of steam chugging past this great symbol of the petrol age, so I stopped and waited for the engine to come into view. As I set my little camera up opposite the main entrance, a police car drew up beside me to investigate. They explained that at a time of major security alerts, an oil refinery was clearly a potential target for bomb threats. However, once they had been reassured I wasn't a terrorist, they got in touch with their HQ to let them know that a traction engine was on the loose on their patch, with a cameraman filming it.

We were due to meet up with the crew and start filming at one o'clock, but it was a warm morning and
driving a traction engine was thirsty work, so by then,
after nearly two hours up on the footplate, Fred was
ready to stop at a pub for a pint. We were nowhere
near our meeting place, and it wasn't looking as
though we were going to get there in time to do most
of the filming we had planned to do there. After his
refreshment stop, Fred drove on through the centre of
Falkirk, telling us a bit about why we had come here:

We're now in Falkirk, which was the place in
Scotland where the Industrial Revolution started.
And here there was a great iron foundry called the
Carron Ironworks that were opened in 1760.
After thirty years, they employed a thousand men
there and became the biggest iron-smelting plant
in the whole of Europe. It was 'ere at the Carron
Ironworks that James Watt's first castings for 'is
earliest engines were manufactured. There's not
much of it left now, but this area was the cradle of
the steam revolution, where Watt built some
of the first steam engines. And Watt wasn't the
only pioneering engineer working in these parts.
One of the other engineers working in this part of
Scotland was William Symington, who built the
world's first commercial steam-powered vessel,
Charlotte Dundas.

Charlotte Dundas was an engineering wonder of its
age, and the place we were heading for had a much

more recent engineering wonder as well, the Falkirk Wheel, the world's only revolving boat lift. It's the centrepiece of the £84.5 million Millennium Link, the UK's largest canal restoration project, developed by British Waterways to reconnect the Union Canal with the Forth and Clyde Canal. Moored just in front of the wheel, there is a three-quarter-sized replica of the *Charlotte Dundas*. This was the main reason we were coming here, but the wheel itself is such a great feat of engineering we knew Fred would want to see it.

Yet again, though, time was against us. Arrangements had been made for us to film Fred taking a trip on the Wheel and to talk to the chief engineer, but it was three o'clock now and we just couldn't do it. I could see that Fred was tired, and he still had to drive the engine back to Bo'ness, because there was nobody else with us who was able to, and there was nowhere here where it could be safely left for the night. It had taken over three hours to get here and it was going to take just as long to get back, so our time was very limited. We just about had time to set the camera up on the canal towpath and for Fred to say a few words about the boat and about the great engineering wonder behind it:

The Scottish engineer William Symington built the vessel for his patron, Lord Dundas, who wanted to use it as a canal tug to draw barges along the Forth and Clyde Canal instead of using horses. The engine was built at Carron Ironworks, where Symington was chief engineer.

The horizontal cylinder steam engine, patented by Symington, were years ahead of its time. Steam engines had been tried on boats before, but *Charlotte Dundas* was the first real steamboat in the world that actually worked. It was propelled by a paddle-wheel at the stern and it went into the record books as the first commercial steamship in the world. In 1803 it pulled two barges laden with 70 ton along a 20-mile stretch of this canal at 3½ mph, which is really faster than what we're doing with the traction engine. But the canal owners were concerned that her wash would damage the canal banks, and it never went into service.

The Falkirk Wheel was opened by the Queen in 2002. It did away with eleven locks that covered a height of 115 feet from the top canal to this canal down here and the revolutionary design means it can turn a huge mass of water and steel using a minimum of energy. It's got two caissons* and each of them can hold four 20-metre-long boats. At each revolution, it moves 600 tons of water with 10 hydraulic motors, and they're unbelievably efficient. But in spite of this, each turn of the wheel uses hardly any water and the same energy as just two boiling kettles. And it's so simple. Makes you wonder why nobody ever thought of it before. Boats entering the wheel's upper gondola are lowered along with the water that they float in, to

* Large watertight containers.

the basin below. At the same time, an equal weight rises up in the other gondola.

It was a great pity we couldn't spend more time here because, despite the Wheel's futuristic looks, Fred clearly appreciated the engineering that had gone into it. Twelve hundred tons of steel had been used in its construction, and one of the reasons Fred would have liked to have had the time to take a closer look at it was the fact that, to make the structure stronger, the steel sections had been bolted together, as opposed to welded. But nothing was going right on this shoot. There were just not enough hours in the day to cope with the constraints imposed by the traction engine and Fred's level of fitness. I wondered how much longer we were going to be able to go on.

On the way back through the rush-hour traffic around Falkirk, Fred brought the engine to a sudden halt. It was the usual problem – water. We needed to find some quickly, and right at the last minute, help was at hand. Just near a roundabout a bit further down the road, Fred spotted a van and some yellow-jacketed men working by the side of the road. They were from the local water board and were carrying out some routine maintenance, and they were only too happy to take Fred's pipe, attach it to the stand-pipe where they were working and fill the engine. There's nothing like getting your water straight from the water board! 'Nearly as thirsty as me and Fred, that,' Alf said as they filled the belly tank. 'Thanks very much, chaps.'

With a tankful of water, they were soon on their way again, but as ever, progress was slow. As well as the speed of the engine, another problem was that Fred didn't know the way. I tried driving slowly in front of him to show him, but the roads were so busy we kept getting split up. At one point, just after crossing a roundabout, I realized that the engine was no longer behind me. Fred must have taken a wrong turning. It took about twenty minutes of crawling around in the heavy traffic to find him; then there was chaos, as we had to hold the traffic up so Fred could make a U-turn to get back on track.

By six o'clock, we were still about 4 miles away from the station at Bo'ness and the railway yard where the engine was going to be parked for the night. We were, however, very close to the hotel we were staying at near Grangemouth, so Fred decided to park up in the hotel car park for the night. The hotel management had no objections and Fred was happy that it would be secure.

When he'd parked up and unhitched the living van, Alf began the nightly ritual of cleaning the engine down. I got Fred a pint of Guinness from the bar, and he sat in front of the engine on a battered old garden chair he'd produced from the living van, supping his pint – the picture of contentment. It was a modern hotel (the sort where businessmen have meetings and sales conferences are held), and the car park was full of shiny executive cars – the BMWs and Mercs of the bosses and the big Fords and Peugeots of their sales forces – but nobody had a vehicle like Fred's. His out-shone them all, and his pride was palpable as he sat there with it that evening. He might have been tired and the engine might not have been performing as well as it should have been, but there was nothing else in that car park that compared with it, or with the pleasure of owning it and knowing that you'd done it all yourself.

As I looked across the car park, a man in a suit approached him, and he was soon engaged in animated conversation. It turned out, Fred informed me later when we were having dinner, that it was the owner of the chain of hotels we were staying in, and he'd given Fred a bottle of fine malt whisky. Not such a bad day, after all!

Next morning, Alf was up before breakfast getting the engine steamed up. With everything to do to get the engine ready for the road, he didn't have time to come in to eat, so I took a cup of tea and some toast out for him. We needed to make an early start, because Fred had to drive the engine to Bo'ness before we could start filming at the foundry we were visiting there.

On the way, there was another problem: this time, it was the lubrication system. Fred explained, 'We ended up with what's termed a "hot box", in locomotive terms. It's all right now; we've put plenty of oil in it and it's cooled down. When it's getting too hot, it starts bubbling.' Luckily, the lubrication problem didn't delay us for very long. Fred made good time and was soon pulling into the foundry yard. He told us all about it as he got down from the engine and went in, with Alf by his side:

This is the foundry we've been heading for – Ballantine's Bo'ness Iron Company. It's been here since 1820 and employs over a hundred people. They've cast everything here, from railings and spiral staircases, to 2-ton cannons for Edinburgh Castle. And their red post boxes and manhole covers can be seen all over Britain. But looking around at the quality of workmanship and the ornamental stuff, there can't be many places as good as what this place is, believe me. They have a range of over 250,000 patterns here that they've got together over the years, including fencing, monuments, post boxes, lamp posts, manhole covers and ornamental pieces. In 1950, there were around two hundred foundries like this in central Scotland. But now this is one of the only ones left.

Ballantine's is still a family business, and after meeting the present-day owner, Ian Ballantine, Fred was introduced to Jim Brooks, the company's buyer, who was going to show him round. Within minutes, we knew why Jim had been chosen for the job. He was a very friendly, talkative fellow, and Fred was soon at ease with him. The first place Jim took him and Alf to was the pattern store, a big room that was stacked up with samples of railings, gates, lamp posts and ornamental ironwork products of every shape, size and design. A lot of it was very ornate and beautiful, and their products must have graced many a famous country house, castle or palace. It was all the sort of stuff that Fred really liked. 'Ah, there's some lovely tackle in here, isn't there?' he said appreciatively as he walked in.

Jim agreed. 'Yes, it's really, really nice. This is just one of the pattern stores we have here. As you can see, we can match up any head with any bar, and these days, that's big business for us, for all the restoration work in parks and what have you. In fact, we've just completed Regent's Park, so that's the kind of scale of job we do. Basically, anything cast iron, we make here. Sadly, we're one of the last places left doing ornamental casting like this, but it does mean we are getting a lot of work.'

'It's the same with places like boiler-makers,' Fred observed. 'There used to be loads of them; now there's only a few of them left, which means that those that are left are getting a lot of work.'

'I don't think we've ever counted them,' Jim continued, 'but I think we've got over a hundred thousand patterns within the foundry. Mainly they date back from when the foundry first started. I would imagine the likes of manholes, gutters and railings would have been the order of the day in the 1820s, and we still have all of those patterns somewhere. We never, ever throw away a pattern.'

Fred went over to have a look at some of the railings and picked up an ornamental post. 'A lot of people don't realize,' he said, 'that every one of these had to be made out of wood before it were made out of aluminium or cast iron. You know, there's some skilled work, isn't there?' This was the cue for Jim to take Fred into the pattern shop. This was like a carpenter's workshop, and three men were working at benches creating beautiful and intricate shapes out of wood.

'This is the pattern shop, lads,' Jim said to Fred and Alf as they walked in. 'Aye. Life starts here. We're one of the last general jobbing foundries that's left these days, and we're sent all sorts of things like postcards, and drawings, and they come here into the pattern shop, and the lads, like Alan here and William and Brian and the boys, sort of turn them into reality. And then, from here, they go down to the shop to be cast. But everything starts its life here.'

'Wood is very durable stuff,' Fred observed. 'It doesn't rot away like steel. I'm just making a pattern for a hubcap for me traction engine. It's the last bit of casting on it, and if I'd known what you do before we came here I'd have brought it with me. And I've just paid £800 for some railings, and they're not very good.'

'You should have come here, Fred,' Jim said, 'and we could have done a deal for you.' Fred looked disappointed that he'd missed out on a bargain, but he was fascinated by the work that was being done by the boys in the pattern shop. It was the sort of craftsmanship that he really appreciated – but there was a lot more to see. The next thing were the moulds that were used for the castings.

As they walked into the shop, Jim explained that a big part of Ballantine's work was street furniture. The moulds were lying in lines on the floor, and amongst them were some very recognizable shapes, including bollards, post boxes and lamp posts. As Jim spoke, one of the moulding-shop workers was walking along one of the lines turning one half of each of the moulds over and laying it on top of the other half, making them ready for the molten metal to be poured in. As he did so, he blew any dust out of the mould to ensure there would be no imperfections in the casting.

For the next stage of the process, metal is heated in a furnace, poured into the mould and left to solidify. Jim took Fred and Alf into the main moulding shop so that they could watch this being done. Here, the moulds were much smaller, but there were many more of them. In a corner, away from all the moulds, there was a big, glowing furnace. A figure clad in a heavy protective cloak with a steel helmet completely covering his head stood by. As he peered into the furnace through his visor, he looked like a medieval knight ready to go into battle.

'So this is the main moulding shop we're going into now,' Jim said. 'That's the molten metal in the furnace over there. All of the impurities in it come to the top, and you can see the furnace man has a thing like Neptune's fork, and he takes all the slag off the top so that we're left with the pure metal. You cannot have any of that slag going into the mould, because the impurities would go into the casting and make a mess of it. There's 3 tons of metal in the furnace.'

As he spoke, a fork-lift truck was driven up to the furnace. On it was a metal container, or ladle, as it is known, which was placed down in front of the furnace. The man at the furnace got up on to a raised platform by the side of it and started to turn a wheel, which tilted the furnace forward. As he did so, the lid came slowly off to reveal the white-hot molten metal bubbling inside.

'So that's it coming now; this'll be ductile iron or spheroidal graphite, but I can't say that with my teeth,' Jim said with a grin. As the metal started to pour out into the ladle, there were sparks everywhere, and a blinding white light filled the dark corner of the foundry.

'That's the magnesium that's making it as bright as you see it there, lads,' Jim explained, 'and that'll bring all the impurities up to the top. You can't have that going into the casting. And there's one ton in that ladle.'

Fred watched intently as the glowing ladle was attached to an overhead crane and moved towards the moulds that had been placed there, ready to be filled. This was heavy, dirty, dangerous and, above all, exciting – everything that Fred liked. Two of the foundry men guided the ladle, full of molten metal, from the furnace towards the bigger moulds. They were going to be filled first.

'Stand well back, lads,' Jim said as the ladle passed close by where they were standing. 'We don't want to be getting in the way of that.' As the ladle moved along the line of moulds laid out on the floor, one of the workers manoeuvred it into position ready to pour the metal into the mould, then a second man turned a wheel on the side of the ladle to make it pour. One false move and the white-hot metal would miss the hole in the mould into which it had to be poured and be all over the floor – and the men's feet.

Once the bigger moulds had been filled, it was time for the foundry men to get the hand ladles out. These looked like metal jugs attached to a long handle. The men took them to the one-ton ladle that was still hanging from the overhead crane to be filled, then carried them along the line of moulds, pouring their contents carefully into each one. It all looked highly skilled, a wonderful blend of strength and precision, and Fred looked on admiringly. As the foundry men poured, the furnace man came along to the big ladle with his fork to stir the molten metal up and make sure it was OK.

'It's all still done in the traditional way with the hand ladles, as you see,' Jim pointed out. 'You've got to be pretty strong to carry one of them about. I think one of the lads was saying there's 56lbs in each of them.'

'And I mean, it's not as though you're just doing one, is it?' Fred noted. 'You've got all them holes to fill up.'

'Yes,' Jim said. 'You've got to be a real man to do that. You think you'd be up for it these days, do you think, Fred?'

'Well, up until me present state of health, I'd have been all right with that,' Fred replied. 'But with this bladder cancer, I'm knackered now. Yeah. Couldn't do it now.'

Jim quickly changed the subject, explaining that the metal is poured through the blow holes and that the secret is to make sure you get a continuous flow of good-quality metal. 'It's certainly an age-old process, and I'm sure we'll be here doing it for a long, long time.'

'Well, this area's very famous for the foundries, isn't it?' Fred said.

'It really is, yes,' Jim replied. 'We've been here since about 1820. The company was started here, and it has been in the Ballantine family ever since. And good news for us, the present Mr Ballantine has a young son, so hopefully he'll come along and join us. He's at university at the minute. The other good thing about Mr Ballantine is that, when he was coming into the business, his father made him come here into the moulding shop first and do this. He made him do the moulding, and he worked in the pattern shop and every other department so he'd have a real insight into the business.'

Fred was still watching the foundry men as they skilfully turned the handles with a twist of their wrists to pour the glowing liquid into the moulds. The job fascinated him, and he wanted to know how long it took one of the young ones to learn the job well enough to be able to be left on his own to do it.

'It's really a five-year apprenticeship,' Jim answered. 'You know, there's a lot of father-and-son combinations in here, so they'll learn the skills from their dad.'

After lunch at the foundry, it was time to go back to the engine to do some driving shots. Although Fred had now been in Bo'ness for two days, we'd not seen him arriving here, so the first thing to do was to film him pulling in at the railway. He drove the engine up the approach to the station and, bringing it to a halt, said, 'We're now heading for the Bo'ness and Kinneil Railway, where they've given me permission to park up me steam traction engine and me caravan. The railway is home to Scotland's largest collection of steam locomotives, dating back over a hundred years.' He'd had a good long run on the engine the previous day, so I asked him how he was feeling about the performance of the engine. His reply was quite positive:

Well, it's getting better. It's running a lot better now. We've 'ad some good spells of maybe 14mph and speeds like that. But we've also 'ad some trouble with the offside back-axle bearing. We ended up with what, in locomotive terms, is called a hot box. It's draining the oil out of the vessel, so we 'ad to stop for a bit for that. It's all right now, because we put plenty of oil in it and it's cooled down. The other thing is, we filled the boiler right up to the top, and we couldn't move the engine, so we 'ad to empty the boiler by blowing it down on to the road. It's my fault for being inexperienced. But, apart from that, it's going like the wind now, brilliant, if you keep 200lbs on the clock. And it seems to accelerate up 'ills now, which it wouldn't do, would it, when we were in Cumbria. I'm quite pleased. There's nothing dropped off it, you know; that's the main thing. The leaks aren't getting any worse on the rivets. So I think we've won. We've had some good hospitality; free ale and free coal. So we'll wrap it up and go for a pint, I think, usual style.

But a traction engine is not like a car, and before Fred and Alf could go to the pub at the end of the day, there was always plenty of work to do. That night at Bo'ness was no different. As well as cleaning the engine down, there were a few nuts that needed tightening.

As Fred worked on the engine, helped by a couple of volunteers from the railway, Alf was busy with his own jobs. Sorting out the coal and water was Alf's department, and by this stage of the journey, he'd got into a bit of a routine, which he explained to us: 'Well, I've just put water in. We've got a bit of coal; we want quite a bit more yet. And there's some polishing to do. Get the fire died down a bit. And sheet it up. That's about it. And then it starts again tomorrow. We'll light the fire and muck it all up again, and then back to square one when we've finished running. That's the way of it.'

When I asked him if he was enjoying it there was no hesitation: 'Yeah, yeah, I am, yeah. We've met some cracking people up here, haven't we? They've given us water, coal, beer – but I don't know whether that's their hospitality or they're trying to get shot of us,' he said with a laugh. 'No, we've met some cracking lads. There's no doubt about it. Anyway, I'll have to get on with me work.'

From Bo'ness, we were going to head back south to England, but before leaving this part of Scotland we'd arranged for Fred to have a look at the Forth Bridges and to drive his engine over the road bridge. Never before had a traction engine done this under its own steam, so it was going to be a notable first for Fred – something he was looking forward to.

The Forth Bridges – the road bridge and the railway bridge – stand side by side as famous Scottish landmarks, great engineering feats from two different centuries. The rail bridge, which I visited with Fred when we were making the *Magnificent Monuments* series, was opened in 1890. It was called the eighth wonder of the world in its time, the greatest civil-engineering triumph of the nineteenth century.

The plan was to film the engine driving to the bridges and then going over the road bridge. Fred was then going to talk to the bridge master and go up to the top of one of the towers before driving the engine back to the railway yard where it was to stay for the night. The schedule had been worked out the week before and, on paper, it looked reasonable. The Forth Bridges were about 8 miles from Bo'ness, so it shouldn't have been too difficult to make the return journey and fit in all the filming at the bridge in a day, especially as Fred reckoned the engine was now capable of doing about 14mph.

We were up early that day, and Fred and Alf had the engine steamed up and ready to drive out of the railway yard not long after ten o'clock. The railway was down at sea level by the side of the Firth of Forth, but to get up to the main road to the bridges, there was a very steep hill. It was the steepest the engine had faced on the journey so far, and it reduced the speed to less than walking pace. It crawled up, taking nearly half an hour to cover the distance a car would have done in a couple of minutes. We were already running late, and we'd not even travelled half a mile.

Once the engine reached the main road, things improved, but it wasn't very long before our regular problem cropped up: water – or, to be precise, the lack of it. So much steam had been needed to get up the hill, and that had used up a lot of water. Fred started to get a bit panicky as he searched for a supply. Fortunately, there was a lay-by about a hundred yards further down the road, and in it there was a hydrant. A very relieved Fred pulled into it and filled the tanks, just in time to avert what would have been a disaster.

The rest of the drive passed without further incident, but it was still lunchtime before the engine got anywhere near the bridges. When they came into view, Fred pulled over into another lay-by to have a look at them. 'Well, there they are, eh?' he said to Alf as they came to a halt. Then, forgetting which century he was in, he added, 'Two together, one built this century and one last century.'

Which was the rail bridge, Alf wanted to know. 'The red 'un,' Fred replied. 'The one they never stop painting. When they built that railway bridge there were fifty-seven men killed. The other one, there were only a couple killed. But there they are. Two of Scotland's greatest landmarks. I've been on top of the rail bridge, you know. Out on the ironwork.'

'Well, if you're going on the ironwork today,' Alf quipped, 'I'm not coming with you.'

Fred studied the bridge. 'I know one thing: instead of it being built out of wrought iron, it were one of the earliest structures built out of steel. I had a book once, with magnificent drawings and pictures in, and I lent it somebody and it never come back. Of the whole construction of it all, as it went on from day to day. It were a right good book that. But I ain't got it no more.'

Fred turned his attention to the road bridge. 'I wonder if they'll let us go over with this. There might be some sort of speed job, you know. You might have to be able to do 20mph, or something like that, which we can't do, can we?'

It was time to find out. Fred took the brakes off and opened the regulator, easing the great engine out of the lay-by and on to the road in the direction of the bridges. The road bridge was still more than a mile away, and by the time we got to the approach road, it was early afternoon.

'There's one thing about it,' Alf said. 'We'll not have to pay a toll, because traction engines won't be on their noticeboards.'

Fred stopped the engine by the side of the road on the wide approach to the toll booths as we sorted out the logistics of filming the engine crossing the bridge. It was only going to be able to make one return journey, so we decided that the crew would be driven along the service road at the side of the main carriageway to a point where they could get a good shot of the engine driving over the bridge. They would then be taken over to the other side of the bridge, where they would join up with Fred and the engine and film the return journey on the southbound carriageway from inside the living van. Meanwhile, I would go to the top of the north tower with a small camera and get some shots of the engine crossing the bridge over 300 feet below me.

The plan was that, after Fred had crossed the bridge, he would then come to the top of the tower and we'd film him talking to the bridge master up there. Fred was looking forward to this; he still got a buzz from being in high places. I'd already been out on the steelwork on top of the rail bridge with him, so this would complete an interesting double for us.

Fred waited with the engine on the approach road just before the toll booth until everybody was in position. I went to the tower with a rigger and, just as with the Humber Bridge, which we'd done a few years earlier, there was a lift. On the Humber Bridge, the lift goes all the way to the top of the towers, but when I stepped out of the lift on the Forth Bridge we were still inside the tower. The last 30 feet or so was up a vertical ladder. I looked at it and knew instantly that Fred wouldn't be able to do it. It was an awful moment as the reality of Fred's condition sank in. In the earlier days of our filming together, he would have raced up, but he would have found it impossible to climb up it now, especially after driving the engine all day. Looking at the ladder, it came home forcefully to me how close to the end of his life Fred was.

Throughout the shoot, Fred was in denial. He would never admit to me how bad he was feeling; he was using the tour to keep himself occupied with something he enjoyed doing and trying to keep all thoughts of death and his failing powers out of his mind. I knew I couldn't bring him up here. Having him face this ladder would have brought it home starkly to him how much he had declined; how close to the end he was. There was going to have to be a change of plan; some excuse for not coming up here with him. In the meantime, though, I had a job to do up there, so I followed the rigger up the ladder and stepped out into the wind, on to a little platform 508 feet above the Firth of Forth. It was a spectacular vantage point, a place way up in the sky, where Fred would have been so much at home.

I set the camera up on a tripod and, looking through the telephoto lens, I could just see the engine setting off up the hill towards the tolls, nearly 2 miles away over on the other side of the bridge. Fred made slow but steady progress across the bridge, and he was soon in the middle and approaching the north tower, where I was stationed. From my vantage point, the engine and the living van were like small toys, but they were a sight worth seeing as they crossed that bridge, and I knew Fred would have been very proud to be at the wheel of the only steam-powered vehicle to cross the Forth Road Bridge. I tilted the camera down as far as it would go until the engine disappeared out of frame and under the tower beneath my feet and then, turning around, followed its progress down the hill and over the Fife shoreline.

The problem with driving the engine across the bridge was that it was all motorway, and it was a long way between the junctions at either end. From the engine's starting point to the middle of the bridge, it was all uphill, and it was a long hill for a traction engine, so it wasn't able to go very fast. Once he got across, Fred had to drive a couple of miles on the Fife side until he reached a roundabout, where he could turn around to make the return journey. Here, he was going to pick up the crew, who had been driven over in one of the bridge's maintenance vehicles. It was a good, simple plan.

I stayed on top of the tower to get some shots of the engine coming back over the bridge. Half an hour at the most, I thought it would take, but half an hour passed and there was no sign of the engine – and the weather was on the turn. I looked to the south, and a band of rain was sweeping towards us from the Pentland Hills. It looked as though we were going to get a soaking up here, exposed to the elements on top of the tower, but the rigger assured me that we wouldn't. He said rain coming up from the south always settled over Edinburgh Airport. He was right, and it was just as well, because we were in for a long wait. Forty-five minutes went by, then an hour, and there was still no sign.

As I waited, I looked over to the railway bridge and thought of happier days, when I'd been up there with Fred, and of some of the other places we'd been to – the top of the Humber Bridge, on the scaffold around the dome of St Paul's, amongst the towers on top of Glamis Castle and in the service tunnel in the middle of the Channel Tunnel. We'd had some good times and gone to a lot of places, like the one I was in now, that most people would never see.

Eventually, after what seemed like an eternity, the engine reappeared, making its way slowly up the hill on the Fife shore, back towards the bridge. I got the shots, came down from the tower and went back over the bridge to meet up with Fred and the crew at the bridge master's office over on the south side. When I got there, the dilemma I faced about Fred and the tower had been solved for me. It was far too late in the day to go up the tower and do any filming. On this one occasion, the slow progress and the poor performance of the engine had come to my aid.

Fred explained what had happened and why it had taken him so long. When he and Alf had got over to the Fife shore, the steam pressure was very low and they couldn't attempt the return across the bridge until they had raised it; hence the long delay. The crew were travelling back to base in Leeds that afternoon, and Fred was supposed to be getting the engine back to the railway at Bo'ness. There was just time to film Fred talking to bridge master Alastair Andrew by his office under the south tower.

Alastair explained that the bridge was just approaching its fortieth anniversary. 'But,' he went on, 'we've got a big problem. Not only do we have to maintain this structure because it's forty years old, but it was designed in the 1950s, when the heaviest commercial vehicle was only 24 tons. And now the European standard is 44. Added to that, last year we carried 24 million vehicles.'

Fred wanted to know if they could put stronger ropes on, but Alastair explained that it wasn't the ropes that were the problem; it was the towers that were reaching their limit. 'In fact,' he said,

we recently put new towers inside the existing towers. We had prefabricated steel sections inserted at river level, and jacked up inside. And the wall thickness of that new steel is about an inch and a half. So you have a column taking an extra 6,000 tons off the existing site. The original vertical cables have been replaced, and we're about to go into the main suspension cables. You've got 11,500 parallel wires in each of those, and we've no idea what's happening inside there, so we're about to force it open, using wooden wedges to look inside and see if there's any serious corrosion in there. What you've got to remember is, it's blowing up quite a gale now, but if the winds got up to 100mph, the centre span would move out 23½ feet in the direction of that wind. So every 60 feet across the deck, you've got a movement joint, and that's where you get the clatter as you move across the bridge. We close at 85mph to all vehicles, because after that point you're starting to get light heads coming off and blowing around, and that's a bit dangerous. Standing where you are now, you would actually see the bridge starting to oscillate in a wind like that. The whole bridge is designed to be flexible. It's hanging on springs, effectively.

When Fred learned from Alastair that the top of the towers were over 500 feet above the river, he said he'd never been up a chimney that big. 'But,' he said, 'we attempted to knock a concrete one down that were 450 foot high, but the bloody thing fell down a day early. It were quite funny, that. Nobody knew what were going to happen. Even the experts. Because concrete chimneys are hard to get rid of. They have a tendency to come straight down. They don't like falling over.'

Fred and Alastair talked a bit more about the bridge, but it was getting late; far too late, in fact, for Fred to drive the engine back to Bo'ness that night. Alastair suggested that the engine could be left parked up in the maintenance yard at the bridge. There was a high level of security there, so it would be safe until the low loader came to collect it to transport it to the north-east for the next stage of the journey the following Monday.

Next day was Saturday, and the Bo'ness and Kinneil Railway was going to be open, with a steam train running on it. I planned to visit the railway the next morning, before driving Fred and Alf back to Bolton in the afternoon.

That evening before dinner, we went to a local pub in Bo'ness for a couple of pints. It was a bit like the old days; a reminder of all the times in years gone by when I'd always go to the pub with Fred at the end of a day's filming. As we walked in, Fred recognized the barman immediately. It was the furnace man from the foundry we'd visited the day before, and Fred was soon deep in conversation with him about his job. A couple of other workers from the foundry came in and joined in. It was the sort of company Fred had always enjoyed. It was a traditional, cosy little pub, the beer was good and so was the company. Fred was relaxed and enjoying himself, listening to the workers' stories and talking about little foundries he remembered in Bolton. It was a good night, but nights like this were getting fewer and fewer.

Next morning after breakfast, we made our way down to the railway. In the yard outside the engine sheds, a little tank engine was being steamed up for a day's work taking visitors along the line to Kinneil and back. Fred soon had a crowd of engine men gathered around him, and he was in his element, regaling them with stories about the building of his engine and his battles with the planning department over the digging of his mine shaft. When the subject of his health came up, he treated it lightly, as he always did with a group of men like this. He had a running gag about his condition, and now, as always, he joked, 'I don't have a dick any more. I have a tap. An' I've got a bag 'ere on me leg to run it off into.' But he was soon back on to the subject of his engine and the saga of the throat plate.

As Fred told his stories, it became clear that there was a problem with the tank engine that he was due to have a ride on. It wasn't going to be able to run, so they were getting a substitute out from the sheds instead. Fred walked over to the station and stood on the platform as a diesel shunter came in. 'While we're here in Bo'ness,' he said, 'we've decided we'll have to have a ride on the railway. It should have been on a steamer, but steam engines are notably temperamental, and they're having trouble with their injectors, like I were with me traction engine the other day, so we've had to resort to the good old diesel engine.'

After a ride up to the Kinneil end of the railway and back down again in the cab of the little diesel, it was time to take Fred and Alf back to Bolton. We'd be back on Monday morning to pick up the engine and do some driving shots on the way down to the north-east for the next stage of the grand tour.

6

Water and Boilers

A long with coal, it was water that was needed to raise the steam that powered Fred's engine on its journey around Britain, so his next port of call was a pumping station that had been built to cater for the ever-increasing demand for water in the Victorian age.

The Industrial Revolution transformed the landscape of Britain. New towns and villages sprang up around mines, factories and railways, and in their turn brought an increasing demand for water, for both domestic and industrial use. This rapid development, without proper planning, left some areas without drains or clean water, and diseases, such as cholera, that are caused by dirty water became common, killing thousands.

Ryhope Pumping Station was built by the Sunderland and South Shields Water Company in 1868. The station ceased operating in 1967 after a century of pumping water, but it still contains two of the finest compound beam engines in Great Britain, and they are maintained in running order by a dedicated bunch of volunteers. Originally developed to pump floodwater out of the Cornish tin mines, beam engines provided the power in the many pumping stations built throughout Britain in the nineteenth century. A beam engine consists of two vertical pistons linked at the top by a beam, which rocks on a central support like a seesaw. The steam cylinder piston is pushed down under the pressure of steam, and the beam, powered by the cylinder piston, pulls up the water-pump piston at the other end.

In 1864, the Sunderland and South Shields Water Company acquired 4 acres of land at Ryhope, and in May of the following year, Thomas Hawksley, in his position as engineer to the company, was asked to provide designs and specifications for the project. The station cost the company £58,416. It has two nearly identical, double-acting, compound, rotative beam engines, which sit parallel to each other. They were made by R. & W. Hawthorn and the cost was £9,000 for the two engines and six boilers. The two 100hp beam engines and their pumps delivered 3 million gallons of water a day from the deep wells at Ryhope. Clean water was pumped from aquifers running through lime rocks 250 feet underground. When the pumping station was in operation, it was not normal to run both engines at the same time; only one was needed, and the other was always on standby, although both could be run in emergencies, and this did happen, particularly during the Second World War. In general, though, each engine was run in alternate weeks, while the standby engine was cleaned and serviced.

We'd arranged secure parking for Fred's engine at the headquarters of Northumbrian Water, and stayed at a nearby hotel. Alf and Alan were up early in the morning to transport the traction engine to the pumping station and get it steamed up ready for me to film Fred driving around the area, prior to the rest of the crew's arrival for the main part of the shoot. The driving was still very important to Fred. Despite all the problems with scheduling around the engine, and the obvious pain it was causing him, he wanted to go on with it wherever there was an opportunity. He'd spent so many years dreaming about getting that engine on the road, and the joy of doing it just seemed to outstrip all the pain. There was a bizarre conflict between the agony you could see he was in and the pleasure he drew from shovelling coal into that engine, covered in oil, and climbing up on it. He was so proud of having made it with his own hands. To have achieved all that and then to have only a couple of months to enjoy it meant that, every single time he drove it anywhere, it was very special, and he wanted to drive it as far as he could.

We did a 4- or 5-mile circuit around Ryhope and, at the end of it, the engine drove into the park-like grounds of the pumping station, coming to a halt next to the cooling pond in front of the elaborately gabled Victorian engine house. It was the perfect setting for

Fred's engine. Its shining brasswork was reflected in the green waters of the pond as Fred and Alf got down to meet Keith Bell from the Ryhope Engines Trust.

'We've come to look at your wonderful engines,' Fred said. 'I've been before, but it were all locked up. There was nobody here. Me and my missus, Sheila. We had a wander around, and she commented on how beautiful it were.'

Keith took Fred and Alf into the engine house, where the two massive compound beam engines stand, symmetrically located on either side of the building. The high standard of the original design and manufacture and the quality of the maintenance over their hundred-year working life means that they are in perfect condition. It's not possible to see an entire engine from any single position, as each occupies three floors within the engine house.

On the ground floor, Fred was shown the hand starting levers for the engine and, on Keith's invitation, he had a go at starting one of these giants of steam. Fred looked excited as he stepped up on to the engine driver's platform and turned the steam valve. Once it was open, he started to operate the regulators that set the engine in motion. It was an awesome sight. Grace and power combined as pump rods, connecting rods and piston rods moved slowly and almost silently in unison.

'These engines are very big,' Keith said once Fred had got the engine running, 'but they are very low on power. They only generate about 100hp. But they did a tremendously effective job. They would pump 80 gallons every stroke, 10 strokes a minute, 24 hours a day. And in that time they pumped about a million gallons of water.'

With the engine in motion, Keith led Fred and Alf up to the middle floor. 'Here,' he said, 'you can look down and see the full size of the cylinders, and you can see the parallel motion. And see how beautifully it works.' Parallel motion is an ingenious device, invented by James Watt, for transferring power from the rocking motion of the engine beam to the vertical motion of the pump rod. He called it parallel motion because both the piston and the pump rod must move vertically, parallel to one another.

The movement of the engine, especially the parallel motion, was quite mesmerizing, and the three men stood watching until Fred broke the silence. 'How many men would it take to work this place?' he wanted to know.

'It would vary,' Keith told him. 'There would probably be an engine man and an engine cleaner, a boilerman and a boiler-cleaner and a supervisor, so probably a team of five during the daytime. That would probably fall back to three in the evening, and only two overnight. But the superintendent lived on site, so they could go and knock on his door if there was a problem. But it would have taken a brave man to turn up on his doorstep in the middle of the night.'

From the topmost floor, the huge rocking beams can be seen and, above them, massive wooden joists support the roof and stiffen the engine-house walls. The beams are like a huge version of a simple garden pump, transmitting steam power via long connecting rods to pumps located at the bottom of a 250-foot-deep shaft. Three Lancashire boilers make steam to drive these engines. 'Aye, that lovely smell of steam, eh?' Fred said as they walked between the two beams. 'How many tons did that beam weigh?' he asked Keith.

'Twenty-two,' Keith replied. 'It took a team of forty-four horses to pull each beam all the way from the banks of the River Tyne, where they were built. Imagine that. And when they got to the Sunderland Bridge, the toll keeper took one look, and he went, "There's no way you're bringing that over my bridge." But they got here somehow, so they must have got across in the dead of night.'

Alf was studying the beams. 'How did they actually get these beams into position?' he wanted to know. 'Because you can see they couldn't get them in through the door.'

'They partly built the engine house to this floor level, winched the beams in, and then built this huge roof over the top. And the roof actually ties the building together as well.' Keith pointed up into the roof of the engine house. 'You see the pulleys and hooks and eyelets there amongst the wooden joists?' he said. 'The idea was that that roof would take the weight of that beam for any engine maintenance work that might have been needed. It was never tried, and I don't think I'd like to try now. But it was designed to do it.'

The top floor was a good vantage point from which to look down on to the huge engine. 'If you look down,' Keith advised, 'you get a lovely view of the cylinder tops. You can see the different size and diameter of the cylinders; wonderful, intricate pieces of metalware. Just watch your head, though, as you look over, so you don't get a clatter from the beam.'

At the heart of any steam engine is the boiler. The three Lancashire boilers they've got at Ryhope date back to 1908, and Keith took Fred and Alf down to the boiler house to have a chat with three of the volunteers. 'There's nothing like sitting down and having a cup of tea in front of one of these boilers,' he said as they settled down.

'Especially in the winter,' Fred agreed, 'when there's snow on the ground and it's nice and warm in here. I'd have liked to have been born then. When I were a kid, there were literally hundreds of these in Bolton. Now there's not even one. You know who invented them, don't you? It were Sir William Fairburn – a Scotsman. Do you know how they made them? They made them stood up on their end. They had a big tower like a pithead gear made out of wood, and at the top some winding gear and a beautiful hook so you could move all 30 ton with one hand.' Fred compared notes about boilers and gave the Ryhope men some tips for getting free fuel. 'Go to Newcastle,' he told them, 'and go round all the places that do replacement windows, and tell them you'll take all the old ones from them, because they have to pay to get rid of them, and they're always glad to find somebody they can give them to. I'm the last man left with any industry in Bolton,' he went on, 'and the council are always threatening me regarding smoke emissions.

There's no chimneys left, only mine, and they should really give me a medal, because I'm the man who knocked them all down.'

After telling them all about his garden, Fred went back to the subject of their boiler house. 'Compared with most boiler installations, this is a bloody palace, innit? You go in some and it's all red rust.'

The volunteers were clearly pleased to hear this praise coming from Fred, and one of them replied jokingly, 'We do keep these boilers very carefully; even better than our wives!'

After Alf had had a go at firing up the boilers, he and Fred paid a visit to the blacksmith's shop next door, where George, the blacksmith, was making a fire bar. He told Fred and Alf that he had worked for forty-three years at a local colliery. 'We used to do a lot of cage work,' he said, 'and for some of the jobs I used to have to get out on the plank across the shaft. I was only sixteen when I started, and I was frightened.'

'Only a plank across the shaft and a black abyss below,' Fred said with relish. 'Those were the days. I don't know what the Health and Safety men would make of it these days. You'd have to have a suit of armour on, or a chain wrapped round you anchored to the Empire State Building; then you could do it. I've had a ride up and down a few shafts on top of the cage. That's exciting. You can see the other one coming up. But people don't realize all that sort of stuff went on in this modern world we live in. People say to me, "You're brave going up a chimney," but that's nothing like working in a mine shaft. Because it's dark, what people don't realize is that a mine shaft is ten times deeper than a chimney.'

Fred asked George whether he'd done many bits and pieces for the boiler next door and then announced, 'Well, gentlemen, we're going to have to leave you. We're on our way to Middlesbrough to look at the transporter bridge. I wonder if they'll let me go across with my traction engine. I opened the visitor centre a few years ago, so I think they will.'

The next morning, Alf was out early again, getting the engine on to the low loader with Alan for the short journey to Middlesbrough. Here, it was unloaded and steamed up for Fred to drive to the transporter bridge, which was opened in 1911 to carry pedestrians and goods across the River Tees. It was hailed as one of the great engineering feats of the time. It still carries 250 foot passengers and 300 vehicles every day.

'And there it is, Elf,' he said as they approached the great steel structure. 'That's Middlesbrough's pride and joy. The biggest transporter bridge that still works in all the world, you know, tall enough to allow ships to pass under it. Yeah, and it were built by William Arrol in Glasgow, who actually built the Forth Railway Bridge. It were made in Glasgow, transported here in big lumps, and then riveted together. When they opened it, they must have had a bit of a ding-dong, and the lord mayor fell in the bloody river. You can just see it with the tall hat floating downstream.'

The bridge provides a regular quarter-hourly service between Middlesbrough and Port Clarence on the northern side of the River Tees for eighteen hours a day. In December 1993, it was awarded the Institution of Mechanical Engineers' highest honour – the Heritage Plaque – for engineering excellence.

The bridge is a cantilever construction with three main bridge spans. It is, effectively, two almost independent structures joined at the centre of the river. Each half of the bridge has an 'anchor' span of 43 metres (140 feet), and then cantilevers across the river from which a travelling car deck, or gondola, is suspended by thirty steel cables. It runs on a wheel-and-track system approximately 43 metres (140 feet) above the river. An electric winder located on the south bank pulls the trolley back and forth, and the bridge's unusual design lets sailing ships with tall masts freely navigate the channel.

When they got closer to the bridge, Fred brought his engine to a halt, and looking at the great steel structure that towered above them, he told Alf a bit more about it. 'As well as having the gondola going across,' he said, 'they had steps, and you could walk across for nothing in the morning when you were on your way to work and come down the other side. If you climbed the ladders, you didn't pay.'

'I heard about one bloke,' Alf said, 'who used to cycle to the bridge, carry his bike up and across, and that way he didn't have to pay.'

'Yeah, I once went up there,' Fred said, 'and it's bad enough on your own, never mind carrying a bike. I've actually seen a list of tariffs from about 1911, and it says a traction engine is the equivalent of 10 shillings.

I'd better go and have a word with the bridge master and see if it still stands.'

Fred and Alf stood on the footplate of the engine, studying the strange-looking structure. 'The men of Middlesbrough are famous for building bridges, you know,' Fred said. 'They built a few up and down the world. I think they did the Sydney Harbour Bridge from here. There's one or two rivets in this one, though, isn't there? There must have been some good riveters around here in the olden days. I'm fed up with rivets, though. There's another sizzling on our boiler. But let's go and have a closer look at it. Are you ready? Brake off.'

'Do you think it'll hold our weight?' Alf asked.

'Yeah,' said Fred confidently. 'There will have been heavier things than us been over it, you can bet.'

When they got to the bridge, the conductor directed the engine on to the gondola then signalled to the driver in the control box on the opposite bank. After assuring himself that the river was clear of shipping, he set the gondola in motion to make its way across to the south bank of the River Tees. As Fred's engine was transported across, he stood up on the footplate beside Alf, clearly enjoying the whole experience.

'Hello, Fred. Want to come and see the workings?' the bridge master asked as they reached the other side. 'They're all original. Haven't changed since 1911.'

'The rope's not so thick for what it's doing,' Fred observed. 'For the weight and distance it travels. How long does it take it to get across?'

'Well, it takes, on average, two minutes,' the bridge

master replied. 'But when I'm not here, you never know what they're up to. They drive a lot faster.'

Fred wanted to know if they always waited for a full load before they took the gondola across. 'No,' the bridge master replied, 'because it's on a schedule: every quarter of an hour. But one of the things that does stop this bridge is high winds. Let's go and look at the control box and see the driver in the cab at the controls.'

Going up the steps, there was a good view of the shipping along the river. Fred was more interested in the structure, though, and he stopped to test the steel cables on his way up. Up in the control box, the driver was ready to start the gondola up for its return trip across the Tees.

'You can see,' the bridge master said, 'driving it is the same principle as driving a tram with one-power control. It's all pretty basic.' So basic was it that they let my daughter Kathryn have a go at driving it. 'In the town,' the bridge master said, 'everybody's proud of the bridge. They call her the old lady.'

'Oh aye,' Fred said. 'I remember that day I came to open the visitor centre, there were great crowds of people all shouting its praises. But I suppose we'd better put our engine on the low loader. The next port of call is Israel Newton's boiler works at Idle, near Bradford. He might be able to stop a few leaks in our boiler.'

By this time, I'd handed some of the directing over to Jon Doyle. Fred got on well with Jon, as did the rest of the team. Fred liked him because he'd taken the trouble to get to know a bit about the engine and the way that it worked, and he'd been around filming all the preparations for Fred's last chimney earlier that year. Nobody had ever done that before, and Fred was pleased that there was a record of it. Jon remembers the filming at the transporter bridge as a particularly good day, because the bridge itself was such an amazing thing, the weather was good and Fred really enjoyed himself.

From Middlesbrough to Idle was about 70 miles, so Alan was standing by with the low loader to transport the engine part of the way. The following day, we'd got some more driving shots scheduled, from Menston to the boiler works at Idle. Before setting off, Fred told us about the importance of good boiler-making:

The backbone of me engine is the boiler, which is needed to raise the steam to make the thing go. Boilers contain steam at a very high pressure, which of course is very dangerous, so the boiler-maker has to make sure that the riveting and the plate work is done to a very high standard, or this could lead to an explosion and create mayhem and havoc over a great area. So at Israel Newton's we'll be looking at one of the most important parts of any steam engine. It's not very long ago that there were boiler-makers all over Britain, and there was even until quite recently a Boiler-makers' Union, but it's a trade that has all but disappeared now. Israel Newton's is now one of the few boiler-makers left in Britain where boilers are still made in the traditional way, using rivets, not welding, as some people are doing now. To me, it's a great privilege to go and watch how they did it in the olden days, being a bit of an amateur boiler-maker myself.

Soon after setting off that day, the problem that seemed to crop up every time we filmed Fred driving the engine raised its head again. Not only was there no coal in the bunker, but the water level was dangerously low. Water was usually quite easy to find, but coal was proving to be a little more difficult to get hold of. Fred talked about the problem:

Roughly, we know how far we can go on a locker-ful of coal. And before it's all gone, you get some more somewhere. Sometimes you can flag a coal lorry down and get some, but when you're out in the sticks, you don't see many. If you're going on a big journey, I've had friends who, before they set off, they know roughly how far they can get, so they arrange with a coal merchant to leave some at a pub or something like that.

We knew the coal problem was coming up again, so Kathryn had gone in search of supplies. Before the shoot, she had drawn up a list of coal merchants all around the country, and on this occasion she was able to buy some from a railway yard and get hold of some sacks from a local builder's merchant, who obligingly agreed to deliver the coal in his Land Rover.

But Fred didn't just need coal; he needed water as well.

As he stopped near what looked like a fire hydrant, Alf got down from the engine and said, 'As you can see, we're empty. We've no coal left. We'll have to fill up with water, and there's a kind gentleman here who's offered to get us some coal.' As Alf got the tackle out of the living van for filling the water tanks, Fred spoke to the man Kathryn had set up to deliver the coal she had bought. 'I might just know a coal yard down the road with a bit of coal,' the man said, in a fine bit of acting. 'Any particular type?'

'Well, the bigger the lumps, the better,' Fred replied.

Recalling the incident, cameraman Rob Taylor said, 'I think I was still under some kind of illusion that this whole thing was all happening for real. I didn't realize how much of it was set up. Jon was very keen to film everything for real, as though Fred was running out of coal and somebody appeared in the nick of time who knew where he could get a couple of bags.'

Then as Alf went to get the water, Fred noticed there was something wrong. 'That, gentlemen, is not a fire hydrant,' he said. 'It's a stop valve.' A class of primary-school children was walking along in line on the other side of the road with their teacher. Fred shouted across somewhat hopefully, 'You don't know if there's any fire hydrants, do you?' Then he added to us and Alf, 'Fire hydrants, as a rule, have a bloody great big letter "H" and are painted yellow.'

All this was being filmed, and Rob said, 'There was some confusion over what was a fire hydrant and, as with the coal, Jon was keen to film this in a real-life way, with a sense of the danger of running out of water. But I think Fred was concerned that we'd look stupid, like we didn't know what we were doing, trying to get water out of the wrong place. It was all a bit frantic for a while that day. A lot of things happened in a rush, all a little bit out of control.'

As it was, there wasn't any great problem with the water. Alf walked off down the road and found a hydrant no more than 50 yards further along. Fred drove the engine to it and they started to fill up. It was always quite a long job, so we got some sandwiches from a nearby bakery and, as Alf stood by the side of the living van eating his, he talked about the problems they were having. 'Nothing seems to have gone right today,' he said. 'We're havin' a lot of bad luck with coal and water, and things don't seem to be going right. We've had this helpfulness everywhere we've been, though, haven't we? Everybody's enjoyed seeing us; talking to us and helping us.'

Just as Alf was saying this, a lady came from a nearby house with cups of tea for him and Fred. 'You see what I mean?' Alf said to us. Fred always drank coffee, so Alf thanked the lady and said to her, 'Just tell him it's Guinness and he'll drink it all.'

As Fred was drinking the tea and finishing his sandwich, a Land Rover drew up behind the engine with two sacks of coal in the back. 'Welsh steam coal, I believe,' the driver said. 'Shall we put it in the back of your engine?'

Alf helped the man to tip the sacks into the coal box and then spotted Kathryn, who had been away all morning getting the coal sorted out. 'Nice to see you've joined us,' he said, thinking she'd been skiving or having a lie-in. 'This helpful man's got us some coal.' She didn't say anything, and let Fred and Alf think they had been saved by this good Samaritan who had appeared on the scene out of the blue.

With the coal and water supplies replenished, they were soon on their way again, but Fred was getting irritated by the leaks that were still appearing all over his boiler barrel. 'These holes are only as big as fly's legs,' he said. 'They're not great big, gaping holes, but they're a bit of a nuisance. When it's not under pressure, there's nowt there; it's dry. But the boiler inspector mustn't think it's going to blow up, so we'll be all right.'

Restoring traction engines is an expensive business, but being a steeplejack, Fred couldn't afford the services of a professional boiler-maker, which is why he built the whole thing himself. At Israel Newton's boiler works, boilers are still made in the traditional way, using traditional plate-bending, flanging and hot-riveting techniques. It's run by Mr Gordon Newton, who is the sixth generation in a family-run business that was founded in 1803.

Fred was looking forward to meeting Gordon and having a look round his boiler works, but progress was slow that afternoon. Jon Doyle remembers particularly the struggle to get up some of the hills. 'The drive from Menston to Idle was a long way. There were some big hills and a lot of traffic, and they were absolutely knackered by the time they got there. Totally exhausted.'

Idle is on top of a hill, and when they finally arrived at the works, it was nearly seven o'clock. Fred was proud of his own boiler-making skills, and when he was greeted by Gordon on his arrival, the first thing he wanted to do was to tell him all about his boiler.

'Aye, we got the rivets from Barnsley for the foundation ring and the new throat plate and round the barrel. The only original plates of the boiler are the top wrapper, the back end and the throat plate. We were ready to rivet the new barrel into it which we made twenty years ago, and a bloody crack appeared.' Fred went on to recount the whole saga of the crack, the new throat plate he had made and the various methods he'd used to stop up all the leaks. Alf had heard it all before, so he lay down on a grassy bank and closed his eyes.

When we went into the works the following day, a huge boiler from a railway locomotive was being lifted by an overhead crane. Fred and Alf wandered around, having a look at everything. It was a hive of activity; just the sort of workshop that Fred loved being in. Red-hot plates were being pressed and shaped in a huge metal press, and sparks were flying in another corner, where somebody was doing some angle grinding. Gordon came over to join them and showed them a bagful of rivets. They were all different sizes, and some of them had names on the rivet head.

'Bending iron,' Alf said to Gordon. 'There's a lot of repetitive stuff, but once you've got it set up right, it's easy then, isn't it?'

FRED DIBNAH'S MADE IN BRITAIN

Gordon agreed. 'Yes,' he said. 'It's the setting up and the thinking behind it that's important.'

This led Fred into a long and detailed technical discussion on the differences in the shape of the fireboxes on Fowlers and Burrells and the tooling that is needed for them.

As Fred and Alf talked to Gordon, they watched plates being put into the press. 'What temperatures do you need to put it in the press and get the job done?' Alf wanted to know.

'You're getting on for 980–1,000°C,' Gordon replied.

I do some press work for other people, and I've got to issue a certificate saying they've been done at a certain temperature. But you go by colour. There's one man who looks after this side of the furnace. But he knows, once the plate is the same colour as the furnaces, it's right. Now, stainless steel is a bit different. It's very stiff material, and you've got to be very quick with the forming process. You've got to have the temperature as high as you can. But it's all dictated by your furnaces. Obviously, you can't go any higher than they will go. The thicker a plate is, the longer it takes to warm up. Historically, all boiler-makers did their own pressing, and when the crash came in 1929, my great-grandfather closed these premises and sacked all his men. He had at that time two sons, and my father was the grandson. And there were quite a few other boiler-makers at the time, and all were affected by this recession. Then in April things got a bit better, so my grandfather started to recruit staff again. But a lot of the other boiler-makers never started again.

They got on to talking about the way men learned to do a job like this. 'My father,' Gordon said, 'always used to say theory is practice written down.' This was a view that was close to Fred's heart; one that he kept coming back to as we went around filming.

The centrepiece of Gordon's workshop was a 1930s press which made the curved plates that were needed for almost every type of boiler. Alf wanted to know what pressure it would squeeze to. 'It's only about 50 ton,' Gordon replied, 'which is amazing. But you don't need any more than that when you are hot pressing. If you're doing cold pressing, you need 500 ton or something like that.'

Fred was fascinated by the place and very interested in the whole history of the business. 'Have you been here a long time?' he wanted to know.

'I've been here since 1960,' Gordon said, 'but the business has been here at this works since 1905. The man who actually started the business was a chap called John Newton. His son was called Israel. They were all engineers, and I'm the sixth generation. My father always used to say when I came to the business, "Never give a man a job to do unless you can do it yourself." And that's how, in my opinion, all businesses should be run. But that's not so any more.'

Gordon then took Fred and Alf on a guided tour of the works to look at the various jobs they had in. They approached a locomotive boiler, and Gordon said, 'This is my pride and joy at the moment. We were approached by the Great Western Society with some very old drawings going back to 1904, to make a brand-new vertical steam rail boiler. The shell or barrel is tapered. This shape took a lot of thinking on the way that it was made, and I'm pleased how it's turned out. There are 415 tubes in it.'

'It'll be a good steamer with all them tubes,' Fred said. He wanted to know what the tubes were made of, and Gordon told him that they were steel. 'People don't realize when they look at one of these things,' Fred went on, 'that for every square inch, there's 160lbs trying to blow it apart.'

They were still looking at the boiler that was being made for the Great Western Society. 'We've been working on this for about two and a half years,' Gordon said, 'and there's no great rush, because they've got to raise the money for it, and it all comes from fund-raising. So they're not pushing me, and I'm quite happy with something like this, where there isn't one like it in the world to copy or have a look at. You've got to take your time. The last one that was made was in 1918, so there's nobody living who's got any experience of building one of these things.'

When Alf wanted to know whether there was a good future in the business, Gordon told him that they had enough work that was ongoing for twelve months, and continued, 'And the type of work we're doing, which is a mix between locomotive work and traction-engine work and also pressing parts for people to put things like fireboxes together, means there is a definite future. And with there being a lack of skills, you'll always get the work.'

'How are you going on about that,' Alf wanted to know, 'about getting people to come in and learn the skills?'

'It's very difficult,' Gordon said. 'You just can't get anybody to . . .' He paused. 'Well, they don't want to wear a boiler suit, for a start,' he continued:

it's not street cred. Sorry about that, but that is a problem. They don't want to dirty their hands. We once had an older generation brought up in a more disciplined manner who were more interested in old things, but that's gone now. I'm now sixty-one, and I've no plans for retirement. Some people can't wait to retire, but I'm not that way inclined. But I'm the last of the Newton family. I've no male heirs, so I've got to make some sort of decision. I can't just say, 'I'll plough on till I drop dead'; you've got to make some sort of plans, so a trust is now being formed. Our business will transfer to this other trust and then, from then on, we can get young people in and try and make boiler-makers of them. People still want traditional type of work. The trust will be the Boiler Skills and Training Trust, and then a subsidiary of the operating company will be Israel Newton 21st Century Ltd. And that's how it'll go.

Fred was reassured. Here was one old skill that wasn't going to be allowed to die out. And as boiler-making headed into the twenty-first century, Fred and Alf were going to head south to visit Sheffield, the city that made the steel for an engine like his.

7

The Road to Steel City

All around the world, the city of Sheffield is associated with steel manufacturing, and it was the advances in steel-making that were made there that made the mass production of steam locomotives, winding engines and traction engines possible. So, from Bradford, Fred was moving on to Sheffield to visit a steelworks.

Iron and steel form the vast majority of Fred's engine, and when it was built, iron was relatively easy to work and could be cast into intricate shapes like the cylinder block and front forks. The problem was, iron is weak. Steel is much stronger, but it's more difficult to make. It's used in the plate work of the boiler and the moving parts, such as the axles and the gears.

It was Monday 21 June, and we'd been filming for

five weeks. Apart from the delays with the engine and the fact that we were not seeing it travelling around the country as much as we would have liked, progress had been good. Fred still appeared to be enjoying the tour, especially when it allowed him to visit places like Israel Newton's boiler works. The main thing was that, despite the fact that he was feeling some pain and discomfort, he still wanted to go on. Focusing on the journey and the places we were visiting was helping him to keep his mind off his illness, at least during the day when we were working, and for some of the time at night, when we were all together having a meal and a drink.

Today was going to be a driving day. We were in the heart of the Pennines, on top of the bleak gritstone moorland between Leeds and Manchester, and it was a little bit of a diversion. Fred had two places near here that he wanted to go to on his engine. Neither of them was related in any way to the building of it, but they were favourite places of his, which he wanted to see while he was on his way around the country. The first was Scammonden Bridge, which carries a minor road through this part of the Pennines across the M62 motorway. 'It's about a hundred foot up in the sky,' Fred said, 'and every time I've been under it on the motorway I've always fancied going over it with a traction engine. It's the biggest single-span bridge in Europe, and it crosses the M62 – the highest motorway in Britain – in spectacular style.'

The second place he wanted to go to was Wainhouse Tower. He'd told me all about it years earlier when we were filming *Magnificent Monuments*:

My favourite tower is one I first found out about as a small boy, when I read in a history book about a man who built a magnificent chimney with what looked like a Victorian solid-silver salt cellar on top of it. It's in the Calder Valley near Halifax, and I well remember as a lad of about fifteen going over Blackstone Edge on a Lambretta scooter to go and look at it. John Edward Wainhouse, who built this ornate folly in the late nineteenth century, worked in his uncle's Washer Lane dye works, and he inherited the works when his uncle died. The dye works caused a lot of pollution through smoke emission, and the tower was originally designed as a chimney for the works, but Wainhouse got a bit carried away. He surrounded the chimney with an octagonal-shaped stone casing that had a staircase of over four hundred steps inside it, leading to a balcony up at the top. Over 9,000 tons of material were used to build this elaborate folly, and Wainhouse himself supervised its construction. But by the time it was completed, it had already become clear that it would never be used as a chimney.

The plan on this bright, sunny midsummer morning was for Fred to drive the engine over the Scammonden Bridge to the Wainhouse Tower. It was a distance of about 10 miles in total from where we were parked, a couple of miles from the bridge.

For Alf, the day started with the two-hour routine of

getting steam up. First, there was the ash box to empty. Alf dropped the ash down on to a tarpaulin that was spread out under the engine. He dragged this out when the box was empty and tipped it on to the ground by the side of the road.

As Alf scattered the ashes to the Pennine breeze, Fred got on with the never-ending job of cleaning the engine. Every time he drove anywhere, it finished up covered in oil and coal dust, so everything had to be wiped down. This morning, there was no Jimmy to help either, because Jimmy was on holiday.

'You can see how they ended up all filthy,' Fred said, 'with an inch of muck stuck to them.'

'It won't be like that in another half-hour,' Alf said as he folded the tarpaulin up. Then there was another, big tarpaulin, which covered the engine at night, to pack away, before he and Fred went back to the polishing. Hours and hours were spent doing this every day; a real labour of love. As they polished they chatted.

'Where are we going next, Fred?' Alf wanted to know.

'There's a lot of steel in an engine like mine,' Fred replied, 'in the axles, piston rods and all the gearing parts, so we're heading for Sheffield, the place that's known all over the world as Steel City. We're going to a forge to see how they used to do it, and how they made stainless steel when they first invented it. And we're going to a rivet and nut and bolt works where I actually got the rivets from when I made the boiler. It'll be nice, that. But first we're going over a rather picturesque bridge over the M62 motorway.'

It was eleven o'clock by the time the engine was steamed up and ready to pull out on to the open road. Although we were in the heart of the Pennines, this stretch of the road we were on, high up, was flat, and the engine was soon bowling along at a cracking pace. With no walls, no buildings and no other traffic, it looked fabulous: the engine with living van in tow steaming along in solitary splendour across this empty landscape.

'How far is it?' Alf wanted to know as they drove along.

'I don't know,' Fred replied. 'Just keep going till we get there.'

It was a quiet road, and with not even any junctions or roundabouts to worry about, Fred was able to enjoy himself and go flat out for a couple of miles. After about twenty minutes, Alf thought he could see the bridge they were heading for.

'Is that the bridge?' he asked Fred. 'It looks high up.'

'It is high up, mate, I'll tell you,' Fred said. 'It's 100 foot.'

'Well, I reckon we should pull up and let a couple of wagons test it first,' was Alf's riposte, 'because I don't fancy being test pilot on a traction engine. Apart from anything else, if we land on the motorway, we might get run over.'

By now they had reached the bridge, and Fred brought his engine to a halt right in the middle of it. Cars and lorries sped underneath.

'It's a long way down,' Alf said. 'They only look

like Dinky cars down there. Belting views of the countryside.'

'Yeah,' Fred agreed. 'It's rather exciting up here. When you're down there, you don't quite realize where you are in relation to this bridge. You can see the road to Halifax over there, and the reservoir that you see when you're coming down the hill. Every time I've come along the M62 and seen this bridge it's always fascinated me and I've often thought, I wonder if it'll hold the weight of a traction engine.'

'Well, if you're in any doubt to it holding weight,' Alf interjected, 'we'd best bloody get going.'

'No, no, no,' Fred reassured him. 'You're all right. I've seen a few six-leggers full of rock coming across, so we're all right.' He looked down at the deep cutting through the rock below them and said, 'When you think they must've shifted a few thousand ton of rock to make this M62, just here,' then added mischievously, 'Concrete bends, you know.'

'Shall we get going before the cracks start appearing?' Alf responded.

After a few more jokes about the bridge collapsing, they were on their way again, heading for Wainhouse Tower. But as always when we were out trying to cover any sort of distance with the engine, the day just slipped away, and at six o'clock, we were still 2 or 3 miles away from the tower.

By this time, we had come down from the moors and had reached the little mill village of Greetland. We needed to stop and take stock of the situation, so Fred drove the engine on to the cobbled forecourt of a former cotton mill. He recognized it immediately. Victoria Mills was the home of Andy Thornton's Architectural Antiques, a place where we'd done some filming for a previous series.

One of the things Fred loved about his engine was the craftsmanship that went into building it. 'The skills of making things in Victorian times were highly valued,' he said. 'Stuff they made like the beginning of locomotive construction and traction engines were much more beautiful and ornate than anything you get today, with lots of fancy work. They did have an eye for nice things, without a shadow of a doubt. I think somehow or another we've lost all that now.'

Whether it was engineering, architecture or the decoration of their buildings, Fred loved the work of the Victorian age, and he knew that here at Andy Thornton's, some of the decorative craft skills that he admired so much were still being kept alive. Fred stood on the footplate of his engine outside the mill and said, 'Well, this behind us is Andy Thornton's, and when the wholesale demolition of our lovely Victorian era started, he started collecting all fancy bits, you see, and of course there's not so many left now, so they've gathered around them a team of craftsmen that are capable of doing fancy wood-carving and all sorts of interesting stuff.'

By now, a crowd had gathered around the engine. Cameras flashed and small children looked at the engine in wonder. But it was all a bit frightening for one tiny boy, who burst into tears when Fred blew a long blast on the whistle.

It was the end of the day, and we were not going to be able to make it to Wainhouse Tower. Fred was disappointed, but he'd had a full day on the engine. He was hot, tired and uncomfortable, and there was an hour's car drive still to come to get to the hotel near Barnsley, close to the nut and bolt works where we were going to be filming the next day. Time to call it a day.

Next morning, Alf was up at the crack of dawn again, taking the covers off the engine and getting it steamed up for a drive from the hotel to the Bolt and Rivet Manufacturing Company. It was a place where they were able to make solid rivets the old-fashioned way, in just the sizes that Fred needed when he was rebuilding the engine.

'When I rebuilt me boiler on me traction engine,' Fred explained, 'I had a great deal of trouble finding rivets, especially ones made of the right material. At one time, every little town and hamlet had its own nut and bolt maker and rivet manufacturer, but the invention of electric arc welding put all these men out of business. Once, rivets were crucial; they held together everything from things like my boiler to the Forth Bridge.'

After breakfast we set off from the hotel. The engine was now running a lot better than it was when he first set out, but there were still all sorts of little things that could go wrong, which meant lots of stops. That morning, Fred was having some problems with the mechanical lubricator again, but it didn't slow him down too much. When he arrived at the Bolt and

Rivet Manufacturing Company he was greeted by the company's managing director, Ron Angus. 'I've brought your rivets back,' Fred called out from the footplate of the engine as he drove into the yard of the little workshop, 'but they're all stuck in my boiler!'

'Ah, good,' Ron said with a smile. 'As long as they do the job well.'

'Aye,' Fred replied. 'We made our hydraulic riveter. We've got one or two leaks, but it's passed the hydraulic test and all that. We've done a tour of half of Scotland, so we're not doing so bad.'

Fred climbed down from the engine and very proudly took Ron round the engine, showing him some of the rivets his firm had made. 'I believe you're going to have a go and make some,' Ron said.

'Aye, that'd be nice.' Fred replied. 'I'll have a go.'

The Bolt and Rivet Manufacturing Company specializes in hot-forging large bolts and solid rivets for the ship-building, bridge-building and boiler-making industries. They make about 400,000 a year. Ron led Fred into the little workshop, saying, 'I'm going to show you the last forging machine in the country making hot-forged rivets.' This was just the sort of place that this series was all about, a little workshop where the skills and techniques that had once made Britain the workshop of the world still survived.

Rivets are made by three men: the heater, who is responsible for getting the metal hot and workable; the forger, who actually bashes it into shape; and the clipper, who trims it to the right size in another machine. The round metal bars that the rivets are made from are each put into a hole in a metal frame, which goes into the forge. This is done by the heater. When the end is white hot, he takes it out and places it into a clamp, which goes into the press that shapes the rivet. Fred had a go at this, then had a go at the forger's and the clipper's jobs. He asked them how many they did in a day and was told that it was between 2,000 and 2,500.

When he'd made a few rivets, it was time to get back on board the engine and head back towards the hotel.

Taking in so much scenery in one afternoon was thirsty work, so on the way back they found a pub to stop at. As they sat outside in the sunshine with their pints, they reflected on the journey so far.

'It's going a lot better than it did in Scotland, innit?' Fred said. 'It's got run in, really in, and it's holding its steam a lot better. We're all right now,' he went on:

I'm enjoying this trip, really. It's very tiring, but it's good fun. Easier than working, but in some ways harder.

Yeah, the Ballantine and Bo'ness Iron Company were really good. It must be one of the best places in Great Britain that makes cast-iron railings and fancy bits. I've seen a lot, and it knocks the wotsits off the Taiwanese rubbish you see. The quality of it were brilliant. And the Falkirk Wheel. That's so simple a thing. It makes you wonder why nobody else thought about it before. But the Scotchmen are very clever. There've been a lot of very clever, brilliant engineers from Scotland. And that were good on the Forth Bridge. We're reputed to be the only traction engine that's ever gone over there under its own steam.

'That was the icing on the cake that day,' Alf said. 'And I told the bridge master not to let anyone else steam over and break our record. I'll tell you what, though. All these beautiful things we've been to and these nice places we've seen and that. If I was asked what was outstanding, I'd say the warmth radiating from the people we've met. We've been made welcome, everywhere, haven't we? That's the highlight for me.'

Fred agreed. 'Yeah. People say to me, "I don't know how you put up with it." But you can't really say, "Go away! I don't really want to talk to you." It's nice to be nice to people.'

We filmed as they sat outside the pub and talked. Jon Doyle, who was directing this particular programme, remembers these times on the road with the engine as the best bits of our filming. 'I was gripped by the reality,' he said:

Retired fellas doing this barmy journey and stopping off at every single pub they could along the way and still trying to make a TV series out of it. For me, the best moments were always out on the road, with Alf and Fred bickering, because they began to bicker like a pair of old women. Alf was just so deadpan, and when Fred used to get a bit hoity-toity, he would just quietly remind him that we were all trying to get a job done. The thing with Fred was, he was in another world; he was in Fred's world, and in Fred's world things just happened for him. So his dinner turned up at five o'clock or whatever and coal just arrived, as if the coal fairy just turned up. He would just drive until they'd run out of coal and just sit by the side of the road until some coal turned up, or until somebody came along who said they knew somewhere we could get some. There was no planning, from Fred's perspective. He was all consumed in getting anywhere, in just going on the engine, getting out of the gate or down the road, or down the next road after that. But he knew that we would sort it out for him.

The following morning, we woke up to overcast skies and the threat of rain. Alf was up first thing, as always, to get the engine ready for the road. Rob Taylor remembers Alf's early-morning shift while we were still in the hotel having our breakfasts. 'I wasn't eating meat,' he said, 'but I'd always ask for bacon and sausage with my breakfast and make a buttie for Alf. They cottoned on to this at this hotel we were staying at near Sheffield and started to take sandwiches out to him on a silver platter. So Alf would be there polishing the engine in the car park, and a waiter would arrive with his breakfast on a silver tray.'

The schedule for that morning was to drive a short distance from the hotel to a spot nearby to meet up with Peter Matchan, a local historian. He was going to tell Fred a bit about the history of steel-making in Sheffield and take him to a hill overlooking the city. From this vantage point, he said, you could really see how the steel industry took off here. We set off along the dual carriageway outside the hotel, but Sheffield is a hilly city, and some of the hills were still a bit of a problem for the engine.

They really slowed things down. Within half an hour of leaving the hotel, the engine ground to a halt as it tried to get up a particularly steep hill. It was a narrow road, and the engine blocked one side of it. As they waited until pressure built up, a long queue of cars formed behind them. After a five-minute delay, Fred was ready to make another attempt on the hill. Alf jumped off to release the chocks and, with a hiss of steam, they were on their way again. But progress was still very slow, and there were some frustrated drivers in that part of Sheffield that morning.

To make matters worse, it started to rain. So far on this trip, we'd been lucky with the weather, which was just as well, because the engine still had no roof on it. On a day like this, Fred and Alf were going to get very wet. They were also now running late for their meeting with Peter Matchan. They were looking for a Second World War tank in a district of Sheffield called Tankersley, which is where we had arranged to meet him. It wasn't very obvious where the tank was, but they did eventually find it on top of a grassy bank by the side of the road. They parked up and ascended the bank to have a closer look.

'It's pretty crudely made, isn't it?' Fred observed. 'Welded. No rivets. By 1940, they'd done away with rivets.'

'Not like your engine, Fred,' a voice said. It was Peter Matchan. He came up the bank to join Fred and Alf by the side of the tank. He introduced himself, and explained that his father had worked in the steel industry.

'It were a traction-engine man that invented tanks,' Fred said to him. 'There were hundreds made by . . .' Fred's voice tailed off. He couldn't remember who had made them. 'I'm going a bit senile,' he went on. 'I can't put a name to it. But it was a very famous traction-engine company made the first tanks. Millions of rivets there were on them, but there's not one rivet on this; more like the crudest of welding. It must have been a lot faster than drilling a lot of holes and knocking a lot of iron pegs in.'

'Well, this is a Churchill tank,' Peter informed Fred. 'These were made here in 1940 under contract from Vauxhall. And these were the workhorses of the Royal Engineers. They made eleven hundred of these in just a few months here at Newton Chambers, the big iron-works round here.'

The tank factory had long since gone, along with much of Sheffield's steel industry. There was nothing much to see where we were, other than modern warehousing and light industrial units, so Peter said he would take them to Wincobank Hill to look down on the Don Valley, which had been the heart of Sheffield's steel industry. They left the tank and chugged off into the driving rain with Peter giving directions from the living van.

As the morning wore on, the hills got steeper and the rain got heavier. It was Sheffield's hills that had provided the city with the necessary raw materials for the industry that led to it becoming known as Steel City: coal, iron and millstone grit for the grinding wheels of its workshops. Its rivers provided the water power it needed in the days before steam, while its forests supplied it with plentiful amounts of wood and charcoal. This meant that, even before the Industrial Revolution got under way, Sheffield was renowned for its manufacture of nails, knives, scissors, scythes, razors, axes and other metal products. It had also established its unique reputation and dominant position in the manufacture of cutlery; a virtual production monopoly that continues in Britain to this day.

Sheffield's success as a steel-producing city really took off in the 1740s, thanks to a breakthrough by Benjamin Huntsman, who operated a foundry at Handsworth, 4 miles to the east of Sheffield. His invention of the crucible steel process made it possible to make much harder, high-quality steel in large quantities. Until 1742, producing steel was a difficult task. The quality of the steel was often unreliable. The steel was made by heating iron bars, which were covered in charcoal. The heating was continued for up to a week, and the material produced was called blister steel. This was turned into shear steel by wrapping blister steel bars up in a bundle and heating them again before forging the bundle. The heat and the action of the forge hammer welded the rods together as they were hammered to the size required. Shear steel was used to make razors, files, knives, swords and the other steel items for which Sheffield became famous. But no more than 200 tons of steel were produced each year in Sheffield using this process. Benjamin Huntsman's crucible steel process changed all that. He was the first person to cast steel ingots. The process produced uniform high-quality steel in reasonably large quantities. The demand for Huntsman's steel increased rapidly and, in 1770, he moved his factory to a new site in Attercliffe in the Don Valley. This area later became the main location for the huge special-steel-making industry of Sheffield.

By the end of the eighteenth century, there were ninety-seven recorded water-powered sites in Sheffield, compared with a third of that number at the beginning of that century. But it was the development of steam power and the bulk production of steel that led to the really massive expansion of the industry and of the city in the nineteenth century. In 1801, 46,000 people lived in Sheffield, a figure that had risen to 135,000 by 1851 and 409,000 in 1901. By this time, Sheffield cutlers counted for 97 per cent of the total nationally. A Sheffield cutler, Thomas Boulsover, devised a means of fusing a thin layer of silver to copper to produce silver plate – the famous 'Sheffield plate', which looked like silver but was far cheaper. This invention took silver-plated cutlery into the dining rooms of almost every middle-class family in the land, and Sheffield's domination of the steel industry was complete.

But the success of its industry was only achieved at huge cost in human suffering and misery. Steel production involved people working long hours, with little protection, in highly unpleasant and dangerous working conditions. As a result of this, Sheffield also became one of the main centres for trade-union organization and agitation in the UK. Sheffield, it was said at the time, was the only town where the decrees of the union were enforced by the blowing-up of factories or shooting capitalists.

Fred and Alf learned some of this history from Peter Matchan as the engine made its way through the rain-swept suburbs of north Sheffield and up Wincobank Hill. As it went further up the hill, the queue of cars behind grew longer and the rain seemed to get heavier. Eventually, they reached a gate. From it, a dirt track led to the viewpoint they were heading for. The track was narrow, with tall grass and bushes on either side. The engine, with the living van in tow, lumbered along through the mist that had now come down.

Fred was beginning to sound a bit dubious about the wisdom of driving the engine along here. 'Is there a pub on the top of this hill?' he asked. But not only was there no pub there, by the time they got to the top, there was no view either. The weather was so bad they couldn't see a thing.

'What we should be able to see from up here,' Fred said, 'is the part of Sheffield that used to be the centre of the steel industry, with forges and steelworkses as far as the eye could see, and of course, all that's gone now. They've built a great supermarket in its place. But today we can't see any of it.'

'What do you want to do?' Alf asked.

'I think we'll go in the van for a bit,' Fred replied, 'till it stops raining. Yeah, I've 'ad enough. So much for our panoramic view of Sheffield. Let's put the kettle on.'

Fred and Alf went into the living van to join Peter, who was still with them. Ever the optimist, Fred looked out and said, 'It looks as though the sun's going to come out. Shall we go and have a look at the view when we've had our coffee in these luxurious surroundings?'

But the weather wasn't about to improve, so they gave up. No time to hang around up here waiting for it to clear, because Fred and Alf had to get the engine down the hill to a Sheffield forge, where we were filming the next day.

Independent Forgings was a company that specialized in the forging of large steel components for the aerospace and oil industries. Their works was the former site of Daniel Doncaster and Sons, one of the oldest forge masters in the world, which dated back to the 1770s. To get to the forge, we had to drive down into the Don Valley towards the centre of Sheffield. It was late afternoon and was very busy. The engine was creating a lot of attention and was a major distraction for homeward-bound drivers. All of a sudden, there was a crash. Four cars on the other side of the road had shunted into each other because the drivers were all looking at the engine instead of concentrating on the road ahead.

'Stuff like this would just go wrong all around us,' Jon Doyle recalled, 'and we'd just keep chuffing on through it all. Fred would bring entire roads and town centres to a standstill, because nobody could do anything if you were driving the engine through the centre of town.'

At the forge the following morning, Fred and Alf looked around the yard. 'There's some fair pieces of iron here,' Alf said. 'What are we going to see here?'

In reply, Fred told him a bit about the forging process. 'Forging,' he said,

is, when the ingot comes from the steel-maker, it's like a bit open-grain, as you might say, and forging into certain shapes consolidates the molecules and makes it much stronger, you see. That's what it's really all about. They do it with hydraulic presses now, and all that. The forging hammer they've got here is, I believe, a 7-ton model made by B. and S. Massey of Manchester. They think it was constructed in the late 1800s, but nobody's really sure. Originally, it was driven by steam power, but two years ago, they had it converted to compressed air. We'll go in an' have a look, shall we?

Inside the forge was a scene that Fred described as 'one of great violence'. Sparks were flying as a huge hydraulic hammer pounded down on to a big lump of white-hot steel. They were, we were informed, forging a ring. The ring was being moved around manually under the hammer by one of the operatives, with a long steel fork. Fred looked on. For him, the fact that these kinds of skills were being lost was a sad reflection on the state of the nation, and as he watched, he gave his views on the subject to one of the workers from the forge:

For everyone who's trying to earn a living in England, there's somebody getting paid £300 a week with a company car saying, 'You can't do that because you don't wear a tin hat.' I were up in Aberdeen a few months ago, and I saw this shackle, and I could have made one meself better in me backyard. It were full of bloody hammer marks. What a mess it were. An' I said, 'Who's made that?' And it were made in Spain. People don't realize how accurate you can get things. Like on that engine, it wants some tapered handles, and I can get a piece of metal for them and *bum, bum, bum, bum*, put it in the lathe and get it perfect.

The ring that Fred was watching them forge was an iron tyre for a tank. But this was exactly the way that the axles or the crankshaft for a traction engine would have been forged. Very little had changed. A hundred years earlier, when Fred's engine was built, there were hundreds of forges like this all over Britain. Now there are no more than a dozen.

Fred joined some of the forge workers when they were having a tea break to talk to them about the job. But first of all he had to tell them about some of the forgings on his engine. Fred was in his element in a gathering like this. Wherever we'd filmed over the years, Fred would always disappear when we arrived on site. But we always knew where to find him – in the little hut where the workers had their brew. Here, one of the workers wanted to know how often Fred made things at home.

'All the time,' Fred said. 'We made an hydraulic riveter for less than 150 quid. Anyway, how long have you worked here, then?'

'About twenty-eight years,' the man replied, 'but I've been in the industry all my life. And I'm sixty-four now. I've been made redundant three times, but there's never been any trouble getting another job. Last time we got made redundant here was in 1999. They closed it down altogether. No work for it. And our managing director bought it and sent for me and Paul, and we've been here for the last four year.'

'It's all these bloody third-rate nations, innit, who cock everything up for us,' Fred interjected. 'In my opinion, for every man in England trying to earn a decent living, there's three men who are paid by the government God knows how much a week and have a car, to say, "You cannot do it this way", "You can't do it that way." But them buggers in foreign countries, it doesn't matter about them. They make as much smoke as they want. Here they sit outside my house waiting for a puff of smoke so they can prosecute me. I'm th'only man in Bolton who's been fined for burning coal in a smoke-controlled area since 1963.'

The man who had been talking went back to what he had been saying. 'Paul's been here about thirty-two, haven't you?'

'Bloody hell,' said Fred, 'that's a lot. Straight from school like? I should imagine being fifteen years old and coming straight from school, it must have been dead scary coming into a place like this.'

'I wish I'd known what I know now,' the man said with a laugh. 'I'd have had thy job. When I came here there were a lot more hammers then. There used to be thirty hammers from 5 hundredweight up. There were two thousand men worked here at one time.'

'It must have been bedlam then, when they were all banging away,' Fred said. 'I bet all the ground were shaking.'

'Well,' the man said, 'there were all houses round here then, and nobody could sleep when the hammers were on at night.'

'It's weird that,' Fred said, 'because I were born next to a marshalling yard, and all night long when I were little, it were like *bang, bang, bang, bang, wuf, wuf, wuf, wuf*, and you just got used to it.'

The worker went back to talking about the jobs they did at the forge. 'This job used to be a good job,' he said, 'but it's crap now. I'm not kidding you. What we get is rubbish for what we do. That's why you don't see many young lads coming into the game now. We came in when we were young lads, because it were good pay.'

'They're like bloody women now,' Fred said. 'They spend so much time beautifying themselves.'

One of the other workers joined in the conversation. 'Lads these days are into computers, aren't they? They don't want to mess around like this.'

'Yeah,' Fred agreed. 'I know what you mean. Somehow or another, I've always been attracted to dangerous, dirty things, you know.' The mention of danger led him straight into: 'Women! Women! I've had three of them, you know. Bloody 'ell. Dodgy business.'

There was laughter all round, and the men were still laughing as they went out of the hut to go back to work. Fred and Alf watched them for another hour or so before repairing to the pub over the road, where Fred talked again about his engine.

'Actually, driving the thing is quite easy. It's just the preparation. It's a good job I've got him,' he said, pointing to Alf. 'I'd be knackered otherwise. The actual working of it is easier than steering. If Elf can get it round the corners, all I've got to do is slow it down and see to the water and the oil. And he's getting a lot better at driving. We can zoom along at 14mph without any fear of landing up on the pavement. And the engine is much improved. I could have been over-critical with it, running down its hill-climbing capabilities, when you can't get up a hill in a swanky bloody Lamborghini unless you change gear. I'm expecting it to do too much, maybe, in top gear. Changing it down to bottom gear, it appears it will go up a mountain, which we did yesterday.'

Fred drank his pint. Today had been good.

Alf had never seen anything like the forge before their visit that morning. 'It were fascinating watching the forging,' he said:

I could have stayed there all day, watching them start with a square block a couple of feet square and keep hammering away. And the rolling and knocking the hole through. It looks so easy, but I'm sure it takes a lot of experience, because a lot of it seemed to be done by eye. I know they've got computers coupled up now, but they did seem to be watching what they were doing, as if their eye were telling them where they were at. I thought it were fantastic. And the other thing I've come across is what a happy workforce it was. They feel they're doing something worthwhile, and they were just a good team, weren't they? We watched the two men at either side of the hammers on the fork-lifts. They can't hear each other; they're just watching one another, and each man knows what the other's going to do next. Everything's co-ordinated.

Fred agreed with everything that Alf had been saying. 'It were really good,' he added. 'I mean, I've never seen anybody making iron tyres before like them men did. I've seen plenty of square blocks, but never seen anyone punching an 'ole through the middle of one. That intrigued me greatly. I might even have a do at that with me own hammer at home.'

Fred and Alf were still in the pub when the shift finished, and the lads from the forge came over to join them for a pint and to continue their chat with them.

'Being something of an amateur blacksmith meself,' Fred said, 'you get a bit of a feel for your job. Yeah. I can hardly write proper, but I made that boiler on the engine meself. I used to be a joiner till I were twenty-two years old. Then I went a bit off when I did the steeplejacking. In the middle of Bolton, there were two hundred chimney stacks, and there'd always be steeple-jacks on them. And I used to go talking to them men, and I based my style on them. Nearly always from Manchester they were; near Strangeways jail. But how have things changed here over the last thirty years?'

'The actual forging methods don't change,' was the reply, 'just the machinery that you work with. When we started, it was all by hand. You brought it from the furnaces with a crane and handled it with chains and levers. It was really hard work.'

'Yeah,' said Fred with relish. 'Everywhere you went there was red-hot iron. Open the furnace door and get that big spoon in there. Hanging on to that must've been exciting, even though it were hard. Basically, the biggest change you've had is the stacker truck job, isn't it? It's that good old stacker truck that takes a lot of the graft out of it now. How long have you been doing it like?'

'Left school at fifteen,' Pete replied. 'My dad didn't particularly want me to go and work at Doncaster's, in a forge, which he'd done all his life. But unbeknownst to him, I went down and had an interview and got a job purely by the fact that all my family already worked there. Two uncles, me dad and, in the past, during the war years, three aunties and a grandma.

'When I went home and told me dad I were working at Doncaster's, two or three days after I'd been for the interview, he went absolutely mad. He didn't want me to go into the industry, but it gets into your blood. Me dad worked nights, and when you do the night shift you get paid on Friday, so he had to get up out of bed on Friday and come down for his pay. If I was off school, he used to take me with him, and I'd stand in that doorway and see the hammers banging away. It were fascinating, and I think that's what got it into me blood. Forging is in your blood, and if it's not in your blood, you'll never do it. I've done it for forty-two years and never looked back, and still enjoy going to work.'

Fred had enjoyed his day, but he was looking tired. The journey and all the work involved in it were taking their toll. More than anything, though, it was his illness, getting worse every day, that was leaving him severely incapacitated. He was a shadow of the man he once was, but he was not going to give in to it and, in fact, he talked that night about getting another hammer for his backyard.

But the reality of Fred's condition was becoming more apparent to everybody around him. I was not in Sheffield that day, but Jon Doyle was becoming increasingly concerned. 'I remember,' he said, 'Fred was really struggling to get on to the engine at this point. His foot was swollen, his boots were not fitting properly and he couldn't move his leg properly. He was having trouble bending it because there was so much fluid in it, and that really affected his mobility.'

But Fred wanted to carry on. He'd seen something of what was left of the steel-making industry in Sheffield that day, and the following day he was going to visit a museum that tells the story of early steel-making in the city.

Abbeydale Industrial Hamlet is the site of Abbeydale Works, an eighteenth-century scythe-making works with water wheels, a tilt hammer, a grinding hull and crucible steel furnaces all restored to working order.

When he arrived there, Fred had a look round with Alf. 'Fascinating place,' he said, and wondered how much of it had been rebuilt. Inside one of the buildings, he found an old tilt hammer and explained to Alf how it worked:

Because steel were difficult and expensive to make, it were mixed with wrought iron. These tilt hammers were used to forge the mixture into blades. A water wheel powers the hammers and bellows. The bellows create a good draught in the fire and get the steel in the forge hot enough to work. What happens is that the water wheel outside turns the flywheel. It lifts up the hammer shaft and, *bang!*, it comes down. It's amazing how it's all survived. I wonder if it works. In this place they made scythe blades in the olden days, when steel was very precious and they could only make a little bit of it. They'd get two pieces of ordinary mild steel or wrought iron and forge-weld a strip of steel in between so the edge were a bit of good stuff. There's still some tool people who make plane irons like that, with a little bit of steel at one end and the rest of it's just mild steel.

As Fred told Alf all about steel-making, they went to have a look at the water-powered bellows, then at a little steam engine next door. Next, it was a visit to the smelting department, where they put the crucibles in the fire. Here, a group of experts from Sheffield University were going to demonstrate the method for making crucible steel.

One of the demonstrators showed Fred and Alf the ingot moulds that go into the fire and explained the process. 'The crucible steel process,' he said, 'starts with the manufacture of special clay pots, or crucibles. These are about 50 centimetres tall and about 20 wide. Each one can hold about 20 kilos of steel. The crucibles are heated in a coke-fired furnace set in the floor of the furnace shop. When they are at white heat, they are filled with broken bars of steel. This has got to be 1,500–1,600°C.'

The demonstrator showed them the bits of steel they were going to be melting. They were pieces of blister steel, he explained. 'It's expensive to make this steel,' he said:

This small piece that I've got would have taken two to three weeks to make. It's Swedish wrought iron, very pure iron, and they would have cooked it in charcoal for two or three weeks. It wouldn't have melted; it would have stayed in this oblong shape, and the carbon and the charcoal would have been slowly absorbed into the iron to turn it into steel. It's called blister steel because of all the lumps on it. Until about the mid-nineteenth century, they couldn't cast artefacts directly. They had to cast it into ingots, and then they'd have to go and forge it and roll it.

Once these bits of blister steel have been put into the white-hot crucible, a lid is then placed over the pot and the furnace is charged with more coke. The steel is then melted for about three hours. The furnace operator keeps adding more coke and checks the melting steel at the same time. To start with, the steel bubbles as it melts. Eventually, the bubbling stops, and the surface of the melt becomes clear. It's then ready to be poured into the moulds.

After the steel has been poured, the crucible is replaced in the furnace and another charge of raw steel is added for melting. Most of the crucibles can be re-used for three melts before becoming too weak, then they are thrown away. Before the 1750s, when Huntsman went into production, they'd got quite dirty steel. But this crucible steel has hardly any slag in it, and the carbon's evenly distributed, so you'd use it for engineering tools. So it was very important material to get the Industrial Revolution going.

'Yeah,' said Fred. 'They stuck it on the end of everything, like drills and chisels and planing machines, and because it was so precious they backed it up with ordinary wrought iron and forged it all together. I've got a very old wooden jack plane at home, and you can see the joint where the steel comes on to the wrought iron.'

The demonstrator explained how the crucible steel process had been developed by Benjamin Huntsman in great secrecy and that many attempts had been made by rival businesses to discover his secret process. One story involved an iron founder called Walker who had a foundry at Grenoside, on the northern outskirts of Sheffield. Walker disguised himself as a tramp and arrived outside Huntsman's works pretending to be ill. It was a very cold night, and snow was falling, so Walker pleaded with the workers to let him in. Taking pity on the beggar, they allowed him to take shelter and sleep in a corner of the workshop. While he pretended to sleep, Walker watched all the operations of the crucible steel process. He discovered that part of the secret involved breaking up some old green bottles, which were then put in the crucibles, on top of the steel. About three months after this cold night, it is claimed that Walker's foundry in Grenoside was also making crucible steel.

The team from the university demonstrated part of the process. The furnace was white hot when they opened the lid, and so was the pot when it was lifted out for the liquid metal to be poured into the mould. The demonstrators kept a respectful distance between themselves and the bubbling melt, lifting the pot out of the furnace with long-handled tongs which grip around the outside of the crucible. The pot was then stood on the furnace-room floor and picked up using another set of tongs, which fit around the middle of the crucible. The molten steel was then poured from the crucible into the cast-iron ingot mould. It would have taken three hours for the steel to solidify and cool down, so Fred was shown another mould which, in true *Blue Peter* style, had been prepared earlier. Here Fred had a go at opening the mould and removing the steel bar that had been cast already.

The filming we'd done in Sheffield had taken Fred through to the halfway stage of the tour. From Sheffield, he was going down into Derbyshire, where he was planning to stay for a few days with his old friend Ian Howard, of Alton Engineering, and visit the workshops of the Midland Railway Centre.

After the demonstration at Abbeydale, Jon wanted to get some shots of Fred driving out of Sheffield and into Derbyshire. The engine had already been steamed up and was ready to go but, as Fred and Alf left the museum, they had a minor accident. 'Outside Abbeydale,' Kate recalls,

Jon made me stop traffic on a main road, where Fred needed to do a three-point turn. While they were doing this, they knocked a massive road sign over. Alf steered the engine into the sign and knocked it over, but all Fred was worried about was whether it had scratched the living van, so he stopped the engine and got off to inspect the damage. The van was fine, but the road sign was wrecked, so Fred got back on to the engine and said, 'Come on, let's get going. Quick! Before anyone sees us.' He was shouting at Alf, blaming him. 'You and your bloody steering,' he kept saying. 'I'll have to get Jack over here to do it.'

Jon remembers the drive that afternoon:

We were driving out of Abbeydale and it was a fantastic day, really bright and sunny. We'd had a rough couple of days just before, coming into Sheffield in all the rain, and it had been hard work. It was a climb coming out of Abbeydale, but by this time the engine was really making tracks, and it was having no problems getting up a hill like the one we were on. In fact, it was becoming a struggle by this time for us to get ahead of them in the car to set up for our shots, because they were travelling so quickly. The drive was wonderful, and even though you could see the pain Fred was in, he was absolutely beaming, because it was a bright day.

After we did that drive, we put the engine on the low loader, and I drove with Fred to the hotel we were staying at in Belper. On the way, the roads were busy and we kept getting stuck in traffic. At one stage, I had to pull up next to the church in a little village in Derbyshire, and I caught Fred out of the corner of my eye, just looking at it. He was having a kind of moment to himself, and he saw me; he clocked that I'd clocked him. Up to this point, Fred had always put a positive spin on things, and he'd never really been honest with me or with himself, to a certain extent, about what he faced. But here there was just this moment where this all turned, stuck in that traffic, in about fifteen or twenty seconds of silence in the car. He looked at me, and I think I even saw a tear in his eye, and he said, 'I miss me steeplejacking days. I'll never climb one of those again.'

For me, that was the moment when he admitted to himself that the end was upon him. And I think there was a change in him after that. Up until then, it was always a bit of a joke and 'Oh, I'll be all right. I'll keep going,' but that was the point when he knew, This is it. When we got to the hotel, I could see the pain, and he was clearly getting worse and worse as the night went on. It was like, here was the man who had spent his life defying death, and now it was staring at him. He was holding on and holding on, but I think that night was the first point he let go.

Fred went to bed early that evening, which was very unusual. However bad he had been feeling up to this stage, he'd always seemed to be able to ignore the pain as he had a few pints and told some of his stories. But not that night.

At about ten o'clock, I got a phone call at home

from Jon. He was very worried about Fred, and he didn't think he would be able to carry on. It sounded as though the inevitable had happened and it was going to be the end of the journey. I drove to Derbyshire early the next morning, getting to the hotel before breakfast. Alf was first down, and he confirmed how bad Fred was. When I saw Fred, he agreed that he couldn't carry on. We sat having breakfast, and there was a really sombre mood. It looked as though Fred's grand tour had come to an end at the halfway stage.

8

Getting to the Palace

It was Saturday 26 June. I drove Fred and Alf back to Bolton and insisted that Fred went to see his doctor straight away. Fred was due to receive his MBE on Wednesday 7 July. It was going to be one of the most important days of his life, and the priority now had got to be to get him better for that.

Forget about any more filming before then, I told him. And I also told him he needn't worry about the engine. Alan had taken it from Sheffield to the Midland Railway Centre the previous afternoon, and it could have secure parking there for as long as we wanted. It would be picked up by the low loader the day before the MBE ceremony and transported to London so that Fred could drive it there.

Back at the office, all the arrangements that had been made for the next six weeks' filming had to be cancelled. The crew were very understanding. They'd lost six weeks' work at very short notice, but they'd spent time with Fred and they understood the reasons. Kathryn got in touch with all the locations and explained the situation. Many were disappointed that we were not going to be able to get there with Fred, but accepted that we would try to fit them into the schedule if Fred got better and his health improved enough to carry on.

By the time I went to visit Fred early the next week, most of the schedule had been cancelled. When I got to the house, though, Fred was looking a lot better. He'd been given some tablets for the swelling in his leg, and they had already started to take effect. He'd also got some stronger painkillers. He was confident that he was going to be all right for his big day at the Palace. But he also wanted to carry on with his grand tour afterwards. I wasn't sure about this.

If we were to complete the series in its original form, at the rate we had been working the previous seven weeks, it would involve at least another two months' filming, as we would have to do it three or four days at a time, with breaks in between for Fred to rest. His condition had already deteriorated since we started the journey, and I just didn't think he would be able to keep going long enough. But that stubbornness and determination and single-mindedness that had characterized Fred throughout his life came through yet again. Completing this journey had become his last great obsession. There were still too many places he wanted to go to; too many friends he still wanted to call in to see. I talked to his wife, Sheila, and to some of Fred's closest friends. There was a feeling that it was this journey that was keeping Fred alive. Everybody felt we should carry on; and nobody more so than Fred himself.

Fred had been awarded his MBE for services to industrial heritage and broadcasting in the 2004 New Year's Honours List. We wanted the tractor to steam up the Mall and through the great gates of the Palace, but the Palace officials decided that the dangers and possible security risks of driving a potential bomb into the grounds were too great, and the Royal Parks Commission were not too keen on the thought of the damage that a 12-ton steam engine might do to the road surface of the Mall. However, the army came to the rescue. The adjutant to the Irish Guards, Alex Turner, offered a parking place for the engine and living van on the parade ground at Wellington Barracks on Birdcage Walk, just a minute's march away from the Palace.

Even as we negotiated with Palace officials and the Metropolitan Police, Fred's condition worsened. A few days before he was due to set off for London, he was feeling very unwell again and stayed in bed all day, sleeping around the clock. It didn't look as though he was going to make it for his big day, after all. The ceremony was scheduled for the Wednesday morning, and Sheila had booked rooms for her and Fred, and for his sons, seventeen-year-old Jack and thirteen-year-old Roger, at the Thistle Westminster Hotel on Buckingham Palace Road, so that Fred would not have far to walk. Sheila was going to drive Fred down on the Tuesday, and Jack and Roger were going to join them at the hotel that evening, having been brought over from the Isle of Man by their mother, Sue.

By Tuesday, Fred was feeling a bit better and insisted that he would be able to travel to London, but the journey was slow, as Sheila had to keep stopping the car to give Fred time to get out and walk around. The tumour was pressing on him and causing him great discomfort, and this was aggravated by having to sit in the same position for many hours cramped up in the car. This was the main reason we were not going to be able to do any more long journeys for our filming – if indeed we were going to be able to carry on at all.

That evening, Fred and Sheila didn't venture out of their hotel, but after breakfast the next morning, they met up with the boys, who had been brought to the hotel by Sue. They were to make up the official party who were going into the Palace to see Fred receive his honour.

I was waiting with the crew outside the gates of the Palace to film Fred's arrival. The day was warm and bright but very windy, and as Fred approached with his family group, Sheila was holding on to her hat. I'd not seen Fred for a few days, and I was amazed to see how well he looked. He was resplendent in top hat and tails, a far cry from the cloth cap and engine driver's jacket we were so used to seeing him in. As he walked up to the gates, he was a very proud man. Fred had always been a great royalist and talked with pride about the days when Britain had an empire, so being made a Member of the British Empire held great significance for him.

However, there were other things on his mind that morning. Fred took me to one side to tell me about a problem he'd got with his braces. They were the old-fashioned kind that needed buttons on the trousers, but the formal trousers he'd hired for the occasion hadn't got any, so Fred showed me some Heath Robinson method of attaching them to the trousers he'd come up with. 'Bloody hell,' he said. 'I hope they hold up, or else I'll be showing me wedding tackle to Her Majesty!'

Then it was time for a bit of acting. 'Is the engine being well looked after?' I asked him.

'Yes,' he replied. 'It's over there in one of Her Majesty's barracks.'

Not to be outdone in the acting stakes, Roger added, 'We've left it being guarded by some soldiers.'

'Yeah,' Fred added. 'It's being looked after really good. No chance of it getting vandalized. After we've done with the Queen, we'll have a ride round town on it.' Then, turning to one of the policemen on the gate, he asked, 'Are we at the right place? I never thought I'd be coming in here like this.' The policeman said they would have to get some ladders up for Fred, to which he replied, 'There's still plenty of room for steeplejacks in London. Where I live, there's nothing standing up no more.'

'Enjoy your day,' the policeman said.

'And no swearing, Fred,' Sheila added as they walked through the great iron gates of the Palace and across the gravelled forecourt, past the guards in their scarlet tunics and bearskins. We'd got press passes to film in the grounds, so we followed Fred through the archway into the great quadrangle at the heart of the Palace, but this was as far as we could go. There was one official television crew who filmed all such occasions, so instead we waited with the assembled media in the courtyard as Fred and his party followed a red cordoned-off walkway to a set of double doors and disappeared into the Palace.

After an hour or so of standing around in the court-yard, people began to appear from the double doors with their medals, their families in attendance. Most stood in the courtyard savouring the moment. When Fred appeared, however, he was pounced upon by officials and ushered over to the waiting media, who were gathered in one corner of the courtyard. The newspaper photographers lined up for pictures of him standing proudly displaying his MBE:

'Fred, just look this way, please!'

'Fred, over here, please!'

'Over here, Fred!'

Fred was loving all the attention, and Jack and Roger looked on in amusement.

One of the photographers was from the *Daily Telegraph*, and he approached Fred, saying, 'You won't remember me, but one of the first pictures I ever did when I was at Bolton School was of you. You were the first person I ever photographed as a school project. It was when you were doing the Swan Mill chimney. I think you knew my brother, Peter Stott.'

'He buggered off to Spain, didn't he?' Fred said.

'No,' the photographer replied, 'that was my dad.'

He then asked Fred if he'd got his cap with him, but it was back at the hotel.

Tim Henman was another celebrity to have been honoured that day, and he was ushered over to the media area to join Fred. He shook Fred's hand and offered his congratulations. 'Aye, pleased to meet you,' Fred said. 'Me recollections of tennis when I were a kid was that they were a load of pansies played it, but it's not so.' Henman smiled politely. Even without his top hat on, he towered above the top of Fred's top hat as they posed together for photographs for the following morning's papers.

When all of the photographers had got the pictures they needed, I asked Fred what the Queen had said to him. 'She said, "You don't still climb up chimneys, do you?"' he replied. 'I thought, Bugger it. No way! But I said, "No, no. It's a young man's business. I'm getting too old for that now, Ma'am." Then it were the hand-shake, and "Bugger off, it's somebody else's turn."'

Sheila stood by Fred's side, smiling. 'You didn't say, "Are you all right, flower?"'

Fred laughed. 'No,' he replied. 'You can't say that to the Queen.'

We had our camera rolling for the whole of this happy occasion, so I asked Fred what he'd got his MBE for officially, to which he responded, 'I don't know, to tell you the truth.' Roger got the official pro-gramme out and read from it: 'Mr Frederick Dibnah for services to heritage and broadcasting.'

Fred surveyed the Palace courtyard. 'We'll nick a couple of these gas lamps for back at base,' he said with a grin. Then, looking up to a frieze above the Corinthian columns, he noticed that they'd done some renovation work and put a new section of stone carving in. 'Nice here, innit?' he said. 'That flagpole is three ladders high. I can tell you that. You could paint that easy.'

'Would you still go up there?' he was asked by a reporter who was standing nearby.

'No. I'm getting too old for that,' he replied a little sadly. 'I'm more of a conservationist now.'

Next it was time for an interview for *Sky News*. 'So what was it like meeting the Queen today?' the reporter asked him.

'I don't know,' was Fred's reply. 'A bit unusual, really. I never envisaged I would end up in Buckingham Palace getting an MBE. A bit of a shock, really. Early days when somebody contacted me, I thought they were taking the wotsit. I thought they were kidding, but they weren't and here I am. I suppose in some ways, this is for services to heritage and broadcasting. Instead of going all round the houses, like you do if you've bin to university, it's pretty easy to say it straight so that the common man can understand it. That's why I do it my way.'

Then Fred embarked on the whole saga of how the BBC first came to film him when he was working on the tower at the top of Bolton town hall. He was about to carry on with his life story, but he paused for breath and the reporter got a chance to get a word in to steer her interview back on track.

'Nowadays,' she said, 'do you think of yourself as

Fred Dibnah, steeplejack, or Fred Dibnah, broad-caster? What's your first love?'

Fred thought about it, before replying, 'Well, neither really. Fred Dibnah, a bit different. I'm a mechanic, a backstreet mechanic. Aberdeen University gave me an honorary degree in backstreet mechanicing, and now Birmingham University have given me a degree in backstreet mechanicing, so it'll do for me, that.'

'And now you've been honoured by the Queen,' the reporter added.

'Oh, aye,' said Fred, 'I've got an MBE as well. The thing is, I've looked at so-called intelligence, and great scholars who've been to university, and they're all very good at standing there and telling you how to do it. But when it comes to actually doing it, they can't do it. I can hardly write, but I can do things. George Stephenson couldn't write proper, but he came up with some good ideas.'

'And you've also got a gift for telling other people and making them understand complicated things,' the reporter said.

'Well, I've always been good at talking.' Then, turning to me, Fred said, 'Right, interview one done. I'm ready for a drink.'

I told him they'd not let us bring any cans of Guinness in with us and asked him if they'd had any in the Palace.

'No, nowt,' he replied, before being asked to do another television interview.

This time, it was for Channel 4. The reporter wanted

to know if it bothered Fred that his MBE had this 'empire' word in it.

'No, no, it doesn't,' said Fred. 'I'm a royalist, mate.'

But the interviewer persisted, saying, 'A lot of people don't take the honour, because of it.'

Fred wasn't having any of it: 'Well, if you look around the world when we were running it,' he said, 'it all seemed to work a lot better than it's working now. Everywhere we were and we've vacated, they're all killing each other now and struggling for power, aren't they?' As Fred displayed his MBE for the Channel 4 cameraman, he told him he'd got a few medals. 'Me granddad were a runner, and he won quite a lot of medals at the turn of the century. They were real solid silver, beautiful things. I don't know whether I'll be able to wear this one when I'm driving the engine or not.'

When all the interviews were over, Fred came over to talk to me. 'I've been to Buckingham Palace before,' he said, 'and only ever stood outside and looked through them railings, an' never thought that I'd end up in the middle of it all. An' it's quite as splendid inside as it is outside.' Then he went on to talk about the picture of the Queen and the Duke of Edinburgh he had in his shed:

Many, many years ago when me shed were just six telegraph poles and a roof, I 'ad visits from an Irish chap, who's now deceased. One day, he arrived with this beautiful photograph of the Queen and Prince Philip in a frame and he said, 'Here, you can have that. I don't want it.' And there were a 6-inch nail sticking out of a telegraph pole, and I hooked it on the nail, and for years it blew about in the wind like a kite when it were very windy. And then, as the years rolled by, the shed got bigger and bigger, and now it takes pride of place right in the middle of the shed. And of course, the Queen and Prince Philip look quite young, because it's a very old picture. It must be fifty years old. I often thought she might have seen it if she watched any of the programmes. What's that doing in this strange place? she would have thought. But I didn't get chance to ask her about it.

By the time we did the filming at the Palace, I had revised the outline for the series to fit in with an amended schedule. Fred's trip to London to receive his MBE was now going to be the last programme in the series, the last of nearly forty programmes I had made with Fred so, there in the courtyard of Buckingham Palace, with his MBE in his hand, I talked to him about the filming we'd done together over the years and about the things he had enjoyed most.

'All of it's been enjoyable,' he said,

but the great drawback with television presenting is you don't get enough time to actually look at a place properly or to study the objects that are there. When we went to the Science Museum here in London they had to keep coming to find me, because I'd wandered away, looking at things that were of great interest to me. I could have spent days there looking at all that stuff, not hours. But, of all the things we've been to, I think the lantern on Ely Cathedral were quite a magnificent piece of woodwork to me. That's why we created that model of it that we did. That were my version of how them men got it all up there in the Middle Ages. Then there were the more modern things, like the Forth Railway Bridge, which is over-engineered, because the Tay Bridge fell down, and even the more modern, modern ones like the suspension bridges made of wire, which are quite fantastic things.

'What about people?' I asked him.

'Of all the people that I've met,' he said, 'the lads who really do it for a living proper, like the steam-hammer men in Sheffield. There was no talking, like a team perfectly rehearsed in every move. The hammer driver, *bum, bum, bum, bum, bum*. Nothing. And when they were placing the punch in the middle of the billet . . .' Fred tailed off into sound effects, a picture of the grimy forge and the white-hot metal in his head. Buckingham Palace was beautiful, but not as beautiful as that. Fred came back to one of his favourite themes – graduates being given management jobs in industry without any practical experience. 'I hope there's not too much of the business "he's left university and he's in charge now",' he went on. 'He's never done it, has he? Not like them men who've done it every day for fifty years. Them men are still there, but they don't get as much money as they did thirty years ago for doing the same job. I just like that style of workman, boilers and riveting and all that sort of thing.'

'Time for a drink now,' I said.

'That's a good idea,' Fred said. 'I were wondering when you'd ask. I could murder a pint.'

After the ceremony, Fred couldn't wait to get out of his posh morning suit and back into his cap and working clothes. We did no more filming with him that day but left him to spend the rest of the time with his family. I'd got work to do, spending most of the afternoon walking the route the traction engine was going to take around central London the next day. This had all been prearranged with the police, and that afternoon we were looking for the best camera positions and working out the best way to get around ourselves to get shots of Fred steaming past the sights.

In the meantime, while we had been at the Palace, Alf had gone on the low loader with Alan to pick up the engine from the Midland Railway Centre, where it had been stored since our filming schedule had been interrupted three weeks earlier. They spent the day transporting it down to London, and by late afternoon, passers-by on Birdcage Walk were witnessing the rather unusual sight of a low loader with traction engine and living van on board making its way down past St James's Park in the direction of the Palace and turning into the gates of Wellington Barracks, where Alan drove it across the parade ground to park at the far end.

By the time they had it parked up for the night and

met us at the hotel we were staying in on the South Bank, Sheila had caught a train back to Bolton, leaving Fred with us for another two days' filming. Jack and Roger were going to be with Fred for the rest of his time in London, so Sue brought them to our hotel, where we had a room booked for them. Until that morning, when she'd been at the Palace Gates to see her sons go in with Fred, I'd never met her.

I talked to Sue about Fred and the boys and about their need to spend some quality time together during these last days of his life. There was a problem, however. Sheila didn't get on with Jack. They'd fallen out a year or so earlier, and she didn't want the boys staying at the house. But there was a solution. Being out on the road with Fred for the next few weeks presented an ideal opportunity for the boys to spend time with their dad on his engine, visiting places, meeting people and doing the things he wanted to do while he was still able. This would leave them with good, positive memories of him during his last days, rather than only seeing him right at the end when he was weak and unable to do anything, so I offered to look after the boys for the rest of our filming. They would be the guests of the production company, which would mean they could be close to Fred. We'd make sure that they were transported around and would book accommodation for them wherever we were staying. Sue was very grateful and readily accepted the offer.

That evening, Fred was in fine spirits; almost back to the Fred I remembered from our earlier filming days. We went for a drink at what Fred could only describe as a 'yuppie' bar, opposite our hotel, and it even brought a change to his drinking habits. They had Guinness on draught, but when I went to the bar for the drinks, I noticed they had the Belgian abbey beer, Leffe, on draught. It's one of my favourites, and as it was very strong, I thought Fred might like it, so I got him a glass. He loved it, and stayed on it for the rest of the night, until we all went off to a nearby restaurant for a meal.

Next morning, we were all up early, especially Alf and Alan, who had to be at the barracks by seven o'clock to get the engine steamed up for Fred's drive round the sights of London.

The rest of us joined them a few hours later. One of the great back-up services that Alan Atkinson provided when we arrived at a location was to do a brew for everyone. He always kept a portable gas stove, kettle, water, tea and coffee in his cab, and when we arrived on the parade ground at Wellington Barracks, he put a brew on, just as he did everywhere else. Fred got his battered old garden chair out of the van and, brew in hand, held court with Alex Turner, the adjutant to the Irish Guards commanding officer who had made all the arrangements for him to park the engine there. Then with the camera rolling and the Irish Guards marching past the van in the drill for the Changing of the Guard, Alf got into acting mode.

He came to Fred and said, 'You'd better go and get some clean togs on. I'll have a look at the engine while you do.' Fred took his cue. Despite the fact that he had already received his MBE, we still had to film him arriving at the Palace to receive it, then cut it in with the footage of the actual day for the television programme. Fred took his cue.

'Yeah. I suppose I'd better get changed,' he said. 'I can't go and see the Queen like this, so I'll go and get me penguin suit on.' With that, he climbed into the living van in his usual attire of cap and oily driver's jacket.

While Fred was in the van getting changed, I talked to Alf as he was getting on with his endless cleaning of the engine. I asked him how he felt about Fred getting this honour.

'Long overdue, I think,' was his reply. 'I feel very proud for him. Very proud. As I'm sure the family do, and the lads and that. Yeah. Well deserved. But I'm not so sure now whether I've to doff me hat, bow or curtsy.' As Alf cleaned the engine, Fred emerged from the living van in all the finery of his morning suit, playing the part of the man who had travelled all the way down to London on his engine to receive his MBE and slept in it next to Buckingham Palace the night before. It was a great moment. The sun shone, the guards marched past the van to the beat of the drum and Fred stood on the steps of the living van, resplendent in his top hat and tails and with a beaming smile lighting up his face. If ever anybody asks me what my outstanding memory of all the filming I did with Fred is, this is it.

After we'd filmed him arriving at the Palace, we had that morning's real business to attend to, and Fred was really looking forward to it. 'We're going to drive round to look at the sights, go over a few bridges and cause general havoc,' he shouted to us as he set off from the barracks.

With Jack standing up beside him as steersman, Roger sitting on the running board of the living van sporting a splendid top hat and Alf looking out from the barn doors of the living van, they made their way past the Institution of Mechanical Engineers, who had provided help and advice over the years for some of our programmes. Steaming on past the Treasury, civil servants, rushing to get to their offices, turned their heads and paused to look at this unusual sight. Then it was into Parliament Square and past Big Ben as it rang ten o'clock. As they drove past the makeshift tents and placards of a group of environmental protesters who were camping out in front of the Houses of Parliament, a woman stood up and started screaming about this 'monstrosity' that was steaming past: 'No respect for our planet,' she shouted. 'You're killing our planet.' But Fred and Jack drove on, oblivious to her protests.

Jack had the difficult task of steering the engine through the busy London traffic, but it was a mark of his skill and confidence in handling the engine that he encountered no problems. In fact, he was clearly enjoying himself, and as well as steering, he was warning his dad of upcoming hazards that he might have to stop for. The engine looked brilliant as it chugged along past the Gothic splendours of the Palace of Westminster. This was an image of Victorian Britain at its best. Sir Charles Barry's great buildings, Pugin's ornamentation and an engine that wouldn't have looked out of place when the buildings were completed in 1860. Again, a combination of all the things Fred loved. But he didn't have any time to stop and admire them now, and with three blasts on the whistle, he was past the Victoria Tower and on his way past the gardens to Lambeth Bridge.

Next, it was over the Thames at Lambeth Bridge, past Lambeth Palace and round the back of St Thomas's Hospital. But there were still some problems with the engine. Fred brought it to a halt next to the hospital. He was, he explained, having a bit of a problem with the axle. It needed a clonk, so Jack got down and rooted around in the locker at the back until he found a hammer.

'We'll have to mend this when we get back to base,' Fred said. 'The engine's running very well. But there's one or two small faults, like this plug on the axle. Every time you go over a bump, it goes further down, and you can't turn it on.'

After a few clonks on the offending part with the hammer, they were back on their way, past Waterloo station and back towards the Thames, where they crossed over Westminster Bridge and approached Big Ben again. A right turn took them on to Victoria Embankment, and they chugged along by the side of the Thames, with the London Eye dominating the skyline over the other side of the river. But it was the paddle steamer *Tattershall Castle* that caught Roger's eye.

The engine was running well, and not causing too much of a hold-up to the London traffic, and Fred drove up Northumberland Avenue, touching the edge of Trafalgar Square as he turned on to Whitehall to drive past the Cenotaph and Downing Street. Cameras that had been busy snapping the Household Cavalry Guards at Horse Guards Parade swung round to get some pictures to take home of the somewhat rarer sight of a 1912 Aveling and Porter making its stately progress past Banqueting House.

At the end of Whitehall, just before going back into Parliament Square, there was a prearranged stop. We were going to do a second circuit, this time with Alf as steersman and the crew shooting from the living van. 'Right. It's time we changed the steering man,' said Fred. 'Go and get Alf.' Alf got out of the living van and swapped places with Jack.

'I thought you'd forgot me,' he said to Fred as he took his place beside him on the footplate. 'I took you halfway round the bloody country!'

Hordes of Japanese tourists crowded round, taking photographs on their mobile phones, and when Fred blew a loud blast on the whistle, they all leapt back in fright. For the changeover, the engine had been parked on double yellow lines, and when a traffic warden came along, Fred explained that they were waiting for the cameraman to get into the right position. Then it was back round the same circuit, with Alf at the wheel.

This time, though, there was a stop, because driving a traction engine round central London on a summer's day was hot, thirsty work, and there were too many nice pubs along the route for Fred to drive past without quenching his thirst. Fred spotted one as he was on his way up Northumberland Avenue, and came to a halt on double yellow lines over the other side of the road. 'Come on,' he said. 'We'll go and have a swift half. Who's guarding the engine?'

'Best thing to do,' Alf said, 'is take one of the kids with you and fetch one over here for me, and I'll stop over here. Then there's an adult here if anybody comes, and I can say I'm just checking something.'

Over at the pub, Fred sat at a table on the pavement outside with Jack and Roger. 'You have got no taller, Mr Dibnah,' a voice said. Fred looked round to see Major Richard Courteney-Harris of the Queen's Lancashire Regiment standing outside the pub.

Quick as a flash, he retorted, 'And you no smaller, Major.' The major had received an MBE from the Queen at the same ceremony as Fred the previous day, and had been out sightseeing with his wife and children when he happened upon Fred and the film crew. 'This man queued up behind me at the Palace,' Fred said, turning to me and the crew.

After a chat about Bolton and some of the people they both knew there, the major left, but we got another pint for Fred and some soft drinks for the boys and carried on filming with them in the sunshine on Northumberland Avenue. 'What about this trip round London today?' Fred asked Roger. 'What did you see that were good?'

'I think we smoked Tony Blair out of Big Ben,' Roger replied.

'No, we didn't,' Fred said. 'We've got some super coal. Radioactive. No smoke.' Then he went on to talk about some of the buildings they'd been past, and about the London Eye. 'When we came and did one of our other television programmes, we saw it halfway across the River Thames,' Fred said, 'stuck when they were erecting it and the winching gear had conked out.' Roger suggested that if he'd been on the traction engine, he could have given them a hand and winched it up for them.

Fred remembered a famous picture of a traction engine like ours and a battleship on its side and a few wire ropes. 'But I don't think the tractor were doing much good, really,' he added. 'What about Big Ben then? We've been up there, you know, right amongst it all, where the big bell is. It has a big crack in it. The first one, the hammer were so big, it cracked it. They had to take it down and melt it. And they reduced the size of the hammer. Then they had another go, and they cracked it again. That crack's still there, but they chiselled it; there were no mechanical grinders then. Then they've turned it through quarter of a turn so the hammer hits it in another place.'

As Fred delivered his little history lesson, a traffic warden appeared by the side of the engine. He walked up and down, looking at the double yellow lines it was parked on. 'What's it doing parked here?' he wanted to know.

Alf looked uncomfortable, but Fred wasn't in the least bit perturbed. He finished his drink, walked over to the engine and explained to the warden that 'the driver of a steam locomotive is entitled to park anywhere in order to attend to his fire or take water'. The warden seemed to accept Fred's explanation and went on his way.

Suitably refreshed, Fred was also ready to move on. Jack decided that he was going to take over the steering again for the drive back to the barracks. For all the tourists along the route, it was an unexpected bonus, and cameras clicked to get shots of the engine *chuff-chuff*ing past the famous sights. But it was time to move on. We were filming at Crossness Engines the next day, and Fred's engine had to be transported there that afternoon so that we could do some driving shots the following morning. Alan was ready with the low loader, and we left Alf with him at the barracks to get the engine loaded.

That evening, we went to Greenwich for a few drinks and a meal. Fred was still in celebratory mood, but when we got there we soon encountered a problem. It was after 8 p.m., and Jack and Roger were with us. All we wanted was a place where we could get a few pints and have something to eat, but British licensing laws being what they are, we found it very difficult to find somewhere they would serve us, because the boys were under age. Eventually, we did find somewhere, but we had to sit outside in a beer garden and, although it was July, it was quite chilly, because by then it was getting late. Was this a taste of things to come over the next few weeks, I wondered.

Next morning, Alf and Alan were, as ever, up early, and they had Fred's engine steamed up and ready for

the road by the time we got to Crossness Pumping
Station. It was going to be the usual routine: a quick
drive round the environs of the location to see Fred
arriving on his engine and departing. Alf had got his
job back as steersman. Roger was perched up on top of
the coal in the tender and Jack was sitting on the board
at the front of the van. From the station, they drove
through the vast wilderness of Thamesmead – all
concrete flyovers, tower blocks and 1960s houses. Fred
pulled into a parking place by the side of Southmere
Lake.

'While we're here on the edges of London,' he said,
'somewhere near here, there's the Crossness Pumping
Station, that's got four great big beam engines in that
have been here since the 1860s. I think we should go
and have a look at them, because they are quite
splendid; the finest Victorian cast-iron work in all of
London. You'd never think it were here, would you?'
he went on, looking across to the four tower blocks on
the other side of the lake. 'It's a magnificent nineteenth-
century building . . . and it has the largest rotative
beam engines in the world. It's something I've wanted
to come and see for some time.'

To get to the huge Victorian engine house, they had
to drive through the security gates of Thames Water
and the modern sewage works. 'This is it,' Fred said as
he drew up outside the ornate building. 'Built in 1865,
when the River Thames were full of pollution and all
the water supply were bad news. And it were part of
three pumping stations which Mr Joseph Bazalgette
built with 80-odd miles of sewers to clean up London.

And he needed pumping stations to help them out. This is the remains of the last one that's still got the engines in. Some of the others are still there, but there's no engines. We'll go and have a look. Disembark. Put the brake on, Roger.'

Alf stayed with the engine while Fred walked into the engine house with Jack and Roger – and what a sight there was to greet them as they entered the engine house! It really was a masterpiece of Victorian decorative ironwork: tall shiny red Corinthian columns and great panels of elaborately decorated metalwork full of leaves, flowers and swirling scrolls, all beautifully restored to their original splendour.

'While Elf's fettling the engine,' Fred said as they were walking in,

I'll show you these brilliant steam engines. These are the biggest beam engines in England, maybe even in the world. Built by James Watt to pump the raw sewage of London. Originally, they had twelve Cornish boilers that burned 5,000 tons of coal every year to make them all go, to provide the steam, and pump the raw sewage of London into the River Thames. By 1920, it were all over with. They were derelict and vandalized and, but for these fine people here who've restored it, it would have gone; it would have disappeared for ever. How can you destroy something as magnificent as this? And yet they did. Everybody destroyed it all. Maybe with a bit more good luck and good fortune, there might be enough money to do up the other three engines, eh? I wonder if they'll let us have a go at playing with the handles?

There were four immense beam engines in the building, built in 1864 as compounds and made even more efficient in 1899, when they were converted to triple expansion.* One of them has been restored to its former glory. 'Magnificent, isn't it?' Fred said as he walked round to the other side of it, where he met John Ridley, one of the volunteers who had been involved in the restoration work.

John explained that it had taken eighteen years to restore this engine, and they were all original parts, polished up using little but elbow grease. 'Would you like to start it?' he asked Fred.

It was just what Fred wanted to hear. Taking hold of the wheel at the front of the control panel, he asked, 'How many turns? We don't want to wreck it.'

'Two turns,' John said, 'but we've got to wait.' Fred was quick to explain that they had to wait for the crank to be wound round into the correct position, because it wouldn't start unless it was in the right shop.

'The piston's got to be in the right position,' John added, 'so that when the steam goes in, you've got a good stroke.' As Fred made a second turn of the wheel, Roger watched intently and observed, 'It's not

---

* Triple expansion engine: a compound steam engine in which the same steam works in three cylinders successively.

like your little engine at home. You don't turn the valve full open.' After another half turn of the wheel, the engine stirred into life, like a sleeping giant that has been roused; it moved slowly and silently, with great powerful strokes. As the engine gathered momentum, John chatted to Fred about the valves. 'A bit bigger than the ones on your engine,' he said.

'Oh aye,' Fred answered. 'Are they like Corliss valves?'*

John confirmed that they were Corliss valves, and invited Fred to have a look at the rest of the engine.

They went up the stairs to the next level and Fred marvelled again at the beauty of all the cast iron. John pointed out the crosshead and then went on, 'This beam here is the grasshopper leg of the parallel link-age mechanism – the original James Watt linkage. I think the fascinating thing about it all is to see that mass of the crosshead coming down and stopping just that much—' He indicated how close it came down to the cylinder.

'Yeah,' said Fred. 'It's about five-eighths of an inch off. I wonder if, when they put it up at first, they had any fun . . . "We'd better take another quarter of an inch off here" like. It'd be interesting to go round with the calipers to see how that gland compares with the one over there.'

* Corliss valve: an American-designed semi-rotary valve which can be opened and closed very quickly, allowing steam into the cylinder without any significant pressure drop (which would lead to the steam cooling, with a consequent loss of power and efficiency).

John went on to talk about the way the piston had to be equally spaced inside the cylinder. As he talked, Roger was studying an elaborate bit of mechanism very closely. It gave a click on every stroke of the engine. 'Is this the top end of the parallel-link motion?' he asked.

'No,' John replied. 'That's the inlet valve, and it has this trip mechanism, and what that does is shut the inlet valve at a certain point in the piston's stroke to conserve steam. It's not the expansion of the steam that matters, it's the giving off of the heat, so they stop the steam inlet off at a certain amount and then, as the steam expands, it gives off heat. And then the steam goes from this cylinder into the other cylinders. So it's used three times. That's why they call it triple expansion.'

'Same as our tractor,' Fred said. 'Is it about a 7-foot stroke?'

'Nine,' John said. 'Fantastic mechanism, isn't it? You could stand and watch it for hours.' He pointed to two other rods that were going up and down near the side of the platform they were on, saying, 'And these two rods are what drove the air pump for the vacuum, and that one drove the water pump that circulated the water through the condenser.'

Fred looked from the bright paint and gleaming metalwork of the restored engine to one of the others. 'You've a lot to do over there, haven't you?' he said. 'Shall we go up to the beam?' Fred went up the wrought-iron staircase that led to the beam gallery with John, closely followed by Jack and Roger.

'There's the beam,' John said as they got to the top. 'All 47 tons of it going up and down. These are the counterbalance weights. It was cast in Birmingham and somehow they got it down here. Probably by canal. When we restored it, what we've done, we've cleaned down to the metal, painted it and tried to decorate not only the engine but the rest of the house as far as we've got, in the same style as the Victorians. So perhaps we can go downstairs and see—'

'Where it's really fancy,' Fred cut in. When they got back down to the ground floor, Fred met Peter Bazalgette, the great-great-great-grandson of Sir Joseph. 'I've read all about your great-grandad,' Fred said, to which Peter replied: 'It's called having shit in the family.'

Looking up at the beam, Peter told Fred that this was the longest they'd ever had this engine going. 'It's now been going an hour and a quarter today,' he said. 'We've only had it going since last year. Six months. Now guess how much London excrement this used to lift every minute when it was really working, in the nineteenth century.'

'Well, I think a few hundred tons maybe,' Fred estimated.

'A hundred and twenty tons a minute,' Peter inform-ed him. 'And dumped it in the river to go out into the North Sea.'

'Was that just one engine,' Fred wanted to know, 'or all of them?'

'That was just the one engine,' Peter said, 'so all four working together, you were right; hundreds and hundreds of tons. I'm a bit proud of this. It cured London of cholera and typhoid.'

'Which was very important,' Fred said, 'because the Thames was very heavily polluted, wasn't it? Seeping into the water supply. And they died in their dozens, didn't they?'

'They called it the Great Stink,' Peter informed him, 'and there was only something done about it when it got so bad outside the House of Commons that the politicians were forced to take it seriously; only when the smell went up their nostrils.' It was a story that fascinated Fred, an epic of Victorian engineering.

'I've read about that,' Fred said. 'They appointed great-grandad to do the job. How many miles of sewers did he do?'

'Hundreds,' Peter replied. 'And can you imagine the disruption to London when they dug the whole of the city up for the system?'

'But have you ever thought, the forethought of our grandfathers, how it's lasted through two generations and it's still working? It's only just now they're having a bit of trouble, and they've built millions of houses since then.'

'He'd have got into trouble these days,' Peter said, 'because he completely over-specified the system. He spent more money on it than we would have done today. That's why it's lasted 150 years. So,' he continued, referring to the engine, 'what do you think of *Prince Consort?*'

'Oh, it's lovely,' Fred enthused. 'Everything's

wonderful. It's a credit to all these volunteers who keep it all going.'

'They named each of the four engines after members of the royal family,' Peter informed him. 'They say the Victorians were very prudish about matters lavatorial, but not when it came to great public work. How does this compare to the size of other engines you've seen?'

'Well,' said Fred, 'this is the biggest beam engine I've ever seen. I've never seen one as big in all the other pumping stations. Round where I live, there's a winding engine on a colliery where the drum will be as big as that, but it's much deeper and weighs 127 tons, but it's quite a modern thing. It were made in 1911. Considering this were just made in sand, it were not machined in any way . . . It's been cast in the sand and erected, and if you take a line on the corner of the window frame, it's maybe only a quarter of an inch out on something so big and so heavy.'

They went on to talk about the volunteers who had restored the engine. 'I've noticed you've got a lot,' Fred observed. 'Up our end, they find it very difficult. There were so many steam engines that people come and join organizations and then disappear, and nothing ever gets done. At least you've got quite a bit done here.'

'We've got about two hundred members and fifty active volunteers, working here twice a week. It's very, very good. We had Prince Charles come and turn it on last September. It's named after his great-great-great-grandfather, and it was originally turned on by his great-great-grandfather. So there's something of a royal tradition.'

'And *Queen Victoria* as well,' Fred added, indicating another one of the engines.

'Yes,' Peter said. 'She's over there. She's a little bit rusty at the moment. We've got to raise two million quid just to restore the building before we can do anything with her.' He talked to Fred about the building and what needed to be done with it, particularly the work that was needed on the roof, before coming back to the engines. 'The other thing that always amazes me about these engines,' he said, 'is that we can stand here and almost talk in a whisper, and it's such a delicate piece of equipment, there's no real noise.'

'More than likely,' Fred said, 'it's had very little done in mechanical maintenance of the main bits that would make the noise, like the main bearings, the big ends an' all that. They're the bits if there is a bit of play that don't half sound bad; like *bang, bang* every revolution. When I were a little lad, I used to go in spinning mills and look at them engines. They'd be bazzing round at quite a lot more revs than this, and some of them were making a terrible row, but it were the end, and no one bothered.'

'The thing I marvel at,' Peter went on, 'is what it takes for people to volunteer; restore a bit of heritage like this that they really love. What is it that makes people do that?'

'Well,' Fred said, smiling, 'I'd have liked to have been here on the first day, when, after all that grafting and scraping and shifting inches of thick grease and everything, the thing actually revolves. It's an un-believable feeling. I spent twenty-seven years doing this here steam tractor, and it were an unbelievable feeling.'

'And,' said Peter, 'it's because of all the fantastic things you've done to help all the steam heritage of Britain and the industrial heritage of Britain, that's why I think you had your visit to the Palace. How do you feel about that?'

'Yeah,' Fred replied, 'I think it rather must be. A bit of a surprise, I can tell you, when I got the letter from Buckingham Palace summonin' me to meet the Queen. Birmingham University have given me an honorary degree, Aberdeen have given me one, and it's all to do with the business of steam and restoration.'

'Did the letter summoning you to the Palace give you the reason?' Peter asked.

'Yeah,' Fred replied. 'Services to heritage an' TV work, or summat like that.'

It was the end of a very good week for us, and for Fred. The break in filming that we'd taken had clearly been good for him, and his visit to the Palace to receive his MBE had raised his spirits. It was a long drive back from south-east London, but Fred seemed happy and contented. And he wanted to get back on the road to continue his grand tour.

9

On the Road Again

The schedule for the rest of the journey involved picking up where we had left off in Derbyshire for a programme on engine building. From here we planned to travel to East Anglia, to look at the origins of the traction engine. At the Museum of East Anglian Life, we had been planning to see a ploughing demonstration using two traction engines, and there Fred would explain how the traction engine developed as an agricultural engine. Then it would be on to the Long Shop at Leiston in Suffolk, a steam museum set in the original buildings of the Richard Garrett Engineering Works. Here Fred would see Britain's first ever purpose-built production line, which was built in 1852 for the manufacture of portable steam engines – the predecessor of the traction engine.

If we had followed the series' original itinerary, from Suffolk, on the way to London to collect his MBE, Fred would have stopped at Colchester to visit Richard Percival, a steam enthusiast who lived in a showman's living van. Richard's next project was to build a steam-driven saw mill, and he wanted to see if Fred could help him find an engine.

After the trip to Buckingham Palace, we had planned to head for the West Country for a programme on what Fred described as 'old-style mechanicing', again with a small diversion en route, this time to visit Ian Woolett, one of the early pioneers in the steam preservation movement, who owned Europe's only working Steam Navvy, a large steam-powered excavating machine. In the West Country, our first stop was to be Tiverton, where we planned to visit Roger Pridham, a boiler-maker who manufactured and repaired steam boilers for traction engines and locomotives. On the edge of Dartmoor, we were to visit Dingles Steam and Fairground Heritage Centre, where Fred would see a selection of steam engines and fairground rides from the era when everything was 'Made in Britain'. The main reason for going to Cornwall, however, was because much of what you see on a traction engine is tin, including the brightly painted outer covering of the boiler, and the great centre of the tin industry was Cornwall. We would not be able to get to any of these destinations in East Anglia and the West Country.

Further on, the route would have taken us to the Forest of Dean, and to Blaenavon in South Wales to look at iron-smelting. Without the great advances in iron-smelting that took place in the eighteenth and nineteenth centuries, the building of engines like Fred's would not have been possible. At Clearwell Caves, Fred was going to see a demonstration of a method of smelting iron using charcoal, in a replica of an early iron-smelting furnace made from mud. Coal and iron-making always went together, and the Forest of Dean still has its own unique tradition of free mining, so Fred was going to visit a true Forest of Dean free mine and meet the miners who had had these ancient rights handed down to them since they had first been granted to their ancestors by Edward I.

From the Forest of Dean, Fred would steam across the Brecon Beacons to Blaenavon and its ironworks. With its evocative remains of early iron-works, railways, waterways, mines, quarries and workers' houses, the Blaenavon Industrial Landscape is one of the best places in Britain to see the course and consequences of the Industrial Revolution. Fred was going to tour the works, which had been at the cutting edge of new technology in the late eighteenth and early nineteenth centuries.

Fred's engine is steered by means of chains, so his next stop was going to be the traditional home of chain-making, the Black Country; then on to the site of Boulton and Watt's Soho Works in Birmingham. Here Fred would tell the story of Matthew Boulton, his partnership with James Watt and the pioneering engineering works they created.

The next stage of the journey was going to take us

to North Wales and a visit to the Welsh Slate Museum at Llanberis to see what Fred regarded as the finest surviving example in the whole of Britain of a big engineering workshop powered entirely by a huge waterwheel. From there, the plan was to drive over Thomas Telford's Menai Suspension Bridge to see the site of what had once been the biggest open-cast copper mine in the world. Then, on his way back to Bolton, he was going to stop at Anderton Boat Lift, the world's first working boat lift, before finishing our filming around Manchester.

Fred still wanted to do all of this, but that was going to be impossible. From this stage on, we would need to stay within a short drive of Bolton, so that we'd be able to get him back to hospital as quickly as possible if necessary. There was also the discomfort he suffered sitting in a vehicle of any kind to take into consideration.

The problems involved in looking after the needs of a sick man and arranging a filming schedule around a traction engine had been enormous. Fred was no longer capable of the long hours and huge physical effort involved in getting the engine from one location to another. Added to this, the filming itself meant working to tight schedules and long hours, which on this series was exacerbated by the complications of steaming up and travelling in the traction engine. Logistics demanded that, from this stage on, we would have to operate as three separate units: Fred, the engine and the production team.

Fred's welfare was of course our primary concern,

so I arranged with Jimmy that he would act as chauffeur, and that Fred would no longer need to be hurried along by the necessity of arriving at a place in sync with the crew. If he needed to stop, he needn't worry, and if he needed to be taken back to Bolton quickly to see a doctor, Jimmy would be able to drive him there immediately.

One of the things that had been giving Fred great pleasure on this trip was driving the engine. It was now performing well, steaming along with relative ease at the 12mph he had originally anticipated, and he was enjoying the experience. 'It's quite strange, really,' he said, 'because I've never owned a traction engine of me own, even though I've driven quite a few dozen belonging to different mates. An' of course it's quite nice when you get a chance to drive your own after twenty-odd years of struggling and restorations to get it into the state that I want it in, like a new one, as you might say.'

However, much as Fred loved being on the engine, his health wouldn't now allow him to drive it long distances or cope with its maintenance. We were lucky that he was being joined for the rest of the trip by his sons, Jack and Roger. Their presence was to be a great source of help and support for Fred over the next few difficult weeks, and without the kindness of Jimmy and his wife, Marlene, who had offered to pick the boys up from the Isle of Man ferry and look after them, none of this would have been possible.

On the morning of Tuesday 13 July, a week after Fred had picked up his MBE, Jimmy drove Fred, Alf,

Jack and Roger to the Great Central Railway at Loughborough. I travelled down separately with the crew. Fred's engine and living van were already there, having been transported from Crossness by Alan the previous Friday after we had done the driving shots there. Preservation railways were proving to be invaluable to us, which is one of the reasons so many of them cropped up in the series. First of all, their yards were secure, so Fred was always happy for his engine to be left at them. As well as this, he was able to stock up with coal and water, and there were also plenty of people with the skills and the tools that were needed if Fred had to do any little running repairs.

Great Central had been a late addition to the schedule, caused by the cancellation of all the stops in the south, south-west and east of England. We'd restructured the series now, and the final programme aired was going to be Fred picking up his MBE, so we added Great Central Railway as a stopping point on the way.

As soon as they arrived at the railway, Alf and Jimmy, with the help of Jack and Roger, set to work on the engine, getting it steamed up while Fred had a look round. With steam up, Fred was able to drive it out of the railway yard at Loughborough and past the station, where he gave what was to be his introduction to the programme:

You could say my engine is a sort of time capsule of Britain's industrial past. All of the parts were invented and built in the United Kingdom. The earliest traction engines were built at a time when Britain was the world's leading industrial power, producing more than half of the world's coal and iron. The traction engine stayed in commercial use for almost a century, but by the 1940s steam engines were going to the scrapyards, and now British manufacturing has been in decline for decades. I've been restoring my engine for twenty-seven years, and I've fulfilled a lifelong dream by getting her on the road and travelling the length and breadth of the country and meeting interesting people. But I've one more long journey to make, all the way to London to meet the Queen and get me MBE, before me grand tour is finished.

On me way, I'm stopping off to visit the Great Central Railway. Its one of our finest preserved railway lines, because it's got a double track like proper railways did have. Most preserved railways are single-line affairs that were once branch lines. This is a proper main-line affair. Great Central Railway is Britain's only main-line steam railway. It's one of the few places in the world where scheduled full-size steam trains operate on double track. Royal assent was given for the construction of the new main line in 1893, and in 1899 the Great Central Line ran its first passenger train from Marylebone station in London. Today the section that has been preserved runs from Loughborough to Leicester. It has over twenty steam locomotives, and many of them are currently being restored. About five hundred volunteers give their time to help run, restore and maintain the railway.

At the station, Fred walked along the platform with Alf, past the maroon carriages of a train waiting to go out. 'In the great days of the railways,' he told him, 'there used to be two routes up England: one up the west coast and one up the east coast. In 1893, the Great Central put one up the middle, and I think it was something like 1899, they got from London to Leicester. An' now it's the only main-line railway that has real steam engines on it and two tracks, and here we are at the locomotive.' The driver was standing by the side of the splendid 04-class locomotive, and introduced himself to Fred and Alf.

'With a big beer belly, you'd never get up there, would you?' Fred remarked to the driver as he squeezed his way on to the footplate. The engine was hauling a scheduled service from Loughborough to the other end of the line at Leicester, and as soon as Fred was on board, the driver tooted the whistle and they were on their way. The 04-class locomotive was one of only two surviving engines from the original Great Central Railway. Built in 1912, it had been restored there in the railway workshops. For Fred, riding on the footplate of a steam locomotive like this never lost its magic. He loved it, especially when it got to the end of the line, where, with no passengers behind them, they let him have a go at driving as they shunted the engine to the other end of the train to hook it up for the journey back to Loughborough. 'It's all the same as me tractor,' Fred said, 'but bigger. And there's a lot more power on this.'

As the wheels screeched and squealed, Fred was reminded of where he grew up and the sounds from the engine sheds and sidings at the bottom of his road. The driver looked on as Fred reversed the loco along the track, giving him instructions when needed. The tricky bit for Fred was braking and stopping in the right place to hook back on to the carriages. But with a bit of a hand from the driver, he did it. Fred enjoyed his little bit of driving, then handed back over to him to make the journey back to Loughborough. While they were waiting for the whistle, Fred helped the fireman out with a bit of stoking and then started to tell him and the driver all about his traction engine. 'New boiler, new bearings, new gears, bloody new everything!' he exclaimed, as they had a brew.

On their way back to Loughborough, Fred told the driver and fireman how it reminded him of when he was a little lad:

Saturday morning treat were to go and climb up the embankment, and I had this uncle who drove an Aspinall,* same as this but smaller, and it'd be pouring down with rain and they'd have sheets hanging over the tender. But he went and died,

* Locomotive designed by John Aspinall. British mechanical engineer who served as locomotive superintendent for the Lancashire and Yorkshire Railway.

and I'd only have been about eight or nine then. I like the Patrick Stirling single-wheeler. I always fancied having a go on that. I like these old-fashioned ones. There's summat about them, isn't there? They all rave about *Mallard* and *Flying Scotsman*, but you get on and it's claustrophobic. You're all hemmed in by all that ironwork. You don't get butterflies on the footplate like you do on this.

As they slowed down and eased on to the platform at Loughborough, Fred watched intently everything the driver and fireman did. 'How many tons have we got behind with the carriages?' he asked.

'Two hundred and thirty,' the driver replied. 'And I reckon we didn't burn more than 5 or 6 hundredweight, did we? I wonder how much diesel fuel it would take to move the same weight?'

When they took the loco back to the engine sheds, Fred met the railway's chief executive, Graham Oliver, who took him to have a look at the workshops where the locomotive he'd just travelled on had been restored. Inside, there were half a dozen engines in various stages of restoration. Graham took Fred over to one side of the shed, where a young man was working on one of them.

'Fred's just been out on the 04,' he said, 'and Craig's the man who restored that engine from a pile of bits. Craig served his apprenticeship with us, and he's learned more about steam while he's been working with us than anybody else here.'

'It's a good thing for a young man, isn't it?' said Fred. 'What exactly did you have to do to it?'

'I had to strip it all down,' Craig informed him. 'Take it to bits. Took the wheels out; took the boiler off. Basically stripped it right down and started afresh. It took me about three years.'

'What a pleasurable thing to do,' Fred commented. 'It's the best way with steam engines. No use thinking, We'll leave that bit, it'll be all right, because it never is. Was there much up with the boiler?'

'Not really,' Craig replied. 'I took all the stays out, and it was just basically a general re-tube.'

These were the sort of conversations that Fred always liked to have, and he was always fascinated to find out about the work that a skilled engineer like Craig had done on a steam engine. 'Did you have much to do with all the bearings and that part of it?' he asked. Craig told him that all the bearings had been replaced, then Fred wanted to know, 'Were there owt wrong with the journals?'

'They were fairly smooth,' Craig told him, 'but we just had them skimmed to get them back to new.'

It never took long during the course of a conversation like this for Fred to get back to the subject of his own engine. 'I'm a bit worried about me tractor,' he said. 'I don't know what I made the front bearings out of, but there's a very weak solution of gold paint coming out with the oil. There's something wrong somewhere. You've got to be careful when you're getting things out of the scrapyard.'

Outside the loco sheds, Fred met up with Graham

Oliver again, and he told him some of the history of the railway. 'The line sweeps along in a nice big curve, and on the journey you had down on that wonderful Robinson 04, the line is so smooth you feel as though you're going a lot faster. This line was built to go all the way through to the Channel Tunnel and Paris, because Sir Edward Watkin, who had the dream of building the Great Central Railway in the first place, had this magnificent dream of connecting Manchester and Sheffield right through to the Channel Tunnel. In fact, he started building a Channel Tunnel, and got about 6 miles under the sea, and then they stopped him, because they said they didn't want those foreigners coming over.'

'Yeah,' Fred said. 'There were, like, three attempts, weren't there? Richard Trevithick had a go. Then there were these railwaymen.'

'Well,' said Graham, 'I think Watkin would have made it, if he'd been allowed to. They closed this line in the late 1950s, and it was such a shame, because in the last decade of this line's existence under British Railways, it carried a tremendous weight of freight. They had named trains like *The South Yorkshireman* and *The Master Cutler*, and it was a real main-line railway, and then they came along with the Beeching plan and closed the whole lot.'

'He's a lot to answer for, Mr Beeching, hasn't he?' Fred interjected.

'If they could have just kept it going that bit longer,' Graham went on, 'with a new Channel Tunnel, who knows?'

Above: By the fifth week of the tour, as Fred reached West Yorkshire, the engine was running smoothly.

Right: Fred always liked to see the engine gleaming, so poor Alf had the never-ending job of polishing it.

Below: How far are we going to get today? A roadside consultation with Jon Doyle and the author, while Alan Atkinson patiently awaits instructions.

Above: It's full steam ahead as Fred prepares to continue his journey after a stop outside Andy Thornton's Architectural Antiques showroom in Elland, West Yorkshire.

Below: Fred arrives at the Bolt and Rivet Manufacturing Company in Worsborough near Barnsley, where they made all the rivets that Fred used when he was rebuilding his engine.

After a long day's filming, the strain on Fred was beginning to show as we reached the Peak District.

PEAK DISTRICT NATIONAL PARK

Below and right: Independent Forgings & Alloys in Sheffield specializes in the forging of large steel components for the aerospace and oil industries. Fred was impressed by the skills of the men who operate the forging hammer.

Above: Fred fulfils another ambition as he drives his engine over Scammonden Bridge, which crosses the M62 in West Yorkshire.

Below: The highlight of the tour: Fred proudly displays his MBE with his sons Roger (*left*) and Jack (*right*) at Buckingham Palace.

Fred on the footplate of the Class 04 locomotive at Great Central Railway.

63601

Above: The early-twentieth-century re-created village at the Black Country Living Museum.

Below: The Bottle and Glass Inn at the museum – always a popular place to stop for a pint during tiring filming schedules.

At the Anderton Boat Lift in Cheshire, Fred met lift operator Gary Hughes (*left*) and Tim Brownrigg (*below*), the engineer who was in charge of the restoration.

After driving down Llanberis Pass (*below*), Fred and Alf enjoy a chat with retired slate-quarry workers Gwillam Jones and Elwyn Wilson-Jones (*left*).

Above: Fred leaves the Welsh Slate Museum at Llanberis, en route to Parys Mountain, Anglesey – once the site of Britain's biggest copper mine.

Below: Fred and Alf meet David Wagstaff of the Parys Mountain Mine Exploration Group (*far left*) and Ian Cuthbertson from Anglesey Mining (*second from left*).

'But you might not have been here then,' Fred said.

'No,' Graham agreed. 'We picked up a main-line railway . . . We've got about fifteen steam engines and six or seven diesels, but they're diesels of the steam age. But there's nothing finer than tanking down this line on a steam engine. We couldn't have achieved all this without volunteers. Many of them are young, so the future looks bright. One of the sad things today is that they are all under pressure to go to university and learn things on computers. But, however long we live, we'll always need people who are fitters and plumbers. We need people who are willing to do these jobs and we've got them here and it's nice to see these lads come along and get practical everyday skills.'

Graham had strayed on to Fred's favourite theme. 'Everybody's not got the same amount of grey stuff in the top of their head, have they?' Fred agreed. 'I find it quite difficult writing a letter, and yet I've got lots of skill in me fingers for making things out of iron, and yet if I had to put in for an exam I'd get nowhere.'

'Yes,' said Graham. 'Everybody is reasonably equal, but they've got different skills, and you need to bring out those different skills.'

With Fred, this was preaching to the converted. 'You get a bloke who's been to university,' he said, 'can do algebra and arithmetic and all those sorts of things, and he's bloody useless if you give him a hammer an' a spanner.'

'Absolutely,' Graham agreed. 'And if people have got skills with their hammers and spanners, let's bring it out of them and let's train them. We've had some really good lads. Craig – he's brilliant. Craig came here straight from school and took an apprenticeship with us, and he's taken to it like a duck to water.'

Back at his engine, Fred sat down in the sunshine with a pint of Guinness, admiring the engine as it was being steamed up for a run he was going to do on it that afternoon. Behind them, a Black Five was steaming up outside the engine shed. For Fred, it was an idyllic situation. It was a warm summer morning, and nowhere could be more suited to Fred than this spot. It seemed to encapsulate his life and all that he loved: an engine shed just like the one he remembered from his childhood; his own traction engine; and his two lads, both as passionate about steam as he had always been – and here he was on the road with them, courtesy of the BBC, travelling round with his engine to places like this.

'It reminds me,' Fred said, 'of when I were little, and I used to go and sneak on to the railway sheds in Bolton, that have all gone now. Yuppie houses all over it now. Happy days. And here we are now sitting miles away from home in Loughborough in a lovely place.'

He talked again about the Saturday mornings he spent with his uncle. When he was about Roger's age, he said, his uncle

used to let me get on it, and I used to spend all Saturday morning in the pouring rain with a sheet off the back of the cab and on to the tender. *Chuff, chuff, chuff*, up and down all morning, shunting coal wagons. And then at twelve o'clock he had to take it back to the engine sheds, so I had to vacate. I had to get back over the fence and go home for me meat pie. But I graduated to the main line. On dark and stormy nights I used to go and buy a penny platform ticket and sit right at the end of the platform where the engine stopped, and Mr Walter Bamburgh, the engine driver – dead and gone now, God bless him – he used to pull up and have a quick shufti up and down to see if there were anybody about, and if there were nobody around ... [Fred's voice trailed off for a moment as he thought about those days so long ago] I used to get on the engine. It were near the end of the great age of steam, and the fireman knew he were going to be out of a job in a couple of years, so he didn't really care about anything; and I used to end up firing the engine all the way up to Rochdale. He used to say to me, 'It doesn't matter what you do as long as you don't lose the shovel; don't let go of the shovel into the fire hole, else we're done for.' And we always went to Rochdale with three carriages, then the fireman took the lamp off round the back and we shunted them into a siding and came back with the light engine backwards. When it got level with Burnden Park football ground, because it was going back to the shed, I had to jump off and climb over the railings and go home.

The house I lived in at Burnden Park, right across the end of the back street, there was the main line from Manchester to God knows where.

Along would come an express train, at two o'clock in the morning, with the fire-hole door open, light shining in the sky, and three of them on the footplate really caning it, and whistle blowing because they were getting near the station. It did keep me awake, but I enjoyed watching it happen. It were incredible. Mr Cuneo's painted a good picture of a locomotive in the dark, with all the fire coming out of the fire-hole door. There were a pub on Manchester Road called the Wagon and Horses, an' it had an iron ladder out of the sidings, down into the backyard of the pub, and I'm not kidding, it was as shiny as the regulator on that engine down there with the usage that it had. All day long it were full of railwaymen either going on duty or coming off duty. An' on a Saturday night and Friday night, it were chock bloody full. You couldn't get a pint. On the big bridge over the main road, there'd be like a Black Five with forty wagons of coal, blowing its head off into the sky, and driver and fireman in the pub: 'We'll just have another before we set off.' Then when they got up the ladder and on the engine, there'd be a blast on the whistle and away they went. They'd all get arrested these days for behaviour like that.

As a kid I used to go to sleep to the sound of the sheds and the marshalling yards, the screeching and the *bang, bang, bang, bang* in the middle of the night. And you never noticed. That's what annoys me about people who complain about noise these days. If you live with it, you don't notice it. They just complain for the sake of complaining, these people.

Fred paused to have a drink of his Guinness before continuing with his reminiscences:

That lamp I've got at home on the mantelpiece, Lancashire and Yorkshire Railway. Manchester Victoria. This guy, he were a shunter, the man with a stick with the hook on the end. And he were in the pub this night, drunk as a rat, with the hat on back of his head, like Will Hay in that film *Oh, Mr Porter!* And I says, 'What are you going to do with your lamp?' And he says, 'Buy us a pint and you can have the bloody thing.' So I bought him a pint and he gave it me. He'll be gone as well now, but I've still got the lamp. It'll be yours some day, Roger. And there are the ones above the lathe in the shed. Ewan Winterbottom got them me for the steamroller, and they were brand-new, those square ones. They're modern, like these on these engines. You can have them as well.

Fred took another swig from his can of Guinness and looked around contentedly, saying again, 'It's nice and peaceful here, isn't it?'

It was a moment that Kathryn remembers very clearly: 'I thought it was one of the nicest, most emotional parts of the whole trip, when Fred told Roger that the lamp would be his one day, particularly as we were all so aware that day wasn't very far away.

Since then, I've often wondered if Roger ever did end up getting that lamp.'

By now, it was lunchtime, and just outside the gates of the railway yard there was a fish and chip shop with a small café attached to it. We all went over for fish and chips and just about filled the place. This was a particular treat for Alf, because fish and chips was his favourite meal. He wasn't too keen on all the fancy stuff we'd been getting in the evenings at some of the places we'd been for meals.

'It was a running joke about Alf and his eating habits,' Kathryn recalls. 'When we went into a restaurant, he would often order a large plate of veg. The reaction of the waiter or waitress would vary, depending on the poshness of the establishment we were in.'

For Fred, there was some driving to do that afternoon. We'd finished lunch, and the engine was steamed up and ready to go. Fred climbed on board. By this stage, he was having to use some little wooden steps that he carried around in the living van to get up and down from the engine. Alf climbed up beside him as steersman, and Jack and Roger sat on the running board at the front of the living van. Jimmy stayed out of the way, because, in the terms of the series, he wasn't supposed to be with us. This stop at Loughborough was being filmed as part of the journey to London, and Jimmy hadn't been there, because he'd still been on his holidays.

Fred drove the engine out of the yard and up past the front of the station for our shots of him arriving at the railway and leaving it. Then, after a circuit of the streets around the station, with their red-brick terraced houses, he drove through the centre of Loughborough and out of town, on the A6, in the direction of Derby. We took care to get some shots of Fred and his engine coming up to the road signs for Shepshed, where we were going to be filming the next day. Then, it was on to a good stretch of dual carriageway, as far as a pub with a big car park, where Alan had the low loader waiting.

Here, with the help of Alf and Jimmy and the boys, he got the engine loaded up, ready to be transported to the Midland Railway Centre in Derbyshire, which was the next place where we'd be doing some driving shots, later that week. I went back to the hotel we were staying at with Fred and the crew.

The place we were staying at, quite appropriately, was the Great Central Hotel, right next to Lough-borough station. It had clearly been a grand railway hotel when the railway itself was in its prime, but now it looked very much what it was – a place that had seen better days. Still, there was a good bar there, and when we arrived I settled down with Fred for a couple of pints at the end of our day's work, as we had always done. These days, though, our bar-room chats were much less carefree than they had been in the past. He had, for the last year or so, been telling me more and more about the problems he was having in his relationship with Sheila, and about some of the advice he'd been getting regarding what he should do about them. He was particularly concerned about the advice he was being given by one friend: to get a divorce. The man in question was somebody he had known as a casual acquaintance for several years and had only become a good friend much more recently. He was an ex-miner who was now a successful businessman; the sort of man Fred had a lot of respect for. Fred had told me on many occasions that this friend had said he should do what they did in the old mining towns and villages, that is, 'Put her things out on the street and throw her out.' But it wasn't what Fred wanted.

'I don't want to be doing that now,' he said 'not in me present state of health. We might fall out an' fight a bit, but she's not that bad, really. I'll say, "We shouldn't be fighting like this, cock," and we'll have a glass of red wine, and then it'll be all right again.' It was clear that divorce was the last thing he wanted to be thinking about at this time, but he was still bothered about the advice he'd been given. As if he didn't have enough to worry about!

Next morning, we went off to the metal-spinner's in Shepshed. With no engine to worry about, it was a fairly short drive from Loughborough to the premises of G. A. Hopkins, the small family business we were visiting. Fred went with Alf and Roger, and once we'd found the place, he announced, 'And here we are; we've come to witness the ancient art of metal-spinning at Mr Hopkins.' In the olden days, you know, they used to make everything metal-spun, like all fancy lamp-shades, pots and pans, and all that sort of thing, and here they do traction-engine chimneytops, and they tell me in here they also made nose cones for Spitfires. There'll not be a great demand for them now, though.'

They walked into the little workshop, where there was a man working on what was clearly taking shape as a traction-engine chimneytop. He leaned over it, applying pressure to it with what looked like a chisel as it spun around on a lathe. The copper that was used when Fred's engine was being built would have been supplied in sheets to a copper-spinner's like this.

'There he is,' said Fred, 'the man who owns the works. Morning, Geoffrey.'

It was Geoff Hopkins, who'd spent a lifetime doing this sort of work.

'Morning, Fred,' he said. 'How are you?'

'Aye, I'm all right, mate,' Fred replied. 'We've come to have a look at your wonderful metal-spinning operation.'

'It's a bit of an old-fashioned trade. We've got an Aveling top we're making at the moment, if you want to come and have a look.'

Fred went over to the work bench to inspect the job that was under way. 'I've done a little bit of metal-spinning myself, in a very amateurish way,' he ventured:

> About twenty years ago, this mate of mine bought a pair of traction-engine lamps at an auction. He paid twenty-five quid for them. He moved away from Bolton, and he rang one day and asked me if I could make a weathervane for him. 'Aye,' I said, 'it'll be twelve hundred quid,'

and he nearly choked on the other end of the phone. So I did a deal with him and agreed to make him a weathervane in exchange for the two lamps, but when he brought them – woe is me – the lamps that had been perfect twenty years before were a mess and I were really disappointed. So I thought, Necessity is the mother of invention. I'll have to learn meself metal-spinning overnight, an' I got this book, *Do It Yourself Metal-Spinning*, an' I made meself a mahogany pattern like a trumpet and had a go. But it wasn't easy, and I got a pile of disasters. In the end I gave up and went to see a proper metal-spinner, and he made it look so easy.

'It's the beading that's the awkward part of the job,' Geoff said. 'We still struggle sometimes. You get used to it, but every now and then one has to go in the bin. It's just one of them jobs. Each spinner has got his own way. I tend to do the bead with a ball bearing, and you can roll the metal round using the bearing. We have got beading wheels, but nobody seems to use them. You learn yourself how to do it.'

'It's like all engineering books that are written by academics who have been to university,' Fred said, getting once more on to his favourite hobby horse. 'And they don't really do a lot of practical stuff. They know how to write about it, but they don't know how to do it.'

Geoff and Fred were both singing from the same hymn sheet. 'A lot of advisers have never left school,' Geoff said:

They've never actually worked on something. They've seen it being done, but they've never done it themselves, never been hands-on. I mean, when you're moving metal, it does all sorts of strange things, particularly non-ferrous brass and copper. Some of it's as hard as nails and some of it's soft. It varies, and you've got to treat it as such. As hand-spinners, you can feel the difference in the material.

It's no good thinking you can spend a couple of days metal-spinning and then you're a metal-spinner. I've been doing it thirty-eight years, and every time a new job comes in, it is a new challenge. Like some of the ornamental work we do – we get instructions from a company who send in maybe a brass or a copper ornament, a finial off the top of a church or a library or whatever, and then you've got to sit and look at it and think how to make it, how to produce it, and how can they fit it, as well. All of these things, you don't learn that out of a book. As I say, at the moment we've got an Aveling top on, so if you want to come and have a look, Tim is going to start spinning it.

'Oh, aye,' said Fred, 'we'll come and have a look at that,' and they walked over to a lathe that had the big round disc of copper firmly attached to one end.

As they looked at it spinning round, Geoff explained the process. 'As you see, we put soap on or oil, and then gently move the metal. You can't force it. It won't go. It just wrinkles up.'

He told Fred how the metal had to be moved with a fairly gentle action, because if you do it too hard, you open the grain in the metal and tear through it. Fred watched intently as Tim turned the flat metal disc into a beautiful copper top for an Aveling engine. As the metal spun on the lathe, Tim pressed on it, then shaped the metal, buffing it and polishing it as he went along. It was very much like watching a skilled wood-turner at work. Then Tim trimmed off any surplus metal with a sharper-edged tool.

As Tim was spinning the metal, Geoff carried on talking us through the process. 'Again,' he said, 'it's one of our primitive turning tools he is using to do this. We've tried all sorts of turning tools, but we always go back to the old stuff. We make these in two halves and join the top to the bottom, either lapping the top over or, if the customer wants, we can join it underneath.'

Alf and Roger were looking on over Fred's shoulder. 'He makes it look so easy,' Alf said admiringly.

'Well, yes,' Geoff agreed. 'He's made a lot of them over the years. It's one of those things you just get used to.'

The job had been completed now, and Alf asked, 'When he was using the tool, he had it under his arm. Did he have to use a lot of pressure?'

'Yes,' Geoff replied. 'I think that's one of the difficulties, judging what pressure to use.'

Fred took the finished chimneytop and examined it.

Then he handed it to Alf. 'Lovely job there, mate,' Alf said.

Now they had watched the demonstration, it was Fred's turn to have a go. Geoff took Fred over to a smaller lathe. Alf and Roger followed them across the little workshop. 'So that's that one,' Geoff said, 'if you want to come and have a go.'

'Yeah,' Fred said enthusiastically. 'I'll try and have a bit of a go!'

Fred might have been having trouble getting round on his engine, but he was still very much up for getting his sleeves rolled up and having a go himself if some craftsman's skill was being demonstrated. Geoff got the lathe started up and put soap on to the piece of metal that Fred was going to be spinning.

'The thing is,' he said, 'years ago, when you were on piece work, you never used to stop the lathe. It'd be going round at about two and a half thousand revs, and you'd take it off and put the blank on as it was spinning round – if you were doing cake tins and things like that. We used to do that type of work for Prestige when they were at Derby, and they'd come along and say, "Here you are, make me them," and you'd have a frying pan, three sizes of saucepan and whatever. We used to turn them in wood, put the aluminium over them, purely for the design people to look at. You'd probably spent a week working on them, and the design bloke would come in and say, "No, they're no good," and walk out.'

Geoff turned to the lathe and adjusted it to get the speed up for Fred to do his little bit of spinning. Fred was raring to go. He picked up the chisel to start, but Geoff took it from him to dip it in oil first. Then Fred was off with Geoff, standing at his shoulder, watching and giving him instructions. The metal was taking shape under Fred's hand. How he did it, I don't know. Wherever we went, and whatever he tried his hand at, he always made a decent fist of it.

'You're getting better now, Fred,' Geoff said encouragingly as Alf and Roger looked on. 'You'll get an order for these at the rate we're going.'

'It feels,' said Fred, 'as if the tool post were an inch or so further this way, it would be better.'

'I know what you mean,' Geoff said. 'But the thing is, what suits one person doesn't suit another. If you were doing it on a regular basis, you'd know where to set the tool post up for yourself. But that's it, job done. We just need to take the soap and the oil off.'

Fred switched the lathe off. 'It's not too bad,' he said, looking at his handiwork. 'It's a perfectly shaped chimneytop for a miniature traction engine.'

'Does that mean we've got to go home and make the rest of the engine?' Roger joked.

Geoff took the completed chimneytop off the lathe and handed it to Alf, who studied Fred's work closely. 'That's lovely that, innit?' he said. 'First-class that, Fred. Knock us a set of candlesticks up!'

'Yeah, all right,' Fred said with a laugh. 'We'll have a go in the shed when we get home. It's that beaded edge that's the awkward bit. It's quite technical, that. But this one's all right. There'll be some poor lad somewhere who's spent about ten years building a model traction engine who'd go over the moon for that.'

While Fred was at the metal-spinner's with Alf and Roger, Jimmy was back at the railway getting something sorted out that had been a problem since we first set off: the fact that the nozzle on the end of the water pipe that Fred had made was too big, and wouldn't fit into the tank properly. 'There was water everywhere when we tried filling it,' Jimmy recalled, 'so I got one of the lads in the workshop at the railway to trim it down for us so that it would fit. And that's when I did the chains on the steering as well. He wouldn't let us tighten them up, but while he was away, I said, "I'm tightening this chain up," and it made a big difference for Alf, because there was that much slack in it he was winding the wheel and nothing was happening. Or you'd go over a bump and it would turn the wheels.'

It had been a fascinating and enjoyable morning at the metal-spinner's. The whole Hopkins family had been there: three generations, Geoff, his son and his grandson, with skills that had been passed on from one generation to the next. It was perfect for the series.

After the little workshop, we were heading for a much bigger one, where they did engineering on a much larger scale. We left Geoff Hopkins' workshop and headed north to Belper in Derbyshire. This was the place we'd reached a few weeks earlier, but the filming had had to be cancelled. Now we were going to have another go at filming Fred at one of the workshops of the Midland Railway in Ripley.

We reached our hotel late that afternoon. It was a smart, comfortable place on the high street with what looked like a decent restaurant and a nice bar. Fred and I were ready for our usual pint when we got there, and Jimmy joined us with some of the crew.

Normally, you couldn't stop Fred talking but, even though he was still putting a brave face on things, he was getting quieter and quieter now. As they finished their drinks, everybody started to drift up to their rooms to have showers and get changed for dinner. I stayed and had another pint with Fred.

'What have I done to deserve all this?' he said, as I came over from the bar with the drinks. 'Why me? Just when I can afford to do all the things I still want to get done in me garden. There's so much I still want to do.' Then he came back to the subject that was causing him nearly as much concern as the cancer that was killing him. It was all this pressure that was being put on him to 'get rid of Sheila' and to 'cut her out of his will'. What should he do?

He wanted my advice, but I couldn't help him very much. Over the years we'd worked together, we'd become good friends, but I'd never got very involved in his personal life. Unlike the earlier films that had been made about him, I'd steered clear of this. It all seemed like a bit of a minefield. I knew Sheila well, and I liked her, but I told him that any decisions he made about who he was leaving things to were his decisions, and he and he alone would have to make them. What I told him he must not do was let himself be swayed by other people. He accepted this, and I was left with the impression that he was happy to keep the will as it was, leaving his house and garden to Sheila, and his engines to Jack and Roger.

When he came down to dinner about an hour later, he seemed to be a lot more cheerful. He had a laugh, as Alf asked for fish and chips when we were ordering our meal, and the waiter said, 'There's a chip shop across the road, sir.' Later that evening, we even saw some glimpses of Fred's old self, as he had a couple of drinks and started to tell a few of his stories to the small crowd who had, inevitably, gathered around him.

Next morning, after an early breakfast, we made our way to the Midland Railway Centre. Alf and Alan had left even earlier. The engine had been parked up there when Alan transported it from Loughborough, and by the time we arrived at the railway, he and Alf had got the engine steamed up, ready for us to do some driving shots. We worked out a route of about 8 miles that would take us along some of the small roads and through a couple of villages close to the railway.

In one of the villages, a crowd of excited children rushed to the railings round the playground of the local primary school to wave as the engine went past, and when Fred stopped in the centre of another, a crowd soon gathered round with cameras and auto-graph books. Obliging as ever, he was happy to wait till every photograph had been taken and every scrap of paper had been signed before moving on. 'Who was the autograph for?' he always wanted to know and then, in his impeccable copperplate hand, he would write 'To Tom' or Jane or whoever, 'Best Wishes, Fred Dibnah, July 2004.'

Now, you could definitely see that there had been a major improvement in the performance of the engine since those first dispiriting days. Alf had become a proficient steersman, and Jimmy travelled along in the living van, standing at the barn door at the front.

As he drove along the leafy lanes of Derbyshire, Fred explained the reasons for visiting the railway he was heading for. 'In the late 1800s and early 1900s, there were hundreds of steam-engine manufacturers based in Great Britain,' he said, 'and of course, they manufactured everything from traction engines to railway locomotives and stationary engines, which were exported to practically every nation in the world. Today, there are very few commercial steam-engine builders and repairers, but now we've reached Derbyshire on our grand tour, and we're going to go to a railway workshop where repairs are done on quite a grand scale, mostly by volunteers, who just do the work for the love of it.'

But on the way to the railway, there was a distraction. Fred spotted the winding gear of an old pit, and with two ex-miners on board, they found it hard to drive past the remains without stopping to investigate. But we had a schedule to stick to. Things had been set up for us at the railway, and there were people waiting there to be filmed with Fred. Maybe we'd have time to look at it after we'd done the filming that had been arranged for that day.

We went straight to the very impressive workshops at the railway centre. The shop we went into was a long engine shed with two tracks running the full length of it, one on either side. On the tracks were locos at various stages of renovation and restoration, and another couple that were in for routine maintenance work. But it wasn't just railway locomotives that were being worked on. Further down the workshop in the middle, between the tracks, there was a boiler from a Ransome's traction engine that had just had a brand-new throat plate put on to it. The far end was a hive of engineering activity, with the bright-blue sparks of a welder at work and another group of workers riveting a boiler – paradise for Fred.

'One of the last steam locomotives to be built in the Midlands is being restored here,' he said. 'It's the only survivor of the last batch of steam engines built at Derby Locomotive Works in 1956. With the decline of steam power, the engine never did much work. It saw only eleven years' service and ended up at the famous Barry Scrapyard in South Wales before being rescued. When it came to Midland Railway Centre, there was a lot of work needed to be done.'

Peter Wood from the workshops was our guide, and he picked up on the loco that Fred was talking about, explaining that they'd had the engine in question, a Standard Class 9F, running on their line, but the problem was that it was a very big locomotive for this railway, because they only had a short length of track.

As they moved on down the workshop, Peter pointed out some of the other locos they had in. After the 9F, there was a 7F class from the Somerset and Dorset Railway. Next in line, there was a Black Five.

They were renewing all the pipe work on this, and changing the brakes from steam brakes to air brakes, which meant that they would always work, even if the engine was low on steam. Getting it registered for main-line use was, Peter explained, the main objective.

Then there was another of those sad moments that brought an abrupt reminder of the state that Fred was in. As they looked at the Black Five, Peter asked Fred if he felt inclined to have a look at the compressors. 'It'll mean climbing up on to it,' he said.

'No,' Fred replied sadly. 'I can't get up on to there now. I'm weary.' He looked at the great black locomotive wistfully, and observed, 'There were plenty of these round where I used to live.' But Fred soon perked up when we got to the far end of the workshop, where there was a lot of activity going on with a hydraulic riveter. Inevitably, it wasn't very long before he managed to get involved in the job and was having a go himself. He was enjoying himself again, all his cares forgotten, totally absorbed in what he was doing.

When we got out of the workshop at the end of our filming, the weather had changed. It was pouring down, and there wasn't a break in the cloud anywhere in sight. It looked as though it had set in for the rest of the day, so there wasn't going to be a chance of investigating the pithead gear Fred had spotted earlier. However, we were going to be back in that part of Derbyshire the following week, so I told Fred we'd try to fit the abandoned mine into that week's schedule.

10

Staying with Friends

The following week, Fred and the boys stayed with an old friend of the family, Ian Howard, at Kirk Ireton in Derbyshire. Ian's business, Alton Engineering, specialized in the restoration and repair of traction engines. Jack and Roger had known Ian's lads since they were small, and it was very much like a home from home for them, and for Fred. We'd got filming to do at Ian's workshops and several other locations nearby, and Ian's house provided a friendly and comfortable base for Fred.

Before he could go back to Derbyshire, however, Fred had another important appointment. On Monday 19 July, he had to go to the University of Birmingham to receive his second honorary degree, for what Fred described as 'backstreet mechanicing'.

Professor Graham Davies of Birmingham University

didn't quite put it like that. 'Fred was given a doctorate,' he said,

> because of his enthusiasm and his promotion of engineering and the history of engineering. He was felt to be one of the foremost enthusiasts for the history of engineering and what it was all about, so it was for his promotion of public understanding of engineering that he was nominated for his doctorate. He came to receive it in his best dungarees, minus cap but with a mortar board instead. By tradition, honorary graduates are asked to give a small speech. For his, Fred didn't go to the lectern. He stood right in front of the audience and delivered a speech right from the heart. It lasted for at least ten minutes, and he kept the audience spellbound with his experiences and his history of engineering. He told the students that he wasn't an educated person, and that he'd come into television and the history of engineering by accident, really, and that everything had grown from there. But it was doing something that he loved, and having the enthusiasm to carry it through; and that was his philosophy for life.

Incredibly, with his cancer at such an advanced stage, Fred was still doing his theatre talks, honouring bookings that had been made the previous year, before the decline in his health had really set in. From Birmingham, Sheila drove him to Nottingham, where he was doing a show that night. They stayed in Nottingham, and Sheila brought him to Ian Howard's to join up with the rest of us the following morning. By the time Sheila dropped Fred off, the lads had got the engine steamed up and we were ready to head off down the lane for some driving shots.

Jack stood proudly up on the engine by his dad's side. He was the steersman now. Alf had been relegated to the living van with Jimmy and Roger. Fred brought the engine to a halt at the junction of two narrow lanes. They were at the bottom of a steep hill. 'We need all this steam,' Fred said, 'to get up the mountain to see two old mates of mine, Ian and Gary Howard, who own a big Fowler Showman's engine. Last year, they had a very bad do, a big fire, and it burnt the shed down and melted all the brass on the engine. But they tell me it's almost finished again now, and now we've got Roger and Jack, me two sons, to help out Alf and Jimmy on our round-the-world tour, so we'll set off up the hill . . . or attempt it. Are you ready, men? Let's see if it'll get up this mountain.'

Alf and Jimmy released the chocks that had been under the wheels while they were stopped, and got up on to the running board beside Roger as the engine moved off with a great *chuff, chuff, chuff* and started to labour up the hill. Progress was very slow, no more than walking pace, but at least the engine kept going. A few weeks earlier, at the beginning of the grand tour, a hill as steep as this would have defeated it. Fortunately, they didn't have far to go and, as they got to the top of the hill, they saw the sign for Alton

Engineering. Jack steered the engine through the gates, and Fred parked up in front of a huge and very new-looking shed.

'It's certainly not steamroller country this, is it?' he said. 'You'd be slurring about a bit, up and down that lot.' Fred got down from the engine and walked in through the big sliding front doors of the shed. He greeted Ian and Gary, who were both up on their great showman's engine, which they were working on all hours.

'Now then,' called Fred. 'Hiya, lads, how you doing? I can see you're doing all right . . . without a shadow of a doubt.'

'Oh, battling on,' Ian replied, 'battling on. Have you had a good run up?'

'Oh aye, yeah,' Fred said, but it was the progress they had made on the restoration and repair of their engine that stopped him in his tracks. 'I–I–I can't believe it,' he stammered. 'You know, from seeing what we all know about twelve months ago, it's incredible, isn't it? You must have worked day and night for that, eh?'

'Aye,' replied Ian, 'we've done a minute or two. Whether another marriage will survive or not, I don't know!'

'Oooh, sshh!' Fred said, and they all laughed as he went on, 'Well, I've tried three times! Steam engines and women are a very hard mix.'

Fred had a good look at the engine as Ian and Gary left the jobs they were doing on it and came down to ground level to join him. 'You've made a brand-new tender,' he said. 'And it didn't do no harm to the boiler.'

'We're hoping not. No,' Ian confirmed. 'We've done all the tests necessary and we've had her in, steam blowing off at two hundred like, and everything's OK.' Fred was anxious to know all about it and was full of questions. 'Is the cylinder block all right? No doubt, it'd bugger the dynamo up, eh? Have you got another? It's mainly the brass bits that suffered, isn't it?'

Ian answered all his questions. The cylinder block was all right, and the dynamo was buggered up, but they had a friend who was trying to repair that for them. 'A lot of people have come forward with spares,' Ian went on. 'The chap who owned it before us still had the Renown nameplate, so we were dead lucky. He's let us have that because that got really badly damaged. I'm still a few bits short, but nothing major or detrimental.' They went on to talk about the fire itself. Seven fire engines were there to tackle the blaze, and it was lucky, they said, that the engine was full of water.

'Yeah,' said Fred. 'I read that it were actually blowing off in the fire. I read how you stopped the fire brigade squirting it with the cylinder, which could've been disastrous, couldn't it?'

Ian took Fred over to the back of the workshop to see some of the things that had melted in the blaze. 'Nightmare corner,' he called it. 'We cried for a fortnight about it,' he said.

'Well, I did as well,' Fred said. 'Well, not for a fortnight, but I couldn't believe it when I heard about it.

When me little lad rung me up and said the Howard brothers have had a terrible accident, I actually cried on the phone. All I could say was they worked that hard, and I've watched them for years with that engine and then to have it all bloody destroyed . . .'

As they talked about the engine and the hours of work they had put into it, I was struck by the dedication of these men. They were men like Fred, men with a magnificent obsession, and it was impossible not to be filled with admiration for all the hard graft they put into preserving these machines they loved.

They talked a bit more about their work on the Showman's engine, then Ian took Fred into another workshop, where two lads and an older man were working on different parts of engines they'd got in for repairs and renovation work. Ian showed Fred a very early Aveling roller dating from 1884 that they were working on. They'd made a new tender for it, and Ian said, 'When it's all whacked together, it'll be the oldest one in steam.' Then they looked at a Marshall that Ian's friend Jack Meaker, who was well known in the traction-engine world, was working on.

'It's got the usual Marshall ailments, hasn't it?' said Fred. 'Why do Marshalls always crack there, while Avelings always crack on the throat plate?'

Ian laughed. 'But Fowlers are perfect. They don't crack nor nothing.'

'When you think about Fowlers,' Fred said, 'Leeds . . . there were more traction-engine builders and loco builders in Leeds than any other city in the land, you know. Yeah. There were dozens of them, weren't there?

All that employment. And now there's nowt left at all, is there? What do we do now? Shopkeepers. Bolton's famous for toilet rolls and incontinence pads, you know! And we used to make boilers and steam engines and all sorts.'

Fred looked around the workshop. Everybody was busy working on big pieces of metal, all showing the sorts of skills he admired so much. 'You've got plenty of work in, then,' Fred said.

'Yeah. It's endless,' Ian replied. 'Next job in is a little narrow-gauge loco. A Fowler, actually. That's going to be an interesting project. Then a Foden traction engine.'

'That's good, isn't it?' Fred commented. 'I mean, there's more of the interest in our hobby. It really grows and grows, doesn't it? So the future's got to be bright for all of us.'

Fred stayed in the workshop for another hour or so, talking to the lads about the jobs they were doing and having a laugh with Jack. Jack's own engine had been destroyed in the fire, as well as Ian and Gary's. 'It hadn't been in steam since the 1960s,' he told Fred, 'and I'd just about got it done, all repainted and everything. I think if things had gone on as they were, I would've been out this year with it. When it had just happened, I didn't know whether to sell the engine, or what to do.'

For Fred, it was like an Aladdin's cave here, with all sorts of interesting engines at various stages of repair and restoration, and he was full of questions about them. 'What's this one?' he wanted to know, pointing to a squat-looking boiler.

'This,' said Ian, 'is another interesting project. It's going to be the firebox for a replica of *Puffing Billy*. It's a project that's going off up at Beamish. We're doing most of the boiler work for that. There's different people doing different projects on it.'

Fred spotted another boiler standing outside at the back of the workshop. 'Aye, it's a bit of a rarity, this one, isn't it?' he said.

'Yeah,' Jack Meaker replied, 'a very early one this . . . 1884. When we get it steaming, it'll be the oldest steamroller steaming. There are some older ones in existence, but they're in museums, and they're not steaming. It'll be an interesting engine.' Fred discussed some of the finer points of the design of the engine with Jack and Ian, working out with them what went where. 'They're only teeny rivets, aren't they?' Fred observed. 'They're not so big.'

For Fred, having his engine somewhere like this at this stage of the journey was very useful. Although it was steaming well now, other faults had started to appear. One that he was getting particularly worried about was the problem he was having with one of the bearings, which had brought him to a halt when he was in London. Jack said he would stay behind and have a look at it when we went out filming the next day. That night, he was staying at Ian Howard's with his dad and Roger.

We on the filming side of things had got a holiday cottage booked just down the road. We were using this as a base and going by car to the places around there where we were filming that week. This was a much more relaxed way of doing things; much more suited to Fred's needs. But we were not going to have the luxury of staying in one place like this for the rest of the shoot. We'd cut out East Anglia and the West Country because of the distances involved, but we were still planning on going to South Wales, the Forest of Dean, the West Midlands, North Wales and a number of locations nearer home in the north-west that Fred was particularly keen to visit. I wondered how many of these places we would be able to get to and how Fred was going to be able to cope.

With Fred at Ian Howard's, we talked about it over a drink and dinner that evening. Everybody was worried about Fred's condition. But the problem was still the pay-off between the pain we knew he was suffering and the general feeling that it was this tour that was keeping him going. Because Fred was on a radio mic when we were filming and he always forgot it was switched on, our sound recordist, Nigel Chatters, would sometimes hear more than the rest of us. Kate Siney recalled: 'I remember Nigel telling me about a time when Fred went to the loo, and Nigel seemed upset because he'd heard how much pain he was in. I remember Fred was hiding it really well, but you could tell he was bad. Having spent a number of weeks with him at the beginning and seen how excited he was about the whole thing and how chatty he was with everybody, you could tell, because he was getting a lot less enthusiastic about things. And also the going to bed early and not drinking very much, you could tell that he wasn't feeling too good.'

It was a real dilemma, but as long as he was insistent about keeping going, and while it was giving him a last chance to see old friends like Jack Meaker and the Howard brothers, it had to be right to carry on.

We'd found a nice little restaurant close to where we were staying which was a bit more expensive than the places we normally ate at, and decided to go there that night. But when we got there and looked at the menu, Alf wasn't very happy with it. He never complained about anything, however early he had to get up and however much work he had to do on the engine, but when he looked at the menu and the prices, he said it just wasn't right. He wasn't going to have any of this fancy food at these fancy prices. I reasoned with him that it didn't matter. All our food, accommodation and travel costs were on the programme budget, and we certainly weren't extravagant. But Alf wouldn't have it. It didn't matter who was paying for it, he said, it was too expensive; and he stuck to his principles. When they came to take the order, he asked if there was something plain and simple they could knock up for him, but it wasn't that sort of place, so he finished up ordering a plate of vegetables.

Next day, Fred was able to leave the engine in the workshop while we went out filming with him. Jack stayed behind to look into the problem with the bearing. He'd learned well from his dad, and he was a skilled mechanic, due to start an engineering apprenticeship with the Isle of Man Railway as soon as the filming had been completed.

As Jack started to work on the wheel, Fred

explained what he was going to be doing that day. 'I'm leaving the engine here today,' he said, 'and going down the road to see Mr David Ragsdale, who's a master at the art of pattern-making.'

David's workshop was round the back of his house in Retford, Nottinghamshire. From Derbyshire, we drove through what was once the heart of the Nottinghamshire coal-field. It took just over an hour, and when we arrived we were warmly welcomed by David, his wife and his dad, who owned several traction engines, which he kept in an outbuilding at the end of the garden. Fred was instantly at home here as well. It was that great traction-engine family again. After tea and biscuits, we set up to film outside David's workshop, where Fred told us a bit about pattern-making:

From ornamental park railings to the cylinder block of a traction engine, everything that was made out of iron had to be cast. The casting were done in a mould, and to create the mould a pattern had to be made. Once they'd made the pattern, they could use it dozens of times. The thing is that, in the 1920s and 1930s, when the demise of the traction engine were very obvious to most people, all the patterns got burnt, so anybody now who buys an engine that's got a dicky part has got to come here and see Mr Ragsdale, who specializes in making patterns from the remains of the original bit, or from a drawing provided by the customer, or the owner of the engine. He's got all sorts of specialist woodworking machines, like circular saws, wood lathes, specialist sanding machines and timber milling machines, and he's a real steam fanatic as well, with six steam engines in the family! About 30 per cent of the patterns 'e makes are for the steam industry. He says there's no component on a steam engine that he hasn't made a pattern for, and there are so many different models. He retains patterns for future use, after the casting. So I'm going to nip in here now and have a chat with him and see what he's up to.

When Fred went into the workshop, David was working at his bench. He was putting the finishing touches to what was clearly the front end of a traction-engine boiler, all beautifully made out of wood. ''Ave you been at it long, like?' Fred asked David as he walked up to the bench.

'Yeah,' David replied, stopping the fine sanding that he was doing. 'I was an apprentice when I was sixteen . . . I've been at it twenty-five years now.'

'People don't realize,' Fred said, 'when they look at our engines and see all these beautiful curved bits, that nearly every one of them had somebody who'd made a wooden pattern for it to get the castings. You're well tooled up with the machinery here.'

David agreed. 'Yes, you've got to have machinery to do our job. You can't do patterns unless you've got the machinery.'

'It's not easy making curved things by hand,' Fred

said. 'I know, having been a joiner from when I was fifteen to twenty-two, if you get machinery that will spin things round, it makes life a lot easier.' He had a good look round the workshop. 'You've got all sorts of interesting projects afoot, haven't you? This is the front end off a convertible like mine, isn't it? When we got the tractor, we had a lot of bother with this front bit.'

David said it was off an Aveling and Porter, quite an early one. As Fred examined the pattern, David explained that it was all made of segments, which are glued together. He pointed to one of the sections and explained that there would be twenty to thirty pieces of wood in that section alone, and a similar number in another section he pointed out. Before going off to the foundry, it would be painted in pattern red. Fred clearly admired the craftsmanship that was involved, and he talked about the way that some people had a feel for this sort of work. David got one of the finished patterns down from a shelf and explained that they were going to take it to the foundry later on. This pattern wasn't for an engine, though. It was for an extension to a copy of a Victorian table. The finished table, he told Fred, would weigh half a ton.

But Fred was more interested in the piece that David was doing for the Aveling. He'd noticed that he'd got the original on the workshop floor, and he spotted straight away the reason the new part was being made: there was a big crack in it. 'People don't realize,' he said, 'how fragile the front of a steam engine is.' Then, looking at the pattern, he observed, 'The bloody skill involved in this, because you've got to make the pattern slightly bigger than the end product, because when the metal solidifies again, it shrinks.'

'That's right,' David said. 'Contraction. We have special rulers to give us an allowance for that. Cast iron's a quarter of an inch in every twelve and a half. Aluminium varies: it's one inch in every seventy-seven. And steel's the greatest, that's one in every forty-eight. It contracts a lot more. Twice as much as cast iron.'

Fred turned his attention to the original front end of the Aveling. 'That's a really nasty crack there, isn't it?' he said. 'It's nearly in two halves, isn't it? Normally, that's the reason that head stock has to be remade, because the chimney base is rotten. Are you going to be painting the pattern all red like they do?'

'Yeah,' David said as he took a newly made pattern down from one of the shelves at the side of his workshop. 'That also has to be finished in pattern red like this one here that we've to take to the foundry. So perhaps we should set sail, should we, and take her and see what they do with it there?'

David took his patterns to a number of local foundries to have the castings made. One man he worked particularly closely with was Barry Bradley from Manor Brass Foundry, which was about 10 miles away, in Ollerton, over on the other side of the A1. When we got there, we found a small workshop in an old industrial unit, not much more than a big shed. The double doors at the front were open. Inside, there were rows of sand moulds neatly laid out on the floor in lines, a big pile of coke and, at one side, a glow from the coke-fired furnace. Castings for things like the cylinder block and the pistons on a traction engine like Fred's were made in small foundries like this, and every casting had to have a pattern.

Today, Barry explained, they were going to be making an engine block for an old Stanley steam wagon that had been built in Massachusetts in 1897. 'What we're going to do first,' he said, 'is to make an impression in sand of the outside of it and of the internal side of it, put it all together and cast it.'

Fred and David stood over the mould and watched Barry place the wooden pattern in it before filling the pattern with sand. Alf, Jimmy and Roger stood a bit further back, looking on. 'That's it,' Barry said. 'That's one half rammed up. To create the casting, I've got to do another mould like this and clamp it on top of this one.' Barry filled the other half of the pattern with sand and clamped it to the first half. Then, when the sand had set, the wooden pattern was taken out, leaving an impression in the sand in the shape of the outside of the casting. 'Right,' Barry said, 'now we're going to light the mould. We set fire to that, and that stops the molten metal penetrating the sand.' As Barry poured some inflammable spirit into the mould and put a match to it, blue flames flickered and spread around it.

'I like this bit,' Fred said. 'Like the Christmas-pudding job!'

'So that's the stage when your fingers catch fire,' Barry said, before putting a solid core into the mould to create the hollow inside of the casting. He repeated the procedure with the other mould, then clamped the two halves together, saying, 'So now we're ready for the final closure. It's all ready for casting, so we've got the molten metal ready.'

'When you're melting brass, you need about 1,000°C, don't you?' David asked. But before Barry had time to answer, Fred broke in.

'I've actually done a bit of brass. We had a little crucible pot, and I made some L-shaped brackets for nailing round lightning conductors. But on the first attempts, I had me mam's hoover running for about an 'our – you know, as a fan – and a funny smell come out of it, and that were the end of it! I graduated to a proper fan later on, you know. Over the years I made quite a few of them, but the demand's gone with the chimneys, like.'

Once the moulds had been filled, the hot metal was left to cool, but that was going to take hours, and Fred had some unfinished business back at David's place. He was going back to meet David's father, Bruce, to have a look at the collection of traction engines he owned. When they got back, Bruce had one of the engines steamed up outside the shed. It was a little three-tonner. 'David showed me a picture of what you started with for this,' Fred said, 'an' it were nothing, were it?'

'Well, no,' Bruce replied, 'it was a heap of little bits and pieces. The cylinder block was a fair challenge because we hadn't got a lot of detail of what it was like. We had a view of the side and the back so, aesthetically, it looks correct, but for the internals we had to get a drawing for a larger engine and reduce the sizes for what it would've been for a three-tonner. But

do you want to have a run on this engine, then, Fred?'
Fred didn't need any persuading, and got up on to the
engine straight away. It was a lot easier than getting on
to his own, because it was so much smaller.

'With it just being a single,' David said, 'she's a bit
on the lively side, but I'm sure you'll get used to her.'

As Fred set off, the little red engine leapt forward.
'Right . . . I see what you mean,' he said. 'Yeah, go on
baby, go on!' Fred drove up from the end of the
garden, towards the house. Alf, Jimmy and Roger
stood by the side of the drive watching. Fred was
enjoying himself, but after a short spin on the engine it
was time to say farewell to the Ragsdale family and
head back to Ian Howard's to see how Jack had been
getting on with the engine.

When we got back, Fred explained to us what Jack
had been doing:

Jack took it upon himself to take off the front
wheel and have a look at a problem we have of the
liquid brass coming out the bearing. We've
known about it for a week or two, and it's in quite
a mess, really. It'll not stop us carrying on, but
there's something terrible happened in between
the brass bearing in the hub of the wheel and the
actual shaft. It's lost about one thirty-secondth
of an inch underneath, with the weight of the
engine resting on it, but when we get back
home we're going to have to do some serious
mechanicing. It's a bit disappointing, but it's one
of the simpler bits of engineering that's somehow

gone completely haywire. I wouldn't like to do another 5,000 miles with it!

Fred's engine had been built in a workshop completely powered by belt-driven machinery, so the following day, we went to a workshop that hadn't changed for a hundred years or more. It was a clock-maker's in Ashbourne, Derbyshire, and the whole place was belt-driven. We were going to see this because clock-making is essentially engineering on a small scale, and clock-makers could be described as the first mechanics.

Again, we left Fred's engine at Ian Howard's and went the short distance to Ashbourne by car. Ashbourne was an important centre of clock-making during the eighteenth and nineteenth centuries, and the family firm of clock-makers we were going to see has been in business since 1826. Back in the eighteenth century, it was the development of these mechanicing skills that led to Britain leading the world in the building of engines like Fred's.

Fred went into the workshop and greeted the present owner, Charles Haycock. 'I've come to have a look at your wonderful workshop,' he said. The workshop was a very interesting place. Line-shafting* ran under the ceiling, with leather belts attached to a series of wheels placed at intervals along the line. Each of these

---

* Line-shafting: long, revolving metal rods suspended from a mill or factory ceiling and running the length of the building. It was part of a system of toothed gears and leather belts that transmitted power from a steam engine or waterwheel to machinery.

wheels was just above a piece of intricate, antique-looking machinery, each one a miniature masterpiece of mechanical engineering, and the belt connected the machine to the line, so that, as the line turned, it operated the machines.

Charles explained that the business went much further back than 1826, because it started under the name of Harlow, in Ashbourne in 1740.

'I see,' said Fred, 'that you've got this wonderful line-shafting that drives all your machinery. Does it all work?'

'Oh yes,' Charles replied, 'it all works. It's a unique survival.' In one corner of the workshop, Charles's son Neil was busy carrying on the family business. He was bent over a workbench, concentrating intently as he worked on a clock. 'There's something in here, Fred, you might be interested in,' Charles said as they walked towards the bench where his son was working. 'That's a new clock movement that Neil's working on.'

'Yeah, brand-new, eh?' Fred said. 'Yeah, it's bonnie, that, isn't it? You've got your number stamped on it. Number 104. Who does the woodwork for you?'

Neil looked up from the intricate work he was doing. 'There's an awful lot of good cabinet-makers about,' he said, 'but finding somebody that's got the eye for proportion for a clock case is completely different, and it's something that's been lost over the years, I think.' Then he drew Fred's attention to the workings of the clock. 'If you look at the pinions inside, they're cut from high-carbon steel in a soft state and then, to make them last several lifetimes, we harden them, but the process of hardening them, quenching them in the oil, distorts them, so they have to be tempered down and then set again by hand by stretching them on the side of a vice and hitting them with a hammer.'

'When you think back to, like, the 1700s,' Fred said, 'when you look at these clocks with these beautiful teeth, how did they do that then?'

'We can show you,' Charles replied. 'We're going to show you how the teeth are cut in the wheels now. We do them on this machine that was built in 1910 in the Black Forest in Germany. We just need to start the line shaft.'

At one time, the line-shafting was powered by a small steam engine, but now, in the only concession to modernity in the workshop, they use electricity. Neil put a blank on to the cutting machine, and his father went to the end of the workshop to start up the line-shafting. When he flicked the switch, the sleeping machinery came to life. The wheels on the line started to turn, slowly at first but quickly gathering pace. The leather belt from the line to the cutting machine started to turn also, and as it did the machine sprang into life, driving the cutting edges and turning the blank round an infinitesimal amount for each new cut as it created a new precision-engineered cog for one of their hand-made clocks.

In the 1890s, the company employed about twenty-five people, but today the demand for hand-made clocks is not as high as it was then. So, as well as their clocks, they now use their precision-engineering skills to make models and replicas of some of the earliest machinery of the Industrial Revolution. Back then, in the late eighteenth century, it was the development of these mechanicing skills that made Britain the world leader in the building of engines like Fred's.

Next day, we were going back to the Midland Railway Centre to have a look at the remains of the coal mine that Fred had spotted the week before, and to have a ride on the footplate of the big 9F locomotive that Fred had seen in the workshops. We stayed at the hotel in Belper that we'd stayed in the previous week. Alf was happy with this. He'd found a fish and chip shop just near the hotel, so that was his tea sorted out for that night; he wasn't having any of the fancy stuff we were having in the hotel restaurant.

The following morning, he left early with Jimmy and Jack to get the engine steamed up. Before they set off, Jack let me know he wasn't happy about his dad having to do this filming. Because he was sharing a family room with him and Roger, he could see what a bad state Fred was in. I tried to explain that we were doing it because it was what his dad wanted, but what Jack had seen had clearly upset him. All he could see was that his dad was suffering, and all this work wasn't going to help him to get any better.

Jack went off with Alf and Jimmy to get the engine ready, but before we could set off for the railway, there was a bit of production work to attend to. Over the previous two weeks, it had not been possible to film many of Fred's scripted pieces to camera telling us where we were and what he was doing there. Just getting around was difficult for him, but having to learn and remember scripts was altogether too much. So we found a quiet room and recorded Fred reading the scripts. It wasn't ideal, but at least it meant that it would be Fred's voice we heard in the programmes. I drove Fred the short distance to the railway, and on the way he talked about all the mithering he was getting about who he was leaving things to and the pressure that was being put on him to change his will. As far as he was concerned, the lads were going to be getting his engines, and that was all he was bothered about. I got him off the subject, reminding him that we'd got a good day ahead of us.

When we got to the railway, the first thing we did was to go and look at the remains of the mine that Fred, Alf and Jimmy had come across the week before. We had found out since that it was what was left of the Western upcast mine that had been closed at the time of the First World War. As they walked towards it they could see a round brick tower that looked a little bit like a windmill, and sticking out of the top of it was a wheel, partly supported by a steel framework that was attached to the tower. As they got closer to it, Jimmy asked Fred how old he reckoned it was. 'It's bloody ancient, that, isn't it?' Fred replied. 'It looks a bit like a flat roper to me.'

They decided that what they were looking at had probably been an old ventilation shaft. 'Look at them,' Fred said. 'Lovely window frames, eh? They've been lovely, them, haven't they, once? Aye, Staffordshire blue bricks, eh. Ready for a coat of renovation, that.'

'It needs pointing,' Jimmy said. 'Have you got any spare time?'

While Fred and Jimmy were admiring the quality of the brickwork, Alf had found a door. It was blocked up, but there were some gaps in the wood, and he was able to see into the tower. 'You can see in here, Fred.'

'Is there any runners for the cage?' Fred wanted to know. Standing next to the tower was a rusting old engine that they went to investigate.

'It's a long time since this saw any work,' Jimmy said.

'Somebody's jacked it up and pinched the brasses out,' said Fred. Then he spotted that it had clearly been a steam engine that had been converted to electric. He could tell because the lump of iron at the bottom was definitely too long for a crankshaft, so that, he deduced, was where the electric motor had been. It was an engine, they decided between them, that had been brought here at a much later date than the original pithead gear. Fred didn't think it had ever run a wire over the big wheel, because it was way out of line. It was perhaps an emergency winder, he decided.

Alf turned and started to walk towards the engine house. 'Let's have a look if there's owt left in th'engine house,' he said. 'Might get lucky.' Fred and Jimmy walked over and joined Alf to investigate.

'You never know,' Fred agreed. 'Might come across a priceless gem.'

The engine house looked as though it was all locked up, but they decided to try the door to see if there was still an engine inside. Much to their surprise, the door was not locked, so they were able to get in, but there was no engine.

'It's dark, innit?' Fred said. 'Pity we haven't got a torch, an' we could see.' He peered into the darkness. 'Eh, look at that there,' he shouted excitedly. 'Look at them lovely window frames. An' there's the indicator board there, see. It's bin a long time since a block of wood went up and down there. Yeah.'

After the little excursion to the remains of the mine, it was time for Fred's ride on the footplate of the 9F. 'When this was being done,' Fred said to the driver as the giant locomotive began to move slowly away from the platform, 'I know you took a great part in the doing up of it. When you were doing it, what were the boiler like?'

'Well, the main barrel was very good,' the driver replied, 'and the front tube plate was the opposite; it was badly corroded. There was stress cracking around the flanges. When we saw the condition it was in once we got the tube down, it had to be condemned, and we had to make a new front tube plate.'

'Yeah. I've seen lots of pictures of it,' Fred said, 'when it were at Barry Island, and it all looked so sad. All the connecting rods had been nicked; all gas axed off. I've got a video at home of them making connecting rods under the big steam hammer. How many years did it take you to do it?'

'Well,' the driver replied, 'it came out of Barry scrapyard in December 1980, and it first ran under its own power this time last year, so that's twenty-three years. It was built in Swindon in October 1959, spent all its working life in South Wales, around Cardiff, and was withdrawn in August 1965, so she wasn't even six years old.'

The line at Midland Railway Centre is a short one, and they were soon at the end of it. Going back, it was Fred's turn to drive – something he'd always dreamed about as a lad. He'd had a go at driving some smaller ones in the past, but never a giant like this from the last days of steam on Britain's railways. He took the brake off and pushed the regulator forward, and the engine started to chug along the line, with Fred in control. 'I'm enjoying this!' he said as he gave a blast on the whistle.

'Yeah, I bet you are!' the driver said.

While Fred was enjoying himself on the footplate, Alf and Jimmy had some work to do. First of all, Fred's engine needed some water. As they filled the tank, Alf said to Jimmy, 'It's time you were back off your bloody holidays! It was going up Wincobank in Sheffield . . . bloody wet through, raining . . . I said we could've been with Jimmy now, sitting on a bloody iceberg on a deck chair with a pint in th'and! 'Ow was th'oliday anyway?' Jimmy had been to Canada and his holiday had included a cruise from Vancouver and along the coast of Alaska.

'It was great,' he replied. 'But I thought I'd come back and give you a bit of a lift.'

'Aye, well, we need another pair of hands,' Alf said. 'Anyway, did you see any whales? And what about icebergs? Did you see any of them?'

'Yeah,' Jimmy replied, 'and we went on a steam

railway at Calgary. Three-foot gauge. 1898 it were built. You want to try it some time.'

'I've no bloody time for running round on this all the time with Fred,' Alf said. 'But did you go to the Rockies?' Yes, Jimmy said, he'd been to the Rockies, Calgary, Montreal and Toronto. 'See any of the Eskimos?' Alf wanted to know.

'No, saw some Indians, though,' Jimmy said.

'Indians?' Alf questioned. 'Not ones with bow and arrows?'

'No,' replied Jimmy. 'They were a bit more advanced than that.'

'They were not shooting at you, then!' Alf said. 'Anyway, I'm glad you're back giving me a lift with the bloody polishing and that . . . I've been bloody calling you every day; have your ears not been burning?'

'No,' said Jimmy. 'Did you ever find that Dire Straits you were looking for?'

'No,' Alf replied. 'We've not found it yet, but I think we've been close to it a time or two.'

Back on the footplate, Fred was still enjoying himself, driving the engine, but he was getting towards the end of the line, and he'd got a task ahead of him that was a bit more challenging than the coasting along he had been doing so far.

'Once you get past the signal box,' the driver said, 'it starts to climb, so . . .'

'. . . Give it a bit more,' Fred said, and that's just what he did. 'Now,' he said, 'the technical bit's stopping in the right place!'

'It's easy to make them go . . .' the driver said.

'Now just slow it down a bit more . . . about twelve on the gauge. We're going to stop just about level with the platform end. Steam brake on now.' Fred brought the huge loco to a halt like a seasoned railwayman. 'Yeah . . . that's it,' the driver said. 'Lovely jubbly . . . I think we'll make something of him yet!'

Fred was beaming as he got down from the footplate. By this time, Alf and Jimmy were sitting on the platform waiting for him. We walked back towards Fred's engine and saw it steaming around the car park. Jack was driving and, beside him, I was amazed to see my daughter Kathryn steering. My heart was in my mouth, but I had no need to worry. It was clear she'd got the hang of it, as she steered expertly between the parked cars and along the little road near the refreshment room. She was clearly enjoying herself, and so was Jack. The sun was shining and Fred looked on contentedly. It was a real moment of happiness and togetherness. A class of seven- or eight-year-olds were playing on the grass, and they waved to Jack and Kathryn as they drove past.

As we packed up at the end of the day, Alf was looking forward to getting back on the road again after the stay at Ian Howard's. 'These are the highlights,' he said. 'All the people waving, speaking to us, taking our photos. I'm going to ask for a cut from Kodak; they must have made a bloody fortune out of us!'

11

Engines at Work

We wanted to see the sort of place where an engine like Fred's would have been built, but there are no great loco works left anywhere today. Now, the only places where you can get any idea of what was involved in building big steam engines on a large scale is at the works of some of the preserved railways. No new engines are being built at them, but a lot of the restoration work that goes on involves stripping engines right down, manufacturing new parts if needed and virtually starting from scratch in building them up again.

One of the biggest workshops is on the Severn Valley Railway at Bridgnorth in Shropshire, which runs trains between Bridgnorth and Kidderminster in Worcestershire, on a line that was built in the mid-1850s. Going there would give us some idea of what a loco works would have been like back in the age of steam railways.

We set off for Bridgnorth on Tuesday 27 July. When we got there, the first job was to get the engine steamed up for some driving shots around the town. In many ways, the driving had become the bane of our life but, along with meeting up with old friends like Jack Meaker and the Howard brothers, getting that engine going and getting it to where he needed to be was still the best bit for Fred. If we'd taken the engine out of the equation, his life would have been so much easier, but there wouldn't have been the smiles, and there wouldn't have been the enjoyment.

We worked out a little circular route around the town from the station. The engine looked particularly good steaming over the old bridge that crossed the River Severn. At one point, we missed a turning, and found ourselves going down an ever-narrowing street in the old part of town. Eventually, we ran out of road as we came to a pedestrian precinct, and Fred and Alf were faced with a very tricky bit of manoeuvring to get the engine turned round so that we could retrace our route. Fred was unperturbed and, amiable as ever, he was happy to sign autographs and pose for photographs for the crowd who had gathered around the engine.

Back at the station, Fred was met by John Robinson, the production manager, who was going to show him around the workshops. First, though, they looked at some of the locos standing outside the sheds.

'Aye,' Fred said as they walked between the engines, 'this reminds me of when I were a kid. I were born near the engine sheds in Bolton, only about a quarter of a mile away. Plenty of smoke and sulphur . . .'

John pointed out one of the locos. 'This is an 8F,'* he said. 'They did all the freight work on BR. This one was out in Persia and Egypt in the Second World War, and it got derailed by a camel. It was pushing a truck, and a camel walked in front of it; the truck came off the rails, and this engine followed it into the desert. We're going to put it back into traffic. We've had the boiler out and a couple of wheels out, and we've done a repair in the firebox.'

They climbed up on to the footplate, and John introduced Fred to Roy, who had been getting the engine steamed up. 'Our friend, Roy,' he said, 'works like a Trojan here, covered in the proverbial.'

'How old is this?' Fred asked. 'When were it knocked up, sort of style?' After a bit of debate, John and Roy decided it was probably 1934, and it lasted until the end of steam in 1968. Then a group was formed and bought it straight out of BR service.

'We've done nearly 130,000 miles with it up and down here,' John said.

'It's a credit to the men who built it,' Fred observed.

'Next time it comes out of service here,' John informed Fred, 'it will have to stay for a while. We hope to put it in our new museum building when we get to build it.'

---

* The London Midland and Scottish Railways 8F class locomotive is a steam locomotive designed for hauling heavy freight.

Fred then got into a discussion about the coal they were using and informed John and Roy that when it's good he calls it radioactive coal. The three of them went on to talk about some of the volunteers without whom it wouldn't be possible to run a railway like this. 'A lot come from far afield,' John said. 'Some from London. They have to get here for eight o'clock in the morning, get the engine ready, drive all day, then they've got to get the fire cleared out before driving all the way back to London, Manchester or wherever.

'The railway works were quite something to see,' John continued, 'because they did everything. When the war came, the government were quite surprised at what the railway workshops could actually do. Of course they started to turn them into working for the war effort, and the railways just had to run as best they could. They were tremendous, the railway factories, they really were. And now we've got nowt.'

'You took the words out of me mouth there,' Fred said. 'Near where I live, there's Horwich loco works, and it's all fragmented off now into bits of tin-pot engineering outfits. You go in and the boiler shop, wheel shop, everything's there with the names all still painted on the walls in the purply red BR paint.'

'I don't think we can make a bean can now,' John observed. 'It's one hell of a state; how the country can survive when it can't make and sell anything! Killing off all the apprenticeship schemes was the worst thing we ever did. It was the way to learn a job. Not like today. You can go to university and learn what you like, but then you need to know how to put the thing together.'

John told Fred that they'd got their own boiler shop where they used traditional repair methods, so they left Roy on the footplate to go and have a look at some of the work that was being done there. In the boiler shop, Fred met the foreman, Graham Beddow, and chatted to him about the boiler he was working on from a Great Western Manor Class locomotive. Fred turned to us and said:

A lot of people would look at this and wouldn't know what the hell it were. What it is is the plate that were inside the firebox that all the tubes go through. They go through the boiler from the firebox to the front tube plate. What Graham is working on is the firebox tube plate – one of the most important plates on the whole machine. It's got the super-heater tubes, which are the big ones; then the smaller tubes are the ordinary smoke tubes. Then the hundreds of small holes down the side are for the stays that stop it going like a loaf of bread when you get steam up, shoving it all out of shape. They're important because they hold the two plates together with 200psi between every one of them. You cannot afford to have any busted ones, or you'd get big bulges coming in it. There's a lot of hard work to put them stays back. In a boiler like this, there are nearly two thousand of them. That's a lot. Our humble little tractor is nothing compared with this, maybe an eighth of it.

Fred then got into a long discussion with Graham about the way he restored the boiler on his traction engine, before walking across the shop to look at another boiler with a copper tube plate. 'Really, for anybody who doesn't know anything about locomotive boilers, this is a wonderful example of explaining it nice and simple.' Fred pointed to a space inside the boiler at the top. 'This big gap round the outside,' he explained,

is full of water, and the stays are these bolts that hold the plates together. If they weren't there, when you lit the fire, it would all go out like a big pudding and bend it and mis-shape it, and no doubt blow up. All the tubes run the full length of the boiler from the front tube plate to the plate at the back that Graham and me have just been looking at. The hole down near the bottom of the boiler is the fire hole where you shovel the coal in, and then there's another plate called the back head, which fills the whole of the back up, and this makes up the wall on the footplate.

Fred spent so long in the boiler shop that by the time he'd left, the last train had departed, so there was no time for any footplate rides on the Severn Valley Railway.

The next day, we went to the Black Country Living Museum in Dudley. The Black Country isn't a place you'll find marked on any map. It's an industrial area to the west of Birmingham that was originally based on coal mining and ironworking and got its name in the nineteenth century, when thousands of chimneys in the area filled the air with smoke and mining turned the ground inside out, creating huge expanses of industrial dereliction.

We were going to the museum to find out how the chains that were linked to the wheels for steering Fred's engine were made. The chain shop there had been built using two hearths from one of the last firms in the area to make hand-made chains, Bloomers of Quarry Bank. The quality of chains made in the Black Country was renowned all over the world, and at the end of the nineteenth century, 90 per cent of all the chain workshops in England and Wales were in the Black Country, most of them in the backyards of workers' houses.

With his engine steamed up, Fred drove over the canal bridge and along the cobbled street, past the shops and houses, the church and the pub of the re-created Black Country village to the chain shop in the Castlefields Ironworks. It was the perfect setting for the engine. Getting off it, Fred said, 'We've come here to the Black Country Museum to see a gentleman making chains in exactly the same way as this chain here on my engine would have been made in 1912, without any fancy electric welding or anything like that. All he's got is a fire, a hammer and a piece of round iron bar.'

When Fred, Alf, Jimmy and Jack reached the chain shop, the chain-maker was hammering a link of a chain on an anvil. 'The Black Country were world famous for the ironwork that they made and, of course, chains were one of the main things. They made everything from chains for the *Titanic*, big links this thick' – Fred spread his arms wide to indicate a huge chain – 'to teeny little chains for tying your dog to the railings. An' Jeff over here, who I've known for quite a few years now, once had me make a link for a chain.'

'I believe a lot of these chains were made in backyards with small family businesses,' Alf said.

'Oh aye,' Fred replied. 'It were ladies who made little dinky ones. But they made some real whoppers as well. I saw some archive film once of making a sling for lifting a locomotive up, and it were fantastic. They had the fire on the floor, and pouring down with rain, it were. Everyone had a Woodbine, all smoking away, and the order were given, and they pulled it out with this overhead lifter like a girder with a pulley wheel on it. It were incredible. I've never seen as many sledgehammers going like that without one hitting the other one. It were quite fascinating watching them. Anyway, I'll go and have a word with Jeff, and we'll watch him make a bit of chain.'

Jeff was working at the forge, taking a bar of red-hot metal from the fire and hammering it on an anvil into the shape of a link for a chain. Fred went over to watch him as he hammered the link on to the end of the chain he was making.

'Ah, beautiful, that, Jeff!' Fred said. 'How many links have you made since I last came to see you?'

'I gave up counting,' Jeff said, laughing.

'I bet!' Fred said. 'You know, I bought some modern chain the other day, and they charged me two hundred and twelve quid, I think it were, for two pieces of chain about that long.' He indicated a length of about 4 feet.

'High-tensile?' Jeff asked him.

'I don't know,' Fred said. 'For steering on me tractor, that's all it amounted to, and I never thought I could have come here and got it for half the bloody price, no doubt. What's the biggest you can do on here?'

'The biggest I can work on this is fifteen-sixteenths,' Jeff said. 'Just below an inch diameter. Then you move up on to the bigger fires. The biggest on the big fires is a 6½-inch diameter.' He pointed to a huge hammer that was standing up against the wall:

And that's when you're swinging hammers like that one. Then it would be two-man hammers, and sometimes three-man hammers as well. Two-man hammers went from 28lbs to 56lbs. Three-man hammers about 140lbs.'

I mentioned to the lads that I once saw them making a big ring with four chains on. There must have been about seven of them, with a hammer each, and you just lost yourself in a sea of sledgehammer heads going one at the side of the other. It were going less and less and less and it were quite lop-sided, and I thought, How are they going to get it back, like? Then another bunch of lads appeared with lumps of 2-inch bar, all sparking on the end, and they each individually shoved them in, and *bang, bang*; and then another guy come and cut the end off with the cutter and sledgehammers, and then they beat it all in. Like when you go to the seaside and you see an anchor lying there, and you see the main spindle and then the curved bits, and in the corners it's all twisted up; and it's all those bits that have been knocked in when it's all white hot. It's really interesting, and most people just wouldn't know.

We went to Sheffield the other day and saw what is reputedly the biggest steam hammer in Western Europe, and it were still working, but on compressed air. They were making, like, doughnuts. Big lumps with a hole in the middle. But when it come down, *bang* . . . all the floor shook 20 yards all round. It were quite exciting.

This was our fourth time filming here at the Black Country Living Museum, and it had always been one of Fred's favourite locations. They have a fine old pub there, and just over the road there's an excellent fish and chip shop.

'This is just the job,' Fred said as he and Alf sat down with a pint in the back room of the pub, while Jimmy had been despatched to the chip shop. 'Not too many customers. Hey, this is like the old-fashioned style, innit?' Fred said when Jimmy returned with their lunch in a three-cornered bag made out of newspaper. 'These must be the best fish and chips in all of England. Good ale and fish 'n' chips in a lovely place.

I bet half of them men in London, with their fancy bloody suits on and their fancy shirts and all that, have longed for this, really. They might make a lot of money, but the bloody stress of it all must be terrible.'

As they ate their fish and chips, Alf said how good it had been at the Severn Valley Railway the day before. 'They're into serious boiler repairs there,' Fred said. 'Yeah, pulling the guts out of them fireboxes. All of that firebox we were looking at had been repaired before, by taking the tube plate out and the back plate. They'd all been screwed in. Originally, the way it would have been made, it would have all been riveted. And somebody 'ad pulled it all apart, and they'd put them screwed ends in.'

Jimmy asked how old the boiler would have been. 'About 1920,' Fred replied. 'I mean, on a locomotive boiler, the wear and tear and the violence of it all is terrific.' Then, looking over to the piano in the corner of the room, he asked Jimmy if he could play it. Jimmy said he could play a bit, and Fred said, 'Playing the piano in a pub is a thing I've always wanted to do. It's weird. Like, me mam used to do it, and we had a piano at home, and she always used to say, "Why don't you go and have piano lessons? You're much more genteel than our Graham," me brother, who's a bricklayer. He went, and the pianoforte teacher, one Mr Robert Grimshaw, said, "Why don't you come? You'd be better than your kid," an' I never ever went. An' our kid can bang a tune out. He learned him. But I never went.

'You'll be like a concert pianist,' he said to Jimmy

when he told Fred he went to lessons for two years.

'No,' Jimmy replied. 'Once I stopped, I never touched it again. I didn't like it. But I wished I'd carried on now.'

'I never did,' Fred said reflectively. 'When me mam died, we got bloody ten quid for the piano. It were a right beautiful thing, an' she polished it every day.'

Alf brought up the subject of the metal-spinning they'd been to see the week before. Jimmy had missed it, so he and Fred told him all about it. 'I think everywhere we've been has been interesting, hasn't it?' Alf said. 'Every single place.'

When they'd finished their pints and their fish and chips, they went out to the engine and rode back over the canal, past the school and the fairground, to the colliery. The ground beneath the museum site was once mined for coal, limestone, fire clay and iron-stone. More than forty mine shafts are shown on old plans, and around one of these shafts, Racecourse Colliery was built as a typical small Black Country coal pit.

'It's not as nice-looking as your headgear,' Alf said when they got off the engine and walked towards the pit. 'There's no shaped sections on it.'

'No,' Fred said. 'Just big blocks of wood. This cage is new since we last came, though.' Fred walked round the headgear with Alf, Jimmy, Jack and Roger. 'All interesting, stuff, isn't it?' he said. Then it was time to look in the engine house. 'This winder in here is the same as the one that were at George's Lane Pit in Horwich,' Fred said. 'It's a pretty ancient piece. It's got the drum outside in another shed. Look here. This is a pulsometer steam pump.'

Jimmy spotted a big spring and wondered what it was. Fred reckoned it was a single eccentric reversing gear. 'In the 1850s and 1860s,' he said, 'they had them like that.' The engine he had restored at Caernarfon, he told them, was very similar to this.

Once Fred had told them all about the Caernarfon engine, they spotted a board on the wall of the engine house with information about the engine and, sure enough, the first thing they saw was that Fred was right about the date. The engine did indeed date from 1860.

The following day, we were going to the headquarters of the North Staffs and Cheshire Traction Engine Club, so we all headed for Burton-on-Trent, which was the nearest place where we could get accommodation. Just over the road from the hotel we were staying in was the Burton Bridge pub, which had its own brewery round the back. Fred had always told me how he used to get a barrel of beer whenever he was going to a rally and set it up on the running board of the living van.

We went over to the pub and had a few pints before going for a meal at a local Italian restaurant, and I ordered a barrel of the brewery's best bitter to set up on the living van the next day. Kathryn remembers getting up early the next morning to go and pay for it and collect it. She recalls the landlord of the pub telling her how he thought that Fred's accent was put on and that no one could really speak the way he did.

She assured him that this wasn't the case, but the man wouldn't have it.

At the club, Fred was going to meet up with a lot of his old mates from the traction-engine world, all people like him who devoted their lives to keeping our steam heritage alive. They were all going to have their engines in steam, many of them working on jobs that needed doing around the site. So far, we'd seen the traction engine as a mode of transport for getting Fred and his team around the country, but these engines were real workhorses, and in their time they were put to a whole variety of uses. This was going to be a day for seeing the traction engine at work.

The club's base was at Draycott in the Clay, in the heart of the Staffordshire countryside. As we set off by car from Burton-on-Trent the next morning, there wasn't a cloud in the sky, and Fred was in good spirits, looking forward to his day with the traction-engine men. When we arrived, his engine was all steamed up and ready for a drive along some of the local roads and round the club site. We didn't go far, but it was enough to see Fred arriving at the site on his engine.

As Fred drove on to the site, he was greeted by Phil Jeffs, the club chairman. 'Aye up, Fred. How are you doing? Have you had a good trip?' he said as Fred got down from his engine. 'Welcome back to Klondyke.'

'It's a few year now since I last came, and things are looking just as nice. It's a lovely place, this, innit? Yeah, you could live in here, you know. I could. How many living vans have you got here altogether?'

Phil looked around the field. There were four or five

engines steamed up in the centre, and all around the edges were living vans like Fred's. 'Ooh, I've never counted,' Phil replied. 'There's probably fifteen or twenty.'

'What a lovely place to leave your living van,' Fred mused. 'If I leave mine on the road, they bloody vandalize it. Horrible people. Peasants. We're breeding more and more, aren't we? What you doing today anyway?'

Phil pointed to a tree over on the other side of the field. 'We're going to pull that dead poplar out,' he said, 'and we want to use the wood for engine chocks. We're going to use the traction engine to winch it out and pull her down. Let's hope it comes down as clean as one of your chimneys! Then we've got the old rack-saw bench to plank it up.'

Fred walked over to the centre of the field with Phil and watched as a steel cable was attached to the winch on a big black traction engine. The other end was attached to the dead tree about 30 yards away. The engine driver started to operate the winch, and the cable went taut. There were a few creaks, but the tree wouldn't budge. Then there was a crack, and the cable went flying into the air as the fastening to the tree broke. Alf and Jimmy made their way over to the tree to have a closer look at it while another cable was being found.

Fred went to look at proceedings as the tree-felling team were securing the cable to the trunk again. 'I reckon if we went further up the tree,' he told them, 'about 15 or 20 foot up, where that dead branch is sticking out, it'd have it easy. But you got a lot of power, that, when it'll bloody pull something like that apart. It will have taken a few ton to do that. Yeah, I tell you what, if we go up 15 foot and it fails again, a double purchase with a snatch block hooked to the back of the engine will do the job.'

Jimmy stepped in to lend a hand, climbing up on to the platform of a hydraulic lift that had appeared on the scene and fixing the cable to the branch that Fred had indicated higher up the tree. This would give a lot more leverage. With the chain firmly fixed higher up the tree, they had another go, and this time they were successful. The tree came crashing down. 'You want to get the stump out now,' Fred said. 'Resort to dynamite, you know.'

The tree was dragged over to the rack-saw bench, which was powered by another traction engine. Fred watched with Phil as the sawing team got to work on it. 'It's amazing,' he said, 'how many different makers there were of these things. Ransome and Son's and Jeffries, Savage's of King's Lynn, Fowler's in Leeds, Aveling and Porter, Green's in Leeds, McLaren's in Leeds. There were literally dozens of these companies making them, some only in a small way, like a village agricultural engineer that bought the castings somewhere else and assembled his own thing.'

As they were sawing the wood, Fred spotted an opportunity to get some good-quality brake blocks made for his engine. He went over to his engine, tape measure in hand, measured the size of his brake blocks, wrote the measurements down on a block of wood, and took them over to Colin, the owner of the mobile saw mill.

'We've got our cutting list here,' he said. 'We couldn't find any paper. Our brake blocks are made of mahogany, and that's the real McCoy, this stuff, isn't it? So if you could be so kind as to cut them for us when you're doing that other big lump of wood. We've made them a bit too big, so we can leave them a few years and let them season. Then when they've shrunk a bit we can get rid of the ones I've got on and replace them with these brand-new ones.'

'All right,' Colin agreed. 'We'll do that then. It'll make a change from doing engine chocks.' Fred thanked him and promised to buy him a pint later. Then he and Phil left to go and watch another job that was being done. There was a gravel roadway all around the perimeter of the site, and a steamroller was at work with a gang doing some roadworks.

'We've got a low spot in the ground here,' Phil explained. 'It's all made-up ground, and it tends to puddle in the winter and everything, so what they're doing is using the club engine, *Lady Hamilton*, that's got a scarifier on, and they're digging the ground up, and we're going to try and level it out and roll it back down and try and get rid of the puddles.'

'It's handy, isn't it, when you've got all your own road-making gear,' Fred said. 'I've got one on mine, but I've never used it. Price's Patent Resilient Scarifier, Broadheath, Manchester. My drive, near where I go in me steamroller shed, is just crushed stone, but it never wears away there. It's always where me tarmac joins on to the cinders, and it keeps bloody disappearing there.'

As Fred and Phil talked, two of the road-repairing gang laid old roofing tiles in the low spots and pot-holes to level the surface. The roller then steamed past them, with the scarifier at the back digging into the uneven road surface, leaving a furrow like a plough would. Next, the workers stepped in to rake the ground and smooth it all out prior to the roller coming back to flatten it. With the work finished, it was time to sit down in the sunshine and relax. By this time, the temperature had reached the low eighties. It was a glorious summer day. The only problem was, there was no shade, so it was getting very hot for filming, especially with four or five steaming traction engines around.

Alf and Jimmy went to the living van to get the barrel of bitter out that I'd ordered the previous evening from the brewery. They set it up on the running board of the van, and a queue of thirsty traction-engine men formed as they started serving. Everyone came along with the pint pots the brewery had provided, asking for a farmer's half in them. As Fred drank his, he looked as though all his cares were forgotten. This was his world; the world that he loved.

'Very good. Excellent,' he said. 'I think, really, bringing this barrel of bitter here has all the potential for a good booze-up, a steam booze-up! In the olden days, we used to arrive at the steam rally with a full barrel of bitter and a load of glasses, and a lot of other people did as well, so it'd save you spending your hard-earned cash at the beer tent, which were always inflated prices. It always led to unbelievable drunkenness. Not done it for a bit, so I'm quite looking forward to this afternoon. I'm going to have a talk with me mates over here.'

Fred got one of the picnic chairs out of the living van and sat, pint in hand, talking to old friends, while Alf and Jimmy pulled the pints. The film crew was forgotten as old stories were told and old friends remembered. They talked of happy times in the past, but they also talked of the future and of a new generation of enthusiasts such as Jack and Roger, who were going to keep the steam movement alive. As I watched Fred with his mates and their engines, I knew it had been the right decision to go on. He'd got his own lads with him, and there couldn't have been a better way to spend his final days.

'It reminds me of my early rally days,' Fred said. 'How's your machine going, Colin? All right?'

'Well, we can't wear it out,' Colin replied. 'We're doing plenty of rallies with it. Trouble is, if you don't do it, the only thing the younger generation know in relation to a steam engine is *Thomas the Tank Engine*, isn't it? And how many people walk up to you and ask, "What were they used for, mister?"'

The group went on to talk about the Steam Apprentices Club. 'We've got 900 kids in the apprentice club now,' one of them said. A younger man who'd been driving the steamroller with the road-repairing gang said he had joined when he was twelve years old and he was twenty-five now.

'It's amazing,' Fred said. 'I don't realize how old I

am. You get blokes come as big as him, and they say, "When I were little, you let me have a ride on your steamroller." '

'That's what starts them off,' an older man said, 'and then they come along and nowadays everything's got to be a bit more controlled and regulated. We've got a log-book scheme, so the youngsters work through a scheme which takes them through the basics of working an engine. I don't say it makes them experts, but it gives them the basics of doing things properly. Of course, when you and I started, we were just allowed to get on and play, but it's got to be a bit more controlled now.'

'It will show the rest of the world what a responsible body of people we are,' Fred said. 'I mean, these machines are bloody dangerous. You know that, and I know that. With the wrong type of person, with not very much mechanical upstairs, it could be a painful thing.'

The man Fred was talking to was the chairman of the Steam Apprentices Club, and he said he'd never known an apprentice get seriously injured. The odd cut on the finger, but nothing serious. 'It started in 1979,' he went on, 'and there's now apprentices from that time who own their own engines, and they're mums and dads themselves, and they send their kids along, so it really is bringing a new generation on.'

'Like me,' the younger man said. 'I started with Colin. I was cleaning brass and polishing and cleaning fires out, and now me and my friend Richard from Severn Valley Railway have restored *Lady Hamilton*.

We've brought her up to what she is, and she's the club's engine, so I'm now custodian of an engine. We go on the road with her; we go where we like, and it's thanks to the Steam Apprentices Club we can do this.'

But for Fred, too many of these skills had been lost. 'Somewhere along the line from the Victorian age, we started to lose it,' he said. 'I think a lot of it's to do with education. I remember a period when they threw all the lathes out of technical colleges, and all the woodwork benches and everything. They replaced it all with theory, and a man can learn how to lay bricks now in six months. That's impossible. Can you imagine lads doing catering, cooking?' Fred almost exploded, incredulous at the idea that a lad might want to cook. 'I know everybody wants to be a chef,' he went on. 'It's all a bit sad in a way. I can't see that teaching a little lad today at school how to bake a cake is any way to run an industrial empire.'

'The problem these days,' the younger man said, 'is that kids are more interested in PlayStations, and steam engines just take a background place, and I'm just glad that the Steam Apprentices Club is bringing it forward, introducing the younger generation to the steam engine, because eventually I'm going to get old, and I want people younger than me following on behind.'

'I think there will be plenty,' Fred said confidently. 'My garden's 12 foot below the level of the road, and I'm messing about in me garden. There's two schools, and they come by me railings, and the sun's shining, and the kids say, "What's that strange thing like Willie Wonka's Chocolate Factory?" And the kids hang on to the railings screaming, "Mam, I don't want to go." It's good that. I enjoy that.'

'Of course, you've got your apprentice driving your engine now,' the chairman remarked. 'That's great!'

'Little'un's only thirteen,' Fred said, 'but Roger can make it go, and Jack took to it like a duck to water. Jack's sort of introduction to steam engines were unavoidable really. I mean, he'd arrived into an household full of steam engines. He's always shown a great and dedicated interest in the world of steam engines. He's smart, and he's started his first job on the Isle of Man Railway Company, so he's not half-heartedly going about it. I'm quite proud of him, really.'

Fred was really proud of his lads, and by this time they had become essential members of the team. They would usually travel around in the cab of the low loader with Alan and Alf so that they could be with the engine all the time, ready to help with loading and unloading it, lighting the fire and getting steam up when we arrived on a location, and cleaning the engine at the end of each day. But much more important than that, they were providing much-needed support for their dad.

Fred thought the world of his lads, and it was a great comfort to him that they were able to be with him on the final stages of his journey. He'd been separated from them for nearly eight years, only seeing them during the school holidays and occasional weekends, so he took real pleasure in going with them to the places he loved and cared about. He positively glowed with pride as he watched them driving and steering the engine, and looking after it. Everywhere we went, he would say to Jack and Roger, 'One day, my engines will be yours.' The engines were the only things he referred to. He didn't talk about money or royalties or even about what was going to happen to his house and garden. For Fred, the only thing that really counted was those two engines that he had devoted so much of his life to, and the fact that they had to go to Jack and Roger.

By four o'clock, we'd done all the filming we needed to do. It was hot and tiring; time to wrap and get back to base. But there was one more thing Fred wanted to do. At the end of a day like this, he said, everybody used to drive their engines to the pub, and he'd like us to film him on his engine, leading all the other engines off site.

One or two engines started to move towards the gate, out on to the main road, but Jack had other ideas. As we waited at the gate, Jack got up on to the engine, but instead of driving it to the head of the line of engines that was forming up, as I expected, he drove it straight on to the back of the low loader, which provoked confusion all round. Jack clearly felt his dad had done enough and wasn't happy that, at the end of a long day, there was still a bit more filming to do with him.

The strain was beginning to tell, and what was becoming clear was that, in my efforts to make sure all of Fred's wishes were being met, other people were being asked to do far too much. Everything was taking far too long, and keeping to schedules was getting more and more difficult. Nobody complained. Everybody wanted to make sure that Fred enjoyed these last days as much as possible.

Surrounding Fred on the journey was a great support team and, without the willingness of everybody involved, we wouldn't have got as far as we had done. The crew and the production team were magnificent, and nobody who was there will ever forget the dedication of Alf, Jimmy and Alan. Nothing was too much trouble for them if it helped their friend to achieve one of his last ambitions. It was a fine example of the sort of friendship that Fred valued so much; the comradeship that men like miners have; the sort of support that comes from depending on your workmates in difficult and dangerous conditions. They were values that had shone through in his programmes; values that he thought had been lost as everybody worked on computers in offices, but nowhere were they more in evidence than here and now.

'The men who really made this happen were Alf and Jimmy and Alan,' Jon Doyle recalls:

Come rain or shine or whatever, they were there, making Fred's dream come true; making it happen for him. He was so reliant on so many people, and they were so happy to be part of it.

Alan was just such a lovely fellow; nothing was ever too much trouble for him, and he was an engine man himself, so he knew the game. No matter what we had to do and whatever the schedule was, he was always on time. He might have had to set off at four o'clock in the morning so that we could start filming at nine with Fred and the engine, just for maybe half an hour's filming, to get it arriving and leaving somewhere. It was an unusual situation for all of us to be in, with us trying to manage schedules and contributors and filming and Fred wanting to spend time with people – private time as well. That was one of his main priorities. But he also had this sense of responsibility that he did have a job to do as well, so he was torn in his own mind about what his priorities were.

But life on the road with Fred had changed. He was a different person, mainly because of the strong painkillers he was on. His speech and everything had started to change. 'He was on some sort of morphine,' Jon remembered,

so he was always yawning, and you'd see his eyes roll. His eyelids would close and he'd just fall asleep. He was really struggling. But there were still such great things we were doing that kept him going.

At this point, though, there were no more late nights at the pub; no more lock-ins. Fred would still have a few drinks at the end of the day, but it would usually be in the bar of the hotel we were staying in. He'd come down and talk over a few pints, and although he'd still tell anybody who cared to listen about the 'twenty-seven years and two divorces', there weren't as many of his stories now. He was frightened by the terrible things that were happening to his body, and he was confused. People were still mithering him, he said, about what he should do with his house and his garden. But generally it was not a subject he wanted to dwell on. Throughout the whole of this period, he was in denial, and thinking about a will or making sure he was happy that his affairs were in order were things he didn't want to be reminded of. For Fred, thinking about these things meant facing up to the inevitability of imminent death, and he wasn't prepared to do this. There were still too many things he'd got to do. Many a time, sitting in the bar at the end of a day's shoot, or sitting at his kitchen table between shooting trips, he would tell me about an article he'd read in the paper about another new drug that offered hope to cancer sufferers. Maybe he'd be able to get it in time.

Throughout all this time, Fred kept this 'clutching at straws' veneer of optimism, but the reality was that his condition was getting worse by the day. By the time we'd done the day's filming at the traction-engine club, we had done thirty-three days' filming with Fred out of the total of sixty that had been scheduled for the series. There was clearly not a chance that he was going to be able to do them all. We'd already cut a lot out of the schedule. Now it was beginning to look as though we would have to cut more.

When we got back to Burton, I had a pint with Fred at the Burton Bridge pub. I talked to him about the rest of the schedule and about how much more he was going to be able to do. We were still planning to go to South Wales and the Forest of Dean, but I thought it was too far for him to travel. If we did the day that was scheduled at the Ffestiniog Railway the next day, and the three days in North Wales that were scheduled for the following week, I said, I thought I would have enough material.

Fred was reluctant to bring the journey to an end, but by now he was in more and more pain, and it was all getting very difficult. He also wanted to be able to spend some time in his garden, as there were still jobs that he wanted to do there. He definitely wanted to do the North Wales trip, because we were planning to steam past Snowdon and over the Pass of Llanberis to the former Dinorwic Slate Quarry, the location of the big engineering workshop powered entirely by a huge waterwheel. All of the line-shafting which connected the wheel with the machinery in the workshops is still intact, and Fred wanted to show us how the sort of Victorian workshop where an engine like his could have been built would have operated.

He also wanted to go to the Forest of Dean, to see the free miners there and to look at some of the ancient ironworkings. As well as this, there were two other places nearer to home that he insisted we should go to. Both of them had played an important part in the building of his engine. Fred had always picked out Bowns Dukinfield Ironworks for special praise. 'Their business is metal pressings,' he said, 'and they made the throat plate and ash pan for my engine. They are a real old-style engineering works that's been in the same family for five generations. The kind of outfit the steam men should support.' Fred wanted to give his support to them by making sure they were included in the series. The other place he didn't want to miss was Smith Bullough's, at Atherton, where they had made nearly all the nuts and bolts for his engine. Despite my misgivings about travelling as far as the Forest of Dean, I assured him that we would get to these places.

Next day, there was a long cross-country journey from Burton-on-Trent to the Ffestiniog Railway. Jimmy drove Fred and Jack, but despite setting off early, it was after lunch before they arrived. By then, the engine had been unloaded and was steamed up and everybody else was there waiting to start filming. Jimmy told me later the reason for the delay. 'On the way over, I asked Fred if he wanted to have a break for a coffee, so we stopped at the Welshpool and Llanfair Light Railway. We were only going to the café at the station, but Jack decided he wanted to have a look in the sheds, so we were well over an hour there. I kept saying, "They're waiting, they're waiting," but Jack had to go and see his mates in the workshop.' It was a difficult situation, but because it was so sensitive, it was not one that we could do anything about. At a time like this, family had to come before any considerations about filming schedules.

'Jack did cause distractions,' Jon recalls, 'but he was a nice lad, and it was good for Fred that he was there. He also knew what he was doing with the engine, and

I think he had quite a lot to do with resolving some of the problems with it. It was hard, because he was very mixed up about the fact that he didn't really see his dad that often and this was an opportunity to spend some time with him, and that meant an awful lot to him.'

The Ffestiniog Railway didn't relate directly to the themes of the programmes, but it was close to some of the places we were filming at in North Wales, and it was one of Fred's favourite little railways; a good place for him to visit with Jack and Roger. By now, Fred's engine-driving had been cut down to no more than a mile or so at most of the locations; just enough to see him arriving and leaving on his engine. It was all a huge amount of effort for Alf and Alan who, with the help of Jack and Roger, were having to get the engine transported to the location and then steamed up when we got there. The drive at Ffestiniog was one of the shortest: out of the gates, a few hundred yards down the road, then back through the gates and into the railway yard. As he brought his engine to a halt and climbed down from it, Fred said, 'Last time we came here, we looked at the passenger side of the Ffestiniog Railway, but this time we've come to look at what it were really built for – the movement of slate – and over here we've got a lovely engine what I'm goin' to have a look at.'

The Ffestiniog Railway was built in 1832 to carry slate from the quarries at Ffestiniog to the sea at Porthmadog. The steam-hauled narrow-gauge railway is one of the most picturesque and spectacular in Britain, running along 13½ miles of track into the heart of the

Snowdonia National Park. The route allowed the slate-filled wagons to run down to the coast by gravity, while horses were used to pull the empty wagons back up the line. Steam locomotives replaced horse power in 1863.

Fred walked over from his engine to a shiny black locomotive in a siding at the yard. He was met by Paul Lewin, the railway's general manager. 'This is a nice one, isn't it?' Fred said. 'I wonder how much of the engine is original?'

'Well, that's always an interesting question,' Paul replied. 'We think the boiler is 113 years old. So does that make it the oldest one in Britain, do you reckon?'

'I don't know,' Fred answered. 'I reckon it's getting a bit that way. No doubt it will have had a bit of treatment, like, but most of it, the boiler barrel, will be original maybe.'

'This ended up in Surrey in the late 1960s,' Paul said. 'Some chap bought it, a guy called Bernard Latham, and he took it and put it in his back garden, and goodness knows what the neighbours thought. But he must have had it there for thirty-odd years. He brought it here in the early nineties, and since then we've been looking after it. I tell you what, Fred, would you like to come with us down to our works and have a look at where we restore them?'

'It would be a pleasure,' Fred replied. 'When I came before, they were building an engine from scratch. They started off with just the funnel and the reversing lever.'

Paul told him that the one he'd seen in the workshop

was operational now, so they would be able to have a look at it. Then he invited Fred to climb aboard, and after blowing the whistle, he released the vacuum brakes and they were on their way out of the siding and on to the main line. 'It runs nice,' Fred said. 'Nice and sweet. What's top speed?'

'The fastest should be about 12 or 13mph,' Paul replied. 'It gets a bit exciting after that.' He blew the whistle as they approached a station. 'I live in the station house here,' he told Fred. 'My missus will probably be out there with a cup of tea for us – or at least we can live in hope.'

As they stopped at the station, Paul's wife was standing on the platform with their baby daughter. 'This is my missus,' he said.

'And the new offspring,' Fred added.

'Yeah,' Paul said proudly. 'She's only three weeks old.' He was the picture of contentment. He'd worked at the railway as a volunteer from a very young age. Now he'd got the perfect job that he'd always dreamed of and was living at the railway with his young family. Fred looked a touch envious as Paul got off the engine to go and set the signals. He promised not to run off with the engine, and chatted to Mrs Lewin from the cab.

'Are you having fun?' she asked.

'Oh aye,' Fred replied. 'I always do. Yeah, easier than working, this messing about, you know.'

Paul came back to the engine. 'Right then, Fred,' he said. 'I've got the token. And you can see the signal's at green now, so we can go back. I have a special whistle code here when I'm going into the station that lets my missus know if I want a cup of tea. It works very well. Providing I'm in her good books.'

'Well, I've had three, you know,' Fred informed him as they went rattling off down the track.

They talked about the performance of the engine. 'She doesn't roll very well,' Paul said, 'even though we're going downhill. The bearings need a bit of a sort-out. The axle boxes are very old and very tired. See that white light?' he said, pointing ahead down the single-line track. 'It tells us the automatic crossing lights are working.' They carried on talking about the railway and about the embankment across the estuary at Porthmadog that they were approaching. 'The place in the trees there,' Paul said, 'is Boston Lodge Works, which is where we are heading for. With a bit of luck, they might have the kettle on.'

When they got to the works, Fred recognized one of the engines that was standing outside. 'Yeah,' he said. 'That's the one that were just a funnel and a reversing lever, is it?' He walked across the tracks with Paul to have a look at it.

'You can see the bogey there that runs on the front is powered, and the one at the back is unpowered,' Paul said. 'Very smooth, very smooth engine, very smooth riding. I think they wore the first one out that they built. It was built in the 1870s, and by 1930 it was completely worn out and they scrapped it, and all that was left was the chimney and the reversing lever that you saw last time you were here. 1999 it was when we did this. Two hundred people gave £5 a month to get the money together to build it. It took about six or seven years to do, but it's done now, and it's a lovely machine. Round the corner here is *Prince*, which is the oldest working steam engine in the world. It dates back to 1863. It was one of the first engines on the line, and when the railway closed in 1946 there was a new boiler for this one sat in the workshops, so when the preservationists came along and reopened it, it was the first engine they got going again, so it has a very special place in Ffestiniog Railway history. Last year, we were opening a new section of our Welsh Highland Railway over on the south side of Snowdon, and we took this engine over there to open that new section, and Prince Charles came along and actually drove this engine, and made his day having a bit of a drive with it.'

Now it was Fred's turn to have a bit of a drive. Paul took him to the station at Porthmadog over on the other side of the embankment, where one of the engines was hitched up to a line of slate wagons. They got on board and Paul invited Fred to take the controls.

'So then, Fred, we said it was all about moving slate around, and here you are, an authentic Ffestiniog Railway slate train – it's all yours, my friend.' Fred was in his element. He was clearly enjoying himself as he took hold of the regulator and the train eased out of the station and over the embankment. 'Now, you've got a speedometer up there, Fred. Anywhere between ten and fifteen is fine. Modern luxury, eh? A speedometer!'

The slate train made a fine sight, chugging across the embankment against a backdrop of the mountains of Snowdonia. 'Well, I don't know about you, Fred,' Paul said, 'but I reckon that's one of the finest views you can get from a footplate.'

'Yeah, beautiful, yeah,' Fred said as he turned to the camera with a broad grin wreathing his face. 'Like Lawrence of Arabia, you know. Do I slow down at this bend that's coming up or just leave it?'

'Well, it's a 15mph limit on the bend,' Paul said, 'and we're only doing 14mph, so we'll be fine. Normally, when we've got a passenger train, we'd be doing 20mph across the embankment, so we'd have to get the brakes on here, but at this speed we're quite happy. Now, whenever you see a "W" sign, you know what to do, don't you?'

Fred didn't know, so Paul told him it was a sign telling him to blow the whistle. Fred didn't need any second invitation, and he was soon tooting happily away. 'I'm enjoying this,' he said. Again, it was one of those moments when all of Fred's troubles seemed to be forgotten. Maybe we could carry on for a few weeks longer while Fred could still enjoy experiences like this.

12

The End of the Road

For the next week, we had scheduled two days' filming in North Wales. On the way back to Bolton,
we planned on stopping at the Anderton Boat Lift
in Cheshire, then to go to Bown's Ironworks at
Dukinfield the next day. But Fred was still driven by
his obsession to get everything done in the garden. So
rather than having a rest between filming, he decided
that his pithead gear needed a coat of creosote.

Despite many offers of help, he insisted on doing
the job himself. He managed to climb the ladder, but
the combined effects of two gruelling cycles of chemotherapy, rapidly failing strength and the painkilling
drugs that he was taking meant that he just wasn't
up to doing the sort of thing that he'd done with
ease throughout his life. As he was up at the top, he
overstretched, the ladder slipped and Fred fell about
20 feet, landing on his back near the top of his mine

shaft. At first, he couldn't move; he'd hurt his back and he was covered from head to toe in creosote. Fortunately, Jack was there, and with his help, Fred managed to get to bed. The next day, he was still finding any movement painful, and his back was covered in a massive bruise, but all he would say to Sheila was, 'Naaa . . . it's nowt, cock.'

Fred was badly hurt, but he wouldn't admit it to himself or anybody else. He was due on location in North Wales the following morning, and he didn't want to miss it. Next morning, he was up early, had his breakfast and was ready and waiting for Jimmy to arrive to transport him to the location. His back was sore, his bladder was causing intense discomfort, but he wasn't going to give in. He certainly wasn't going to let me know, for fear that the trip would be cancelled.

When I got to the car park at the top of Llanberis Pass, the clouds were hanging low over Snowdon. Up there at the top of the pass, we were just below the cloud line. The engine had already been unloaded from the low loader, but the tanks were empty, and Alan and the boys were looking for somewhere they could get water. Fred had just arrived with Jimmy, but he didn't mention anything to me about his accident. There was no indication from him that there was a problem. It was Jack who told me about it, and the condition his dad was in. When I broached the subject with Fred, he dismissed it. 'Naa, it's nowt. I'll be all right. I'm looking forward to driving through the mountains.'

It was July, the middle of the summer holidays, and

the car park was busy. It was the starting point for one of the paths to the top of Snowdon, so there were a lot of walkers there, and many others who had come for the scenic drive through the mountains of Snowdonia. Fred was soon surrounded by fans, and while Alan and the boys were trying to sort out the problem with the water, Fred was busy signing autographs and posing for photographs. The only place they could get water was from a tap in the café, but even then there was still a problem.

Fred looked up from signing another autograph and explained, 'We haven't got a hosepipe long enough. And then, the taps are them you have to keep your thumb on all the time to keep them running. Water must be desperate on top of this mountain.'

I spoke to Alf about Fred's accident and the extent of his injuries, and he confirmed that he was in a bad way. But this, he said, was where he wanted to be and what he wanted to be doing. He was still determined to carry on and get round to as many places as possible. Fred did, after a while, tell me a little bit about what had happened.

'I had a bit of an accident this weekend,' he said. 'I fell off the top of the headgear in the back garden, and on Sunday I couldn't walk. I spent all Sunday in bed, and Monday weren't much different. Now I can just about walk. But I'm in a worse state now than last time you saw me.' Then he laughed. 'I'm bloody near dead, really.' Still laughing, he turned away to sign another autograph. 'A N G I E, is it? Sorry about the oily fingermarks. It'll make it more authentic.'

Whenever he was in these situations, he was always very open about having cancer. He didn't quite make a joke of it, but whenever he was asked about it, he would treat it quite lightly. People would come up to him and say, 'You're looking well, Fred,' and he would just say, 'Yeah, but I've got this bladder cancer, you know,' and leave it at that.

Alf and Jimmy were now helping to get the water tanks filled. Because they couldn't attach their hose-pipe to the taps in the café and keep them running, they had to use buckets and anything else they could lay their hands on to get the water. And it takes a lot of buckets to fill a 160-gallon tank. Jack got hold of a big plastic container, and he went backwards and forwards from the tap in the café to the engine, filling up the green tank on the side of the boiler. As they filled the tanks, they started to get the engine steamed up, but by this time it was late morning and the boys were getting hungry. Roger had brought some potatoes with him that he was going to bake in the old traction-engine-men's way – in the boiler. As he wrapped the potatoes in tinfoil, he held his hands up. They were black with soot and grime from the engine. 'Best hands in the world for doing this,' he said with a grin. 'I'll make a chef in no time.'

Roger was as cheerful as ever. I asked him if he often cooked his dinner this way, and whether this was what he normally put in the boiler. 'People put roast lamb in,' he said with a laugh, 'spare ribs, bacon in there. You can do baked beans on the cylinder block. Spaghetti rings on the cylinder block. Eggs and bacon on the shovel. I never tried toast, but we could.'

While Roger worked on lunch, Jack worked on getting the engine ready for the road. With steam up and Alf on the footplate beside him as steersman, Fred set off down the Llanberis Pass. Slate has been quarried from these mountains for over 1,800 years. But it was with the coming of the Industrial Revolution that the Welsh slate industry really took off. Fred and his team were on their way to see a Victorian workshop at the Welsh Slate Museum in Llanberis. It was the kind of place where an engine like Fred's would have been built.

It was 6 or 7 miles from the top of the pass to the museum. It turned out to be one of the last long drives that Fred would do, and it was the most spectacular. At least it was downhill all the way, so there were no problems with the engine. And what a fine sight it was as it steamed down the pass through the scenic splendour of Snowdonia. Mountains towered on either side, dwarfing the engine itself. Sheep scattered as Fred blasted on the whistle, and Roger sat on top of the tender doffing the old top hat he was wearing to passing motorists.

After driving for 5 miles, Fred was thirsty and wanted a pint. Towards the bottom of the pass, he spotted a pub, but it was closed. Jack opened the inspection door on the front of the boiler and got the potatoes out to see if they were baked. Alf tried one, but it was too hot.

'Do you want a knife and fork for it?' Jack asked him.

'A set of teeth would be all reet,' Alf replied with a grin.

Roger got a blackened specimen and tried to peel the burnt skin off it. 'Get the carbon off it and it'll be all right,' he said.

As Alf and the boys ate their simple feast, Fred talked about his engine. 'Now that the engine has been run in,' he said, 'it will do 15mph with ease. If it's in top gear, it goes very fast. You should never try and change gear on a hill like the one we've just bin on. I mean, you read all sorts of horrific stories about these super-duper men in the old days being able to change gear on the run. I don't think I fancy trying that. Maybe on the level it's not so bad, but on any hills like these round here, it's a bit fatal, I think.'

With the potatoes finished and no sign of the pub opening, the boys were soon on their way again. Within half an hour, they had arrived at the Welsh Slate Museum, and there was a great photo opportunity for some of the visitors as Fred drove by the side of the Lake Padern Railway on his approach and a little train pulled by a miniature saddle-tank engine chugged along the narrow-gauge railway alongside Fred's engine.

'I said I'd come back,' Fred declared as he drove through the imposing stone archway into the courtyard of the quarry's workshops and offices. The last time we'd been to the museum with Fred, he'd had a go at dressing the slate, but on this trip it was the workshops he was interested in. They catered for all the repair and maintenance work of the quarry, which at its height, in the late 1880s, employed over three thousand men. The power came from a huge waterwheel built by the De Winton Company in Caernarfon, and Fred had always said it was the best surviving example he'd ever seen of an engineering workshop driven by belts and line-shafting. The whole site was so big it had its own railway. It was self-sufficient, right down to casting their own machine tools in the foundry. It operated from 1809 to 1969, and during this time thousands of tons of slate were exported to the four corners of the world. The quarrymen hacked away at the mountain, creating different levels linked by inclines. The weight of trucks loaded with slate going down the mountain was used to haul the empties back up again.

'Really,' Fred said as he looked round the courtyard, 'it would be wonderful to be let loose in here with about 60 ton of iron plates of different thicknesses, and about 50 ton of coke, a few 45-gallon drums full of oil, and there would be no bloody end to what you could make in a workshop like this, because there's a machine tool of every description that you could ever wish to have. It's a pity it's a bit too big for our shed! There used to be hundreds of engineering workshops like this around the country, and it's the sort of Victorian workshop where my engine would have been built.'

The first workshop Fred walked into with Alf looked as though the last shift had just finished minutes earlier. Everything had been left exactly as it would have been. It was full of the sort of engineering machinery that fascinated Fred. 'All of it,' he told Alf as he pointed out the long metal rods that ran the length of the workshop, 'is driven by this line shaft, which is ⅛ mile long, and all driven by the waterwheel at the other end. How's that for a lathe over there! *Boyoi-oi-oing!* It's a fair one. And this radial arm drill here. Let's go and have a look at it.'

He walked over to the drill to take a closer look. 'Bloomin' 'eck!' he exclaimed. 'You'd never believe it, would you? Made in America. The Americans were quite famous for making machine tools, you know, in the early days. Must have been about 1890 or something like that.'

Fred was clearly excited by all that he was seeing, and all his pain seemed to be forgotten. This ancient-looking workshop inspired him, and all his old enthusiasm was back. He walked over to a workbench in front of a leaded window. Above it, there was a pulley wheel. 'They used a lot of these pulley wheels in quarries,' he told Alf, 'with overhead ropeways and all of that.' Then, looking at some of the things on the bench, he said, 'We've got lots of these at home, haven't we? Antiques, and dies, and things.' Fred pointed into the next room. 'Look at that over there – a locomotive boiler. We'll have a look at that in a bit.'

Alf spotted another machine. 'Is it for milling, that?' he asked Fred.

'No, it's a drilling machine,' Fred replied. 'It's just a drill. The table doesn't traverse anywhere. If it were a milling machine, it would. They didn't have milling machines in the olden days. That drilling machine, though, is about the same size as ours. An' look at these – antique chain blocks. Who's got one of these, cock? Yes, we have, rusting merrily in our shed. Just the same. Maybe a little bit bigger than this. We've got a shaper as well, similar to that, but two sizes down.'

They walked on a bit further and saw another little lathe. 'That,' decided Fred, 'would be for all the little locomotive wheels.' Then something else caught his attention. 'Look at these. Ropeways. They'd have been for those wire ways they had. Hey, these are brake wheels. They've got wooden inserts inside. Can you see?' He wandered round, fascinated by every rusting bit of metal in the workshop, muttering all the time, more to himself than to Alf, 'Yeah, that's interesting, innit?' He was totally engrossed, oblivious to the camera and anybody else who was there.

In the middle of the workshop, Fred spotted something else. 'Yeah. I know what this is for,' he said. 'It's a portable slate saw. They've got one of these at Glyncliffon, near Caernarfon, where we did the steam engine up. Just the same as this. You put the block on the table, an' it goes along these railway lines and cuts it to shape.' He walked on to another piece of machinery. 'Hey, come and have a look at this shaper over here,' he called to Alf. 'It's a big 'un, innit? You can do owt you want with this.'

Alf came over to have a look. 'Could you have used this for making parts for the traction engine?' he enquired.

'Yeah,' Fred replied, 'we did. You've seen it, haven't you? The Butler one. All the valve-chest covers were made on our shaper. And there's other things where I just can't put my finger on it. When we were doing the boiler and we 'ad to make that piece with the slant on it, we planed the slant on it with the shaper. It's really a planing machine. But there were bigger ones than this. There might be one somewhere.'

Fred was off now on his favourite subject: the things he could do with some of this machinery if he had it in his garden, and he couldn't stop talking excitedly about it as he and Alf walked through into the next room. Then, spotting a 'No Smoking' sign on the wall, he went on, 'Yeah. Bloomin' 'eck. Look at that, even in the olden days, no smoking. You'd have thought they'd all be going with their pipes and that sort of thing. Yeah, look at this here, a loco boiler. It don't look in bad nick, that, does it? It's nice, innit? You could make one of them here with all the tackle that they've got.'

Fred recognized nearly everything in the workshops straight away, and was able to explain to Alf what each of the machines was and what it was used for. But some things took a bit more working out than others. 'What's this one?' he asked, looking at one strangely shaped piece of ironwork. 'We don't know what this is. It's a mystery.' But after studying it for a bit, Fred decided that it was a mechanical bellows. As he went from one room to another, there was one common cry from him that kept coming up: 'Look at that. Same as one we've got at home.'

The Welsh Slate Museum is a fascinating place, where you can learn a lot about what was once one of Wales's major industries. At its height, Wales was producing nearly half a million tons of slate a year, four-fifths of all British slate. But this level of production came at a price. Life was tough for a quarryman. The hours were long, pay was poor and many workers died before their time due to ill health and accidents. During blasting work, rock could fall without warning, burying men alive or driving them over the cliff. Between 1822 and 1969, 362 men were killed, most in rock-falls. Many thousands more were injured. A custom-built hospital was opened to treat quarrymen who had had accidents, and long before the NHS, the 'hospital shilling' was kept back from the men's pay so that any quarryman could be treated in hospital.

Later that afternoon, Fred sat with Alf, having a pint in the bar of the pub we were staying at. 'I told you it were a good workshop, that,' he said. 'You've got everything you would need for building a loco-motive. I wish it were all mine. I'd live in one corner.'

Dinorwic Quarry closed in 1969, but some of the workers still lived around Llanberis, and we'd arrang-ed for Fred and Alf to meet two of them at the pub. Gwillam Jones and Elwyn Wilson-Jones had worked at the quarry since the early 1950s. 'That's where I served my time as a fitter,'* Elwyn told them. 'I started in 1953.'

'There must have been a lot of opportunity for fitting and mending things,' Fred said.

---

* Engineer responsible for the manufacture and installation of machinery components.

'You're telling me,' Elwyn replied. 'I remember where you were today, where the museum is situated, there used to be about sixty people working in there alone.'

Alf asked Gwillam if he had worked there as well, and he told him that he had worked in the quarry itself, with 3,400 other men. 'I blasted things,' he said when Alf asked him what he did there.

'Yeah,' Fred said. 'There's some nice pictures in there of blokes on bosun's chairs drilling holes in rock-faces. Makes you wonder what happened to it all. It's still the world's best roofing material, compared with all the modern rubbish they've come up with. There's nowt can beat a piece of slate.'

'When this quarry closed in 1969,' Elwyn broke in, 'they said at the time there was a lack of demand for slate, which is rubbish. I think there was a lot of politics involved. In 1969, they built the big power station inside the mountain, and I think they wanted the mountain for that purpose. We'll never know.'

It was a view that Fred concurred with. 'Nobody ever tells us,' he said. 'It's like the coal industry. It just disappeared.'

In reply to a question from Alf about the accident rate in the quarry, Gwillam told him it was very high. 'They had their own quarry hospital with a surgeon there.' The work was clearly dangerous, but Fred saw it as something that would have been fun as well.

'Them inclined planes always fascinated me,' he said. 'I bet you had lots of fun with them.'

'Yes,' Elwyn replied. 'Sometimes they forgot to hook

the full wagons at the top, and they came running down and all the wagons would be in smithereens at the bottom.'

It was clear that this had caught Fred's interest. He'd always liked a good story about disaster. 'Yeah, smashed-up wood and twisted metal,' he said with relish. 'Anyone down at the bottom would be legging it pretty fast.'

Fred had a great fascination for anything to do with mining, but he was even more interested in the workshops. Gwillam said his father had been chief engineer, and he remembered a time when there were six blacksmiths in the workshop, all working flat out. When he told Fred how he'd learned about doing brass castings from an old foundryman, it was the cue for Fred to return to one of his perennial themes, for what turned out to be the last time on film. 'Well, that's the best way,' he said. 'Having an old man stood at the side of you saying "You're making a bugger of that" is the best way to learn, and you can't get that out of a book.' He recounted the tale of going to Birmingham University to receive his honorary degree. 'They were all Chinamen there,' he said. 'Hundreds of them coming up for their diplomas. And seven-eighths of them were girls as well! Young lasses, all with a degree in engineering! So what's going to happen to us? We'll just be shopkeepers and tourist attractions in a bit.'

Elwyn and Gwillam were in general agreement with Fred but we'd strayed a long way from them telling us about their working lives, so Alf asked them if they had any stories to tell. Gwillam was the first with one. 'The winter of 1947,' he began,

> was a very hard one, and I started with my father to learn how to blast the rock down. We used to light the fuse with a cigarette always. Not with the matches. Because we were paying for everything – the fuse, the powder and the caps. We used to go twice a week to the top of the mountain to the powder house. And I was coming down once with a bag of powder on my back, a fuse round my neck and some caps in my pocket, and I stopped behind the quarry hospital to have a smoke. Well, the doctor was in the window. He saw me, but I didn't see him. I carried on down with the powder, and we had to call into the office to see the manager. 'Oh, Gwillam,' he said when I went in. 'You've got to have three days off. We're not going to sack you, but I'll give you three days off.' But I'm still here, after smoking while I was carrying the powder and the fuses.

Then Elwyn joined in. 'There's a true story,' he said,

> about a chap from Caernarfon working in the quarry. When somebody came looking for a job then, they had to knock on the door of the manager's office, and when he said, 'Come in,' they had to take their caps off to show respect for the manager. Well, this chap from Caernarfon came in, to look for a job. He knocked on the

door, and the manager said, 'Come in,' and he walked in with his cap still on his head. So the manager said, 'Do you know what you're supposed to do when you walk into the manager's office? You take your cap off.' So the chap from Caernarfon said, 'I've come here for a job, not for a bloody haircut.'

I was pleased we'd made it to the workshops with Fred that afternoon. It had always been one of his favourite places, and that day while he was in there with Alf, he was totally absorbed in everything, his illness far from his mind. It was getting to places like this that was keeping him going. He'd always said that, for him, making the programmes was like a big holiday, with the BBC paying him to go to all sorts of lovely places he wanted to visit. This trip was no different, and he wanted to make the most of it while he still had time.

But Fred was now tiring very quickly, and he was clearly in a lot of pain, wincing visibly as he tried to sit down or stand up. It had to be bad, because Fred had always given the impression that he was completely oblivious to pain. Jack expressed his concern to me again. Sharing a room with their dad, he and Roger could see the extent of the bruising on his back from the fall and were more aware of the effects of the tumour than anyone else. I told Fred that he shouldn't be doing this, that he should have let me know about the accident as soon as it happened. There would be no problem postponing the rest of the filming until the bruising on his back had gone down and he could move around more comfortably. But, again, he insisted on going on.

The next day, we went to Anglesey to see a mine, which would have produced a lot of the copper for a traction engine like Fred's. Before the Industrial Revolution, Wales was a rural country, with a population of only half a million. But slate quarrying, lead mining and copper mining transformed it into the great industrial nation which it became in the Victorian era. The Isle of Anglesey became famous because of the Parys Mountain, which at one time was the largest copper mine in the world. Along with the nearby Mona mine, it dominated the world's markets in the late 1700s.

Parys Mountain was a bleak-looking open moorland, and when we arrived there, everything was shrouded in mist. As I drove into the car park, I could just about make out the shapes of Fred's engine, the living van and the low loader that had transported them there from Llanberis. Alf and Alan had everything off to a fine art now, and the engine was steamed up and ready for Fred to drive a mile or so up and down the road. The steps were got out of the living van, and Fred climbed slowly up on to the engine. Every time he did this now, it seemed to be getting more and more difficult for him. With Alf by his side, he drove out of the car park, and we set up the camera by the side of the road. It was cold and damp, but we didn't have to wait long before the engine emerged from the mist in a cloud of smoke and steam.

'Copper was used in great abundance for the manufacturing of locomotives and all sorts of other types of
steam engines,' explained Fred:

The high-pressure steam pipes are all made from
copper, and the bearings and the fancy bits – the
name plates and all such as that – are made from an
alloy of copper and tin and lead mixed together.
This is Parys Mountain I've come to in North
Wales, and you wouldn't think it now, but this was
once the biggest copper mine in the world. What
we'll do now, we'll take the van off, and we'll go
over exploring the mountains with a light engine,
because we might end up somewhere where we
can't turn it round, if we've got the van on.

With the van unhitched, Fred drove the engine up a
track and into the mist. Alf was steering, and Jack and
Roger were both hanging on wherever they could get a
foothold. They drove across a bare moonscape until
they came to the edge of a huge crater. 'Look at that
down there,' Fred said. 'Yeah, we'll leave the engine
here an' go an' have a look over the edge.' They all
climbed down from the engine and walked to the edge
of the crater.

'That's one big hole, innit?' Alf commented. 'It
looks like a roadway down there, and a tunnel.'

'Aye, bloomin' 'eck,' Fred responded, 'that's a fair
hole, innit? They've shifted a ton or two out of there.
You wonder if like . . . well,' he pondered, 'obviously
they've open-casted it, but . . . look at all them

different colours. Yeah, it's like a lunar landscape, innit? That's, like, natural rock formation there. Let's go and see if we can find an engine house ... there's one somewhere on this site. I've seen it from down below, you know. Come on, we'll go and have a look.'

Today, the great mine is an impressive chasm, opened up at an early stage of mining after a collapse of other workings. But there are still many abandoned workings, which are being explored by a mine-exploration group. Fred had always been fascinated by old mine workings, but he wasn't fit to go underground, so we'd arranged for him to meet Ian Cuthbertson from Anglesey Mining, the company that owned the site, and David Wagstaff from the mine-exploration group. He drove the engine back to the car park and left it with Alan, while we went by car to an old engine house on the other side of the site, where we'd arranged to hold our meeting.

David told Fred that the engine house was one of the oldest in Wales. The engine, he said, was put in it back in 1819. 'It'd be nice to get it back again,' he said, 'but nobody knows where it's gone now.'

'It'll have been made into knives and forks about twenty-seven times,' Fred said. 'But at least the masonry's still here, innit?'

Alf spotted a shaft and wanted to know if it was the one that was associated with the engine house and whether it was still open and the workings were still accessible. David told him they were, and that the Parys Underground Group went down every Wednesday night to the 45-fathom level (nearly 300 feet down). Ian picked up on this, and said that they were able to go down much deeper into new areas since draining the water out the year before. In answer to a question from Fred about how they had managed that, David answered, 'A company came and pumped it out, and this was to save Amlwch from flooding. If the dam had gone that was holding it back, it would have washed straight down the valley.'

Ian told Fred that there were eighty-five shafts on this site, and that the workings went back almost four thousand years, but the mine had been at its peak towards the end of the eighteenth century. 'It was very successful,' he said,

and it was run by a man called Thomas Williams, from the other side of Anglesey, who became a major entrepreneur in the early stages of the Industrial Revolution. He corresponded with Matthew Boulton and the Wedgwoods, and all the others who were involved in the Industrial Revolution, and he not only mined here, he got the smelters as well, and when he'd smelted the copper he made it into sheets, or he made it into blanks, and he delivered it to people who needed it. He ran a whole concern all the way from primary production to sale and almost to the end use, which was very unusual in those days. The Cornish mines were used to selling their ore at the gate of the mine, and they thought it was cheating to actually own the smelters and rollers. He became known as the copper king, and this was his copper kingdom. In fact, the road that you can see is what is known as the copper road, which goes down to Port Amlwch. Horses and carts took the copper all the way down this road and later, the smelters were down there, and when they first laid this road, they laid it with zinc. They didn't know how to smelt it. It was one of the most expensive roads in Europe. And when they realized what they'd done, they ripped it up.

Fred wanted to know whether there was any truth in a story he'd heard about the reward given to the guy who had discovered the copper deposits in the mountain. 'Yes,' David answered, 'the story goes that, on 2 March 1768, after four years of searching on the mountain and just as they were about to give up, the great discovery was made, and Roland Pugh, a Welsh miner, got the credit for that discovery, and he got a bottle of brandy and rent-free cottage for life.'

'Amlwch became the biggest town in Wales at the time,' Ian said, 'and they had fires all over the mountains they were smelting on.'

They all moved on from the engine house to the steps where the miners used to go down into the mine. It was, David told Fred, the way the mine-exploration group goes in now. 'It goes down,' he said, 'to the first level at 10 fathoms, about 60 feet. Then it goes down another 300 feet, which is as far as we can go at the moment.'

That afternoon, we went to a nearby pub to talk to David and another member of the mine-exploration group who had brought along some photographs of the underground workings. But for Fred, it was too much. Over the last few weeks, we'd watched as the terrible illness had taken its toll; we'd seen his energy fail and his passion and enthusiasm fade. This afternoon in a little pub on Anglesey, it seemed to be extinguished. Fred was exhausted, and you could see the effects of the high dosages of morphine he was taking to keep himself going. As we set up the camera and lights to film his chat, Fred struggled to keep his eyes open, and dropped off to sleep. We couldn't go on any longer. It had to be the end of Fred's brave battle to carry on with his grand tour.

We talked about it that evening over a pint or two in the bar of the hotel we were staying in. He was still reluctant to give in, and he wanted to battle on. The journey and the filming had been a sort of therapy for him. They had kept him going, and accepting that he couldn't do any more was accepting the inevitability of death not being far away. He still clutched at straws. There was another new drug he'd read about. Maybe he'd be able to get it in time to save him, or at least give him a few years' grace to get on with unfinished business. 'There's so much to do,' he said, and then, 'What have I done to deserve this?' He was desperate for somebody to give him some hope; to assure him that it wasn't all over just yet. I tried to reassure him that we'd be able to get the rest of the filming done when he was feeling a bit better, but I knew it wasn't going to happen.

We agreed to stop at Anderton Boat Lift on the way

back the next day, but the filming at Smith Bullough and Dukinfield Ironworks would have to be put off. Jimmy wasn't with us, so the next morning I drove Fred from Anglesey and along the North Wales coast. Over the years, we'd done a lot of filming in North Wales, so it was a journey we'd made many times before. As we approached the Marble Church at Bodelwyddan, I slowed down. It was Fred's favourite steeple; he had always enthused about the grace and beauty of it and the skills of the man who had built it. He didn't say anything as he looked over to the beautiful little church we'd filmed at in happier times, but I think he was finally accepting that the end was near.

As we drove away up the hill towards Queensferry and Chester, Fred started to talk about his garden. 'I don't know why everyone's so bothered about me garden and about who's going to have it all. It's not worth owt really. Just a pile of junk that I've assembled over the years and rescued from the scrapman.'

We carried on to the boat lift, and as we got closer, Fred perked up a bit. He was looking forward to seeing it and having a go on it. The structure is a black and white Victorian masterpiece with a chequered history. It was built as an alternative to a series of locks, to bridge the 51-foot height difference between the River Weaver and the Trent and Mersey Canal. The initial plan to build a flight of locks was abandoned due to lack of space and the amount of water that would be lost from the canal into the river. When we arrived there, we went through what had become the usual routine. The engine had already been unloaded and steamed up, and Fred gamely drove it up and down the lane that led to the lift.

'On our way back to Bolton,' Fred said as he brought the engine to a halt in the car park, 'we're going to stop off at the world's first boat lift. The Anderton Boat Lift was built in 1875 to solve the expensive problem of getting goods from the River Weaver navigation up to the Trent and Mersey Canal. The goods mainly were pottery from Staffordshire, and salt from Cheshire going back the other way. It was taken out of use in 1983, and extensively restored. Then, in 2002, it re-opened to the public after a £7 million refurb. I'm now going off to see Tim and Gary, who are going to give me a ride on the thing.'

Gary Hughes, who was one of the lift operators, was there to meet Fred. He was going to be showing him around. Fred walked over to the lift with Gary, and together they walked along a gangway on the top level of the lift. Gary explained that the lift has two caissons and that each caisson could accommodate two narrow boats.

'I've seen it a lot in picture books and read about the restoration part of it, but I didn't think I'd end up standing on top of it,' Fred said. From his reading about it, Fred said he knew that all the structure above him was not needed now. 'It's only been kept here for cosmetic reasons, to give it the look of how it used to be when it was first built.' Fred looked down on the caissons and there were barges in each one on either side of the lift: one going up, the other on its way down from the canal to the river.

'Each of the caissons,' Gary said, 'are 250 tons with the water in them, and counterweights on either side lift them up.'

'So the weight of that one with a couple of boats in goes down and pushes this other tank up, does it?' Fred asked.

'Yes, that's it,' Gary said. 'We just add a little bit of power in between to overcome the friction on the seals. That's basically how it worked when they first did it back in 1875. And it's very economical as well, because it uses very little power. Marvellous engineers in that day.'

'Oh, aye,' Fred agreed. 'We have a lot to answer to our granddads how good they were. They were bloody brilliant men, weren't they? Compared with the modern world we live in. What's the biggest boat you can get in?'

'The caissons are 75 feet long,' Gary replied, 'so we can accommodate a 72-foot narrow boat, which is consistent with local canals. In 1875, when it was first built, it was hydraulic, but they were bombarded with all sorts of problems, so it went to electric operation in 1908. This allowed them to operate the two caissons independently, which brought about a faster transit of materials, with the boats able to go straight through without waiting for one coming the other way. The reason we've gone back to hydraulics now is to get rid of all this weight we're carrying upstairs. The wheels up there are 3 tons each, and there's seventy-two of them.'

Next, it was time for Fred to have a ride on the lift.

He went over to a barge that was moored by the side of the canal near the lift, and climbed on board to be taken down to the lower level. He sat at the front of the barge with Tim Brownrigg, the engineer who was in charge of the restoration.

'It's a wonderful creation, innit?' Fred enthused as they glided over the aqueduct that led into one of the caissons.

'What we're doing at the moment,' Tim said,

is going in the aqueduct, which was built in 1875. This is the original wrought iron. When we were doing the refurbishment, we had to do a lot of calculations to work out how strong these girders were. Victorian engineers were good, but they weren't quite that good. We had to put quite a bit of extra metal on the caissons to make them strong enough. The large A frames up above us and the upper-gear deck were added to the structure when the lift was converted to electric in 1908, after corrosion damaged the original hydraulic mechanism beyond repair. We've seen from the photographs how they built this 1908 part of the structure. They had small derrick cranes, steam-driven ones on trestles, which they raised up as they built it. We're still not entirely sure how they got the main beams up. They weigh about 20 tons each.

'They were very ingenious men,' Fred said. 'Not like the modern man, because we've got easy ways to do things, big cranes and all that. They hadn't got any of that. It was all ropes, blocks, sticks, winches and snatch blocks.'

By this point, they were in the caisson and on their way down to the lower level 51 feet below. As they descended, Tim told Fred about the restoration that had brought the lift back to hydraulic operation. 'They took the main A frames off as one piece, like giant Meccano,' he said. 'Then re-erected it about a year later, once everything had been refurbished.' Fred asked him how heavy the caissons were when they were full of water. 'Well,' Tim replied, 'a caisson full of water weighs about 250 tons. Both caissons are balanced at the moment, and all we do is transfer the oil from one piston to another.'

At the bottom of the lift, the barge sailed out of the caisson into the Anderton basin and then out on to the River Weaver. As Fred enjoyed his boat trip and chatted to Tim about the engineering expertise that had gone into the building of the lift, Alf was looking after the engine. It was the end of a long trip, and his thoughts were turning to home. 'Well, it'll be nice to get home and see how the missus is coping,' he said. 'It wasn't work. It was an enjoyable holiday and a once-in-a- lifetime experience. Traction engines are just such amazing machines, a lovely sight. You've got to take your hat off to people who keep them going, keep them on the road.'

For Fred's engine, this was almost the end of the road. The filming that had been scheduled for the following week in South Wales and the Forest of Dean had been cancelled, and although there were going to be a couple more days' filming around Bolton, this was the end of the grand tour around Britain. When Fred got back from his boat trip, the engine was being driven up on to the low loader by Jack, to be taken back to Fred's garden. I had already left and had asked Jon to direct this last day's filming. I needed to start editing the film, but also, I just didn't want to be there for what I knew was going to be the end.

13

Back Home

Fred was now back at home, too unwell to do any more long trips. The grand tour was over. It was the second week in August, exactly three months after we had set out, and there had been a massive deterioration in Fred's health. He had driven himself on because he wanted desperately to get round the country and visit all the places we had planned to go to, but he just hadn't been able to endure the levels of work he had been subjecting himself to any longer. The dream of doing it the way the traction-engine men of old had done it, staying in the living van by the side of the road, had never really been feasible, but at least he'd got round to a lot of the places he wanted to visit and seen a lot of old friends for the last time.

Although we couldn't travel any long distances or be away from home for more than a day at a time, there were still three places close to Bolton he wanted to go to. All of them had provided important parts for his engine, and he wanted to visit them on it. Budenberg Gauge Company had supplied the pressure gauge; most of the nuts and bolts that held the engine together had come from Smith Bullough's; and his new throat plate had been made at Bown's Dukinfield Ironworks.

We made arrangements to film at Smith Bullough's and Budenberg's on consecutive days in mid-August, but there was a problem with the ironworks. They had just started their annual holidays, and the works was closed down until the first week in September, so we couldn't do anything there until then.

Smith Bullough's was in Atherton, which was no more than 4 miles from Bolton. The people at the works were great friends of Fred's, so he wanted to drive there on the engine to let them see it. The Budenberg Gauge Company was a bit further away, in Irlam, so the plan was to go there by car the following day.

On the morning of Tuesday 10 August, Fred got up early. Alf went round to the house at seven thirty and helped Fred to get the engine steamed up. By nine thirty, the crew had arrived, and they were ready to set off on the short journey to Atherton. Fred was in good spirits as he drove the engine through the centre of Bolton and out on the road we had travelled on back in May on our first day of the journey. Now, with all the teething troubles behind it, the engine was performing much better, and he was able to get up the hill out of Bolton without any of the problems he'd had the first time. He even had time to stop to visit the site of the Pretoria pit disaster in Atherton that he'd wanted to visit on our first day on the road in May.

Back on the engine, it took less than half an hour to get to the nut and bolt works. One of the biggest problems Fred had faced when he was building the engine was finding places that could supply him with the parts that he needed. This was particularly true of some of the smallest parts, such as the nuts, bolts and rivets needed to hold the engine together. At one time, nearly every town around the country had little work-shops where things like this were made, but now almost all of them have disappeared. Fred lamented the fact and spoke about it frequently.

Thomas Smith's, or Smith and Bullough's, as it's now known, is one of the old-time nut and bolt works, and produces about eight hundred bolts a day. One of the problems that steam enthusiasts have is that nuts and bolts are produced in metric sizes these days, but the beauty of Smith and Bullough's workshop is that they still make the old-style imperial thread sizes that a traction engine like Fred's needs. As he pulled into the yard of the works, Fred told us about the place.

'Smith and Bullough's nut and bolt works,' he said, 'is one of the few remaining bolt manufacturers in Britain, and they specialize in making one-offs in old thread types like Whitworth. Great big bolts with funny threads and big square heads, and any shape you want. "Whitworth" is a word that's practically non-existent now, but you can get Whitworth nuts and bolts here.'

Alf got the steps out of the living van and Fred

climbed down from the engine. Before going into the works, he told us a bit more about Whitworth. 'In Manchester,' he said,

Sir Joseph Whitworth perfected the standardization of screw threads, so everybody could make nuts and bolts that were all practically the same. From the beginning of the Industrial Revolution, each workshop had its own system and its own sizes. Nuts and bolts were all individually made, with many different screw threads. I've actually worked on machinery where each nut was made to fit the bolt, and when you screwed them on they waggled about as they went down, until they actually landed on the face that they were intended to go on. Whitworth realized that if it were possible for all engineers to use the same system, machined parts would be made much better and mass production would be possible. Whitworth's micrometer was able to measure to an accuracy of one-hundred-thousandth of an inch, and by 1860 his specifications for sizes of screw threads were accepted through all of England.

Fred walked across the yard to a door with Alf.

'There don't look to be anybody about,' Alf said. 'Shall I ring the bell?'

But Fred felt too much at home here for that. 'No,' he replied, 'we don't need to do that. I know them all in here. They're all nice lads. I know the way upstairs.'

Fred let himself and Alf in, and went up the stairs to the office. 'Hello, chaps,' he said cheerily as he walked in. 'Is it all right if we show the BBC where all the nuts and bolts come from that hold our traction engine together? We'll not fall in any nut and bolt machines or owt like that. We know where they all are, so we'll go and have a look round. You all keeping all right, are you?'

Down on the works floor, Fred looked as though he was born to be there. The dark, soot-stained little workshop, with the flames of a furnace lighting up one corner, was the sort of place that had always fascinated him, from the time he was a little lad. It was what he meant when he talked about backstreet mechanicing. Fred leaned on a pile of grimy-looking sacks stacked up against the wall and said, 'I'm going to have a go at making a bolt for me engine. You start by hot forging a blank bolt, cutting it to size and screwing it up on a special machine.'

Fred walked over to a press, where one of the operatives was at work. 'Hiya, Tony. How are you, mate?' he said. 'Can we get some new threads put on here? We used all them inch-and-a-half screws what hold all the tyres on the tractor. We had the back wheels in the back kitchen drilling all the holes and putting threads down the holes for them to screw in, but I'm pleased to say none of them have come loose, and it's had a beating. I was polishing round them only last night. Yeah, me tractor's more or less held together by Mr Smith's nuts and bolts. I can't remember whether I paid for them or whether they give them me.'

'I think it were three postcards we got for that,' Tony said, 'with your picture on. That's what it cost you.'

Fred laughed. 'I'd forgotten about that,' he said. 'Aye, you've been here a long time now, haven't you?' Then, looking at the bolt that Tony was making, he asked what size it was. 'It just happens that our bolt's the same,' he said when Tony told him they were 24mil.

'Do you want to put the thread on it?' Tony asked him. 'Just bring it up to the die.'

As Fred took the bolt and put it in the die, he asked if it put the thread on in one cut, then had a go at doing the job himself. 'Bloomin' 'eck,' he said as he took the bolt out of the cutting machine. 'That looks good. A few weeks' practice, and I'll be all right. Thank you very much. I remember coming by here about twenty years ago, and all the shafting were lying out in the yard, and I come in, and I think it were you I talked to. I said, "I've got to have some of that," and I got quite a lot. Then I come back and took some more out of the mechanics shop. And I've been coming here ever since. It's all going round now, you know. It drives eighteen pieces of machinery in me garden. Next stop, we'll go and see John in the store, because he gave me all the set screws on me traction engine. See you later. Thanks very much.'

Fred left the workshop, carrying the giant bolt he had just helped to make. He and Alf walked down a narrow passageway between two buildings. Fred clearly knew his way round, and it was very apparent that he was used to getting a lot of the things he needed for his engines here. 'We should get a few drawer-bar spindles while we're here,' he said to Alf, 'but we don't know what diameter it is.'

'Where are we going now?' Alf asked.

'I think we're going to the stores,' Fred replied. 'After that, we'll go home and see what's what in the back garden.' In the stores, boxes of nuts and bolts were stacked up on steel shelves; all sorts of shapes and sizes. 'Aye, it's all happening in here,' Fred said as he looked around.

'Look at the size of that, Fred,' Alf said as he picked a big bolt out of one of the boxes.

'Aye, it's nice, innit?' Fred said. 'Beautiful. Made in Atherton.'

John, the store man, was sorting through some boxes at the far end of the stores. 'Now then, John,' Fred said familiarly when he spotted him.

'Now then, Fred,' John replied. 'What can we do you for this time?' Fred was amongst friends here.

'We're scrounging again for our tractor,' he replied.

'Do you fancy a cuppa while we sort something out?' John asked him.

'Aye, we'll have a brew,' Fred replied. 'Coffee. One sugar.' John brought mugs of tea and coffee over to a table and sat down with Fred and Alf.

'There's some history in here,' John said. 'And we keep managing to keep going.'

'Aye,' Fred said. 'I've been coming here for twenty-odd years. All your rivals have really gone. I remember the mill just down the road, nearer to Bolton, and we were doing some downspouts, and there was the big, long shop doing them big nuts – *bang, bang, bang,*

bang. That's empty and derelict now. George Parker's – that's another that's gone. It were famous, Atherton, weren't it, for nuts and bolts?'

'All you could hear at half past seven in the morning in the olden days, coming down Bank Lane on the other side of Atherton, were the clogs of all the women,' John reminisced. 'And they put a monument up in the valley not far from here, because that's where the original nut and bolt works started. I don't know why the Bulloughs settled into this area. You've got the pits, I suppose. There were pits every half-mile. Then you'd got all your cotton factories.'

'A lot of people don't realize,' Fred said, 'that the heads on bolts before the '14 war were much bigger than what they were after. In an attempt to save metal, they reduced them down to modern size. But they don't look as good now; they're not as nice. I were lucky, really, when I were looking for bolts for my engine. There was one day I went in the scrapyard and somebody had pulled this stainless-steel food machine to bits. It must have been pre-war, because they were pre-war five-eighths, stainless-steel nuts, all polished, with the corners off and everything, and I got a bucket-ful. All the plates and the cylinder-end covers, and the valve-chest covers and the safety-valve covers, are all held on with just five-eighths mild-steel stainless-steel nuts.'

They carried on talking about nuts and bolts, a subject close to Fred's heart. John said their biggest market was for imperial. 'The metric market is a dead market.'

'When you're saying imperial is your bestseller, are you meaning it's making a comeback from metric?' Alf enquired. 'Are we going back to imperial?'

'No,' John replied, 'but nobody's stocking imperial now, so when somebody needs it, we get the orders. But the demand is a growing demand. People don't think they can get the Whitworths, but when they find out they can get them from us, you've cornered that market. You're supplying a happy customer.'

Fred finished off his coffee. 'There's no manufacturing now,' he said. 'Mr Napoleon were right: we're all a bunch of shopkeepers, or we will be in a bit. Anyway, we'd better make a move.'

'Nice seeing you, Fred,' John said. 'Pop in any time.'

'We'll come when we want to scrounge some more,' Fred replied.

As he went back to his engine for the short drive home, Fred said there was another reason why he'd wanted to make sure that we filmed with him at Smith Bullough's. 'As small workshops like this modernized in the 1970s and 1980s,' he said, 'they had to do away with the old technology like the line-shafting that once drove all the machines. I remember coming by here about twenty-odd years ago, and it was all lying in the yard, and the boss said I could have whatever I wanted. So I was able to provide a good home for all that line-shafting.'

The following day, we went to Budenberg's, in Irlam. Steam pressure gauges are still hand-made at Budenberg's, as they have been for over 150 years, under a patented design filed by them in 1849. As Fred and Alf had travelled around on the engine over the previous three months, they'd always had to know what the steam pressure was and how much water they had in the tank. If the pressure had got too high or the water level too low, the consequences would have been disastrous. So the pressure and water gauges were absolutely vital.

'My engine is fitted with a very important safety device,' Fred said as he stood by it before leaving home next morning. He pointed out the pressure gauge on his engine. 'This pressure gauge,' he said, 'indicates the pressure of steam in the boiler. I've had a few from Budenberg's in Manchester. They make everything; all the works inside the body of the thing, and the casings. The only thing they don't do is the glass window in the front. In its heyday, the company employed over five hundred people, but now they're down to just sixty-odd workers.'

It was a short drive to Irlam, and we were soon parking outside a unit on a modern industrial estate. 'Victorian workshops, where this sort of specialist work used to be done, no longer exist,' Fred said as he looked at it, 'but the old skills are still there. Even if the work is done now in a modern industrial unit like this.'

He was met by the works manager, Len Weedon, and as they walked across the factory floor, Fred told him that he'd got a shed full of pressure gauges. He'd acquired them, he said, over the years since being a kid and sneaking into disused boiler houses.

'Most of them will probably be Budenberg gauges,'

Len said. 'We came to Manchester in 1850. We had various locations throughout Manchester, and we went to Broadheath in 1914.' Fred said he thought the pressure gauge on his tractor was from about that period.

Len took Fred over to a workbench where a gauge was being assembled which dated from 1906. He told him that they still made a lot of old-style gauges. When they looked in an old catalogue to check the price of it then, it would have cost 21 shillings.

'It's a bit like clock-making, isn't it?' Fred observed.

Len agreed. 'It certainly is. Just one stage up. All done by hand and, basically, the principle hasn't changed from the early days, from the 1850s and 1860s.'

'People don't realize,' Fred said, 'there's about three thousand and odd steam-driven road vehicles in England. A lot of them haven't got their original ones on. They're like more modern replacements. If you can find one with the name on like Marshall's or Fowler's, it adds to the authenticity of the machine.'

While Fred was there, he was given a demonstration of how the teeth are cut on one of the parts of the gauge – the quadrant. The machines this is done on are Microns – Swiss machines – and all the ones they had at the works were pre-1900. Brass was being cut when we were there, but the machines also cut stainless steel.

Fred appreciated the precision of the work and, as he watched, he gave his explanation of what a pressure gauge was and how it worked. 'The pressure gauge,' he said, 'consists of an open tube that's been bent into a circle. An' the steam is offered into one end of the tube, and on the other end, which is blanked off, there's a linkage that goes to a needle and tells you how many pounds per square inch of steam there is in the boiler.'

Before leaving the factory, Fred had a story to tell. 'One day,' he said,

about fifteen years since, or something like that, we stopped for lunch in Knutsford, or somewhere that road – Cheshire, like – at this pub. And the pressure gauge was one we'd done the case ourselves. It had got 'Fred Dibnah, Bolton' on it. And this guy came in with a yellow silk cravat with red spots on and a big 'tache, and he says, 'I see you've not got one of our gauges on your machine,' and I says, 'Who are you, Mr Budenberg?', and he says, 'As a matter of fact, yeah.' An' I said, 'Well, I'll tell you what, mate, at home I've got one, a lovely one with special traction-engine gauge on it, but it's really badly damaged.' The bezel were cracked, and all the glass were cracked, and the bottom were black, and he says, 'You bloody chaps are all the same, you want it for nothing, I suppose,' and then we had a pint and I bid him good day. But before I left, he said, 'I'll send a man,' and it must have been months later, this guy just appeared, and he said, 'I've come from Budenberg Gauge Company for your pressure gauge,' and we give it him. He took it away, and it came back quite a long time after, and it were like brand-new, all shined-up new glass, new everything.

Later that week, we did one more day's filming with the engine. With the limited time we'd had with it out on the road, we'd not been able to get any of the close-ups of moving parts that were needed to edit the driving sequences. So we arranged to take the engine to a disused airfield near Southport, get it steamed up and shoot all the driving shots we needed, including close-ups of Fred and Alf as they were bowling along. Alan came to pick the engine up and transport it to the airfield on the low loader, and Fred had an enjoyable day putting his engine through its paces without having to worry about any traffic.

By this time, I had started to edit the programmes, so Jon was there directing. 'The runway,' he recalls,

had a service road, which was rather anony-mously positioned against some trees, so the background was always green, or the blue of the sky. It was perfect for what we wanted, and in the space of one day we could get all the cut-aways that we hadn't been able to get on the road. We spent the whole day there, and there was Jack and Roger, Alf, Jimmy and Alan and the whole crew. The day worked out brilliantly, because it was one of those days where there was blue sky, then a storm came in and it got cloudy and rained, so we had every conceivable background that we could need for all the shots we needed to get.

I was having a field day, and I wasn't the only one, because Fred had never really had the opportunity to drive the engine at full bore before on the road, because he couldn't stop it quickly. It was always too dangerous, because there was always a corner coming up, or some traffic lights, or some other reason why he could never really open it out. So this was the first time he had a truly open road in front of him, and he could let it go. We didn't need the living van for these close-up shots, so he could just go full throttle. We were doing car-to-engine tracking shots, and he was just shouting to us in the car, 'How fast are we going? How fast are we going?' I looked at the speedometer, and we were doing nearly 25mph. That was as fast as it had ever got, and it just made Fred's day. He'd always said it should go 20-odd mph, and now, for the first time ever, it was.

At last, Fred was happy with his engine. But after that, there was no more filming, other than the one day that had been arranged at the Dukinfield Iron-works for the first week in September, and by then, Fred was very ill. He was on extremely strong pain-killers, and something called Tramadol, which, along with the morphine he was on, had the side effect of making him act strangely. He spent longer and longer in bed, but some days were better than others. On these, he spent his time pottering about in the garden, doing whatever jobs he was still able to do, with Alf and Fred's faithful boiler tender and general help, Ian Thompson, there with him every day.

One day, I went over to talk to Alf about the time

he'd spent working with Fred in the garden and travelling round on the engine:

Me and Fred work well together. Fred's very easy to get on with. He'd all this hanging over him, the terminal illness, but he insisted on keeping going. He were determined he'd get round to as many people as possible, and there are some lovely memories. The highlights were how the public reacted to us. The joy on their faces; all the snapping they did; they just loved Fred. Every time we stopped, people would descend on us. They'd ask how old the engine was, where we were going, where we'd come from. I've never known him refuse to give an autograph or let people snap his picture or talk to anybody. He had his off days, because he weren't a well man at this time, but he insisted on keeping going, and I'm sure it meant everything to him. The engine had a good run round, and I'm sure that took his mind off his own problems. He just wanted to be out there doing a nice day's driving, and a nice chat in the evening with people out of the workses we'd been to and the general public. We must have talked to thousands of people.

You wouldn't have suspected there was anything wrong with him a lot of the time. He didn't bloody complain, so most of the time you'd think he was all right. I knew he was ill, but he didn't show it much; he did hide it a lot. Towards the end of the day, you could see he were feeling a bit tired and looking a bit jaded, but after a wash and brush-up and getting in the restaurant or the pub and talking to people, he seemed to come alive again. There were some happy times, there really were, but as we got to the later programmes, it was getting more and more difficult for Fred to climb on the engine. We carried a short ladder with us so that he could climb up to the level of the engine platform. And when we had a stop, we got into the habit of getting a chair out of the living van for him to sit on.

By the end of August, Fred was fading rapidly and, as his health deteriorated, more and more people who'd enjoyed his company over the years were coming to the house to spend some time with him. The one day's filming for the series that Fred was still desperately keen to do was at Bown's Dukinfield Ironworks.

'There are hardly any left now,' he said, 'but this is a real old-style engineering works that's been in the same family for five generations. Their business is metal pressings, and they make large pressure vessels for oil and gas fields. But the main reason I want to go is because they made the throat plate and ash pan for me engine. Hot steel plates that weigh up to 5 tons are heated in gas furnaces there, and great big hydraulic presses apply forces of up to 800 tons to press huge plates into dished ends – the way they've done it for over a hundred years.'

Places like this had always been particularly important to Fred, and the programmes I made with him allowed him to show people that these traditional skills still existed. Many people just didn't know that; they didn't know that there were forges still operating; they didn't know that rivets were being made or imperial nuts or bolts, or the fact that there are traditional boiler-makers still operating in the country where steam engines can be repaired in the traditional manner. Fred just showed people what was in that shed on the industrial estate that was making all that noise and racket, and he showed people how we came to be where we are. He also showed that engineering was something not to be hidden away but something to be proud of. For Fred, Dukinfield Ironworks illustrated all of this perfectly, which is why, even though he was fading fast, he insisted on being taken there for that one last day.

A date was set for 2 September. Alan Atkinson would take the engine with Alf, and I'd drive from Bolton with Fred and Jimmy. I went over to Bolton the afternoon before to see how Fred was. I'd been on holiday and hadn't seen him for a couple of weeks. The change was dramatic. Gone was the bluff, cheerful, healthy-looking Fred I used to know. Now he was pale and sombre, and there was a distant look about him. Ian had lit the fire in his boiler, and Fred was sitting by it with the old leather jacket on that he normally saved for the coldest days in the garden. It was late afternoon, and the first leaves of autumn were beginning to flutter down on to the garden and the shed roofs.

Alf and Ian left, and I sat with Fred as he looked into the fire. He was frightened and confused, and the effect of the morphine and all the rest of the drugs he was taking was causing him to hallucinate. He was seeing things from the past, but everything was very mixed up. He talked about his engines and his back-yard, but the timescale of when he'd done things and which wife he had been with at the time was unclear. What he was clear about was that he still wanted to go to the ironworks the next day to show everybody where the throat plate and ash pan for his beloved tractor had been pressed. 'Them men deserve to be seen,' he said. But a lot of the time he wasn't very coherent, and he looked so ill that any filming we did with him now would be unusable. I knew I needed to cancel the filming, but I couldn't tell him we wouldn't do it. It would have been like a death sentence to him; it really would have been the end.

It was getting dark, and before I left I said I'd go to the off-licence to get him some cans of Guinness. As I went out of the gate, I recognized Fred's old friend Michael Webber. He'd known Fred since he was a lad, when he used to go round to help Fred with the roller and act as steersman whenever he took it out on to the road to go to a rally. Michael was standing outside the gate, not sure how to get in, and he was worried about the reception he might get from Sheila, who had stopped him from seeing Fred in the past. 'You'd better go in and see him,' I said as I opened the gate for him.

I went to the off-licence for the Guinness, and

Michael sat down by the boiler with Fred and chatted with him about old times. Apart from a chance meeting when we'd been filming *Age of Steam*, he'd not seen Fred for a long time, and he was shocked to see how bad Fred was. I brought the Guinness back and took my leave, promising Fred that I'd be back early the next day for the filming.

When I arrived the next morning, Michael was there with Alf and Alan getting the engine steamed up and on to the low loader. The three of them set off for Dukinfield, and Jimmy took Fred in his car, with me following in mine. Fred insisted he knew the way, but when we got to the eastern side of Manchester city centre, Fred couldn't remember the road out, so we drove backwards and forwards along an inner ring road, crossing and re-crossing the same roads. 'If he'd let me go on the motorway,' Jimmy said, 'I could have found my way there, because I'd been over with the throat plate and collected it from there, so I knew where I was going. But he wouldn't go on the motorway. He said, "I don't like motorways, so we'll go this way. Keep turning left. I used to be able to find my way by chimneys, but they're all gone."'

Eventually, we got to the ironworks. The engine was already steamed up and ready to go when we arrived and, not surprisingly, Fred wanted to drive it. I think everybody there was worried, because nobody was very sure how heavily drugged he was and whether he was in any fit state to be in charge of any vehicle, let alone something that could be as difficult and dangerous as a traction engine. But Fred insisted he was all right and climbed up on to the engine beside Alf for what was going to be the last time. They set off on a little circuit of the streets of Dukinfield, and Alf recalls what happened as they were on their way round. 'There were some steeplejacks on a church steeple,' he said, 'and Fred blew the whistle. They looked down, and they were waving, and he was waving to them, and we'd just left them when he said to me, "I've had enough of this," and then I realized he was a lot more ill than what he'd been letting on, because I'd never heard him say anything like that before. I was a bit concerned then, and I was watching him in case I had to grab his levers to stop us.'

Alf's steering was good, but he'd never had any practice driving the engine, so when Fred had to stop in traffic, he agreed to let Michael Webber take over the driving to get Fred back to the ironworks. Michael drove the engine down the road with Fred standing by his side, a reversal of their roles nearly forty years earlier, when Michael had his first ride on the roller as a schoolboy.

It was to be Fred's last trip on the engine. When they got back, we went through the motions of doing a little bit of filming in the works, as Fred stood watching a pressing. It was the sort of work that he had always admired so much, and they were the last shots that were ever taken of him. His journey was over. Within a few days of filming at the ironworks that had made such an important contribution to the building of his engine, he was admitted to Bolton Hospice, where he spent his last days.

Index

The full-length collector's edition of *Made in Britain* is available as a set of twelve DVDs. For details of these and all of Fred's programmes on DVD contact PO Box 15, The View from the North Ltd, Appleby, Cumbria CA16 6WY or visit:

www.theviewfromthenorth.co.uk

Fred: The Definitive Biography of Fred Dibnah

David Hall

FRED DIBNAH WON the hearts of millions of viewers with his television programmes about his life as a steeplejack, and his passion for the industrial history of Britain. With his trademark flat cap, enthusiasm and knowledge of the country's steam past, his gift for storytelling, and his cry of 'Did you like that?' as another giant chimney slid to earth behind him, he quickly became a genuine favourite with viewers.

This is an intimate portrait of Fred, from his childhood in Bolton, to his days as a steeplejack – the job he was to love above all others - and on to his successful television career. We discover all the different sides of Fred's personality – engineer, steeplejack, artist, craftsman, steam enthusiast, inventor, storyteller and eccentric. This definitive biography will delight Fred's many fans.

'Fred Dibnah, philosopher and steeplejack, has been representing the people for nearly 20 years'
SUNDAY TELEGRAPH

'Dibnah, a true man of the people . . . you can almost hear the echoes and smell the oil and smoke in this affectionate delve into his life'
MANCHESTER EVENING NEWS

9780552154888

Fred Dibnah's Buildings
Of Britain

David Hall

HAVE YOU EVER looked at one of our great historical buildings and wondered how on earth it was built? Well now you can get the answer from a man who devoted his life to that question, Fred Dibnah.

Fred takes us to some of the country's most famous castles, cathedrals, abbeys, great houses and bridges, and gives precise explanations of how they were constructed at a time when technology was limited and there were no power tools, no concrete, no steel, no engines and no heavy machinery. Illustrated with Fred's own beautifully executed drawings, published here for the first time, we explore engineering marvels such as St Paul's Cathedral, the Humber Bridge and Blackpool Tower. Fred's passion for the traditional skills of builders, carpenters, stonemasons and structural engineers shines through on every page.

Fred Dibnah's *Buildings of Britain* is a celebration of the architectural and engineering feats that made Britain great.

'Straight talking, frank speaking – with Fred Dibnah
you got what it says on the tin'
DAILY TELEGRAPH

9780593061824

Manchester's Finest:
How The Munich Air Disaster Broke the Heart of a Great City

David Hall

ON 6 FEBRUARY 1958, British European Airways flight 609 crashed in a blizzard on its third attempt to take off from an icy runway in Munich. On board were the Manchester United football team, the Busby Babes. Seven of their players were killed instantly in the crash, the great Duncan Edwards died three weeks later, and two other players were so severely injured that they were never able to play again.

News of the tragedy sent shockwaves around the world. *Manchester's Finest* tells of this terrible air crash, but it is also the story of the immediate aftermath of the disaster and its effect on the city of Manchester. David Hall's poignant and very personal memoir remembers a season long gone when a patched-up team, carried along on a great wave of emotion, came to embody the heart and soul of a great city.

'Not only the best book on Munich, but one of the very best books on the United . . . A totally refreshing account'
MICHAEL CRICK, author of THE BOSS:
THE MANY SIDES OF ALEX FERGUSON

9780552156301

Fred Dibnah's Victorian Heroes

David Hall

FRED DIBNAH WAS a man born out of his time. His era should have been the 'magnificent age of British engineering' – the nineteenth century – and his heroes were the great industrial engineers of the period whose prolific innovations and dedicated work ethic inspired a national mood of optimism and captured the hearts of the British public.

Fred Dibnah's Victorian Heroes tells the stories of some of these men – including George and Robert Stephenson, Isambard Kingdom Brunel and Joseph Whitworth – and what it was that made them such inspirational figures to Fred. What were their backgrounds? Where did their drive and vision come from? What sort of people were they at work and at home? And what was their contribution to the history of industry and engineering?

Most of them – like Fred – were colourful, larger-than-life characters for whom no challenge was too great. Taking these fascinating characters as inspiration, *Fred Dibnah's Victorian Heroes* gets to the very heart of what allowed nineteenth-century Britannia to rule the waves . . .

9780593064900